BEYOND

BAD

[GIRLS

BEYOND

BAD

GIRLS

{ gender, violence and hype }

MEDA CHESNEY-LIND AND KATHERINE IRWIN

Routledge
Taylor & Francis Group
New York   London

Routledge
Taylor & Francis Group
270 Madison Avenue
New York, NY 10016

Routledge
Taylor & Francis Group
2 Park Square
Milton Park, Abingdon
Oxon OX14 4RN

© 2008 by Taylor & Francis Group, LLC
Routledge is an imprint of Taylor & Francis Group, an Informa business

Printed in the United States of America on acid-free paper
10 9 8 7 6 5 4 3 2 1

International Standard Book Number-13: 978-0-415-94828-9 (Softcover) 978-0-415-94827-2 (Hardcover)

Library of Congress Cataloging-in-Publication Data

Chesney-Lind, Meda.
    Beyond bad girls : gender, violence and hype / Meda Chesney-Lind and Katherine Irwin.
        p. cm.
    Includes bibliographical references.
    ISBN 978-0-415-94827-2 (cloth) -- ISBN 978-0-415-94828-9 (pbk.)
    1. Girls--United States--Psychology. 2. Mass media and girls--United States. 3. Violence in children--United States. 4. Violence in adolescence--United States. I. Irwin, Katherine. II. Title.

HQ777.C535 2007
305.23082'0973--dc22   2006102808

Visit the Taylor & Francis Web site at
http://www.taylorandfrancis.com

and the Routledge Web site at
http://www.routledge.com

To Margaret Renton Chesney, my mother, for encouraging me to ask questions

Meda Chesney-Lind

and

To my parents Fran, Marsha, and John for all your support through the years

Katherine Irwin

Contents

ACKNOWLEDGMENTS   ix

1   GIRLS GONE WILD?   1

2   THE NEW BAD GIRL:
    CONSTRUCTING MEAN AND VIOLENT GIRLS   11

3   SPEAKING OF GIRLS   33

4   GROWING UP FEMALE: FAMILIES AND
    THE REGULATION OF GIRLHOOD   67

5   POLICING GIRLS' PEER GROUPS:
    COLUMBINE AND THE HUNT FOR GIRL BULLIES   89

6   PATHOLOGIZING GIRLS?: RELATIONAL AGGRESSION
    AND VIOLENCE PREVENTION   107

7   POLICING GIRLHOOD: SEXISM, SCHOOLS,
    AND THE ANTI-VIOLENCE MOVEMENT   129

8   STILL "THE BEST PLACE TO CONQUER GIRLS":
    GIRLS AND THE JUVENILE JUSTICE SYSTEM   157

9   POLICING GONE WILD   183

REFERENCES   189
APPENDIX   215
NOTES   217
INDEX   223

Acknowledgments

We have long felt the need for a book that presents the facts, such as we know them, about girls' violence, while also "talking back" to the media images of "bad girls" that bombard us daily. We also wanted to chronicle the serious and real world consequences of this misogynistic framing of girlhood for all girls, but most particularly girls of color. Fortunately for us, many at Routledge shared our sense that this was an important project, and they have been incredibly supportive and helpful. In fact, because it took us far longer than we expected to pull this effort together, we have had the good fortune to work with three editors. Thanks, initially, to Ilene Kalish who was so supportive and helpful in the development of the idea of this book, and who helped us sail through the early prospectus review process. David McBride kept us on track, and Gerhard Boomgaarden ultimately helped us pull the project together. Thanks also to Anne Horowitz, Heather Yarrow, Amy Rodriguez, Christian Munoz, and others at Routledge for their support and efficiency in the many layers of production and promotion of the book. Finally, thanks to the reviewers at both ends of the process who provided us with much needed scholarly and intellectual guidance.

We have also received wonderful support from colleagues and friends at the University of Hawaii and elsewhere. We would specifically like to acknowledge the support of the Departments of Sociology, the Women's Studies Program, and the Asian Pacific Islander Youth Violence Center at the University of Hawaii. Here, thanks particularly to Janet Davidson, Konia Freitas, Susan Hippensteele, David Johnson, David Mayeda, Scott Okamoto, Lisa Pasko (now at the University of Denver), and Karen Umemoto. University of Hawaii graduate students such as Corey Adler, Michael Dziesinski, Amanda Hall, Amy Matsen, Vickie Paramore, RaeDeen R. Karasuda, Kristina Lawyer, and Jonathan Jarvis were especially interested in and supportive of our research and for this we are very appreciative. Rachel Bradshaw provided outstanding advice and assistance while editing early drafts of several chapters. Katy's siblings, Jeanette Irwin, Anne Irwin, Johnny Irwin, Dave Mosick, and Cliff Sarkin lent their insights and space in their homes for this project. We deeply appreciate that.

We also want to thank the staff at Girls Court in Hawaii who also let us see that sometimes good things happen, even in your own back yard: here many thanks to Judge Frances Wong, Judge Karen Radius, and Rachel Yuen for believing in girls' programming in Hawaii. We would like to recognize the important but largely informal national network of academics, policy activists, and practitioners who have tirelessly encouraged and nurtured a national focus on girls in the juvenile justice system. Special thanks from us to Sibylla Artz, Barbara Bloom, Lyn Mikel Brown, Jeff Ferrell, Russ Immarigeon, Dan Macallair, Rebecca Maniglia, Merry Morash, Kathy Nesteby, Barbara Owen, Lori Rinehart, Robin Robinson, Paula Schaefer, Randy Shelden, Melissa Sickmund, Nan Stein, Giovanna Taormina, and Mary Scully Whitaker. Finally, many thanks to the girls and young women who spoke with us for this book, and who have spoken to us in the past about their lives and their experiences with the juvenile justice system. In truth, this book is for all of you!

For helping to provide a healthy balance between work and home, we also want to thank Ian Lind for his unfailing support over the years, and Lou Ortiz for his endless patience, understanding, and humor.

1

GIRLS GONE WILD?

It seems like the news about girls is increasingly grim, at least if you rely on the mass media. While we've always known about "bad" girls, in the past decade we've been jolted by media images of "gangster" girls, every bit as menacing as their male counterparts, even portrayed as peering at the world over the barrel of a gun. As we entered the twenty-first century, popular culture suddenly discovered "mean" girls, backstabbing their way to popularity, and now, only a few years later, it seems as though our mean girls have suddenly turned violent. Do we now need to worry about girls committing "savagery in the suburbs" as one recent headline in Newsweek announced (Meadows and Johnson 2003)?

While girls' aggression and violence have dominated girl culture literature in the new millennium, keep in mind that a few years previously we were worried about girls for a different reason. Piqued by Pipher's *Reviving Ophelia* (1994), which railed against girls' plummeting self-esteem during adolescence, adults in the nineties were concerned with the poisoned and sexist culture that encouraged girls to fall behind boys in a number of ways. Girls, more than boys, for example, lost self-esteem during adolescence, monitored and felt badly about their looks and their bodies (Brumberg 1997), and were sexually harassed at school (Orenstein 1994; Stein 1999). Now, instead of falling behind boys, girls are said to be catching up with boys in dangerous ways. But are today's girls really seeking equality with boys in crime the same way they have in soccer? The notion has a clear intuitive appeal. It seems obvious to many that as girls seek "equality" with boys, they run the risk of picking up the downsides of masculinity, including aggression and violence.

This book aims to fully explore this question, and in the process, take a close look at aspects of controlling girlhood both historically and currently. As criminologists, we both have a long-standing interest in criminalized girls and have done research on their actual behavior and problems; we have also both carefully studied the system that was established to formally control girls, the juvenile justice system. Both of these research experiences set the stage for this book.

Initially, though, it was the distance between the reality of the lives of girls in trouble with the law and the media constructions of those same girls that first prompted us to think about writing this book. In short, very much of what is being said in the media about girls and their problems seems oddly disconnected from the reality of girls' lives and their very real problems. Moreover, while there has always been a gap between media claims about girls and their real lives, this contemporary gap seems especially problematic and punitive. In the *Reviving Ophelia* era, for example, the target of blame was a hyper-sexualized, sexist, and physically violent culture that poisoned girlhood. The target of blame has increasingly become girls themselves, rather than a poisoned culture. Worse, the fact that current misinformation is widely believed by those who have substantial power over girls makes the need to set the record straight all the more apparent.

This book is our modest effort to do just that. In it, we will first explore the dimensions of the media images and constructions of girls' aggression and violence. We will then explore the actual trends in girls' delinquency and violence, as well as the more recent concern about girls' indirect or covert aggression. Finally, we will explore the ways that popular images of female defiance presage increased control of girlhood, especially when those controls dovetail with long standing societal interests in the control of people of color and economically marginal populations. Here, we work from a moral panics paradigm (Cohen 1972; Hall et al. 1978; Jenkins 1998) by understanding popular representations of aggressive and violent girls to have touched off a series of institutional sanctions against girls. In short, ideas about certain groups, even if misinformed, can have real social consequences if they are widely believed; we argue in this book that this is precisely what is happening in the current public fears about girlhood.

It will be our contention that masculinized images of bad girls (so common within the current "bad girl" hype) serve a number of important societal purposes. Notably, they serve to warn all girls and women of the negative consequences of seeking political and social equality with men while also justifying harsh new controls on certain girls—the daughters of the powerless. In a race and class biased society, the demonization of certain girls and women as gender outlaws justifies their harsh control and punishment, all the while cautioning the daughters of the powerful about the downside of challenging male dominance.

The masculinization of female defiance also brings the role of race and class forward. In a society that has long sought to keep all women in line with negative images, breaking gender norms has very real consequences for all girls who are seen as challenging their assigned place. While the role of popular negative stereotypes in girls' lives will also be a focus of this work, we will examine the racialized and class-based consequences of policies and practices crafted in response to real or imagined shifts in the aggression of all girls. Again, as criminologists with an interest in gender, we examine the role of the juvenile justice system in the enforcement of girls' place in a society that does not necessarily seek the best and fullest childhood for all its girls.

In subsequent chapters of this book, we look at two mechanisms of social control: the paternalistic system that, in the name of protecting girls, occasionally punishes them, and the retributive system that segregates and incapacitates girls from the youthful underclass. These two mechanisms of control are interlocking in key ways, such that we feel that it is impossible to advance a comprehensive analysis of contemporary constructions of "bad girls" without also accounting for the race and class effects of our responses to wayward youth in general. The increased social control of girls that we currently observe has its roots and is warranted, so we are told, because girls are becoming increasingly violent. In chapter 2, we begin by undertaking a review of the popular claims made in the media about girls' violence and aggression and, most importantly, we critically review the evidence offered to support the notion that girls are becoming more violent.

First, we locate the "mean girl" and the "violent girl" media narratives as part of a historic trend to identify and publicly denounce "bad girls." Since at least the 1950s, the media has identified different "bad girls" who break feminine norms and seemingly threaten the moral fiber of American society. While the type of bad girl has changed throughout time—from the sexually promiscuous girls of the fifties to the revolutionary of the seventies, the girl gangster of the eighties, the mean girl at the turn of the century, and the "violent" girl of the new millennia—the theme is the same: more bad news about girls and girlhood. All girls, no matter what their race or class, are subjected to misogynistic popular narratives about the bad and destructive nature of girls.

We then turn to the evidence that the media and trade books rely on, like *See Jane Hit* (Garbarino 2006), to justify the countless stories about girls' violence. Here, we suggest that despite significant increases in girls' arrests for certain offenses, notably simple assault, there are many reasons to be skeptical. In fact, virtually all other available measures of girls' violence (including self-report studies, victimization studies, and even other arrest trends) fail to show big increases in girls' violence. Some even show declines. How can this be? This book will answer this key question by documenting that the real trends that are occurring are more complex, and more about the policing and controlling of girls than about their behaviors.

Certainly, we are not the first people to argue that the reality of girls' aggression and violence is more complicated than the media has presented (see also Alder and Worral 2004; Artz 1998; Bjorkqvist and Niemela 1992; Brown 2003; Brown, Chesney-Lind, and Stein 2005; Campbell 1993; Morash and Chesney-Lind forthcoming; Steffensmeier et al. 2005). However, in this book, we contribute to and extend the critical literature of girls' violence and aggression by documenting how specific changes in family, school, and peer contexts have resulted in girls' everyday lives being increasingly monitored and, thus, their misbehaviors being more likely than in the past to result in formal justice system involvement.

Interestingly, what we find is not a widening "net" (wherein the juvenile justice system simply expands control over girls) as some have suggested (see Steffensmeier 2005). Instead, we argue that the institutions that have historically socialized and controlled girls *informally* (families, schools, peer groups) are changing the way they monitor and control girls—with bad consequences for girls. Egged on by media hype about a supposed increase in girls' aggression and violence, adults in these settings are intensely monitoring girls, recognizing their misbehaviors (which are usually minor), and then sending them into the juvenile justice system in increasing numbers because of the "aggression" and "violence" they have "discovered."

What do girls themselves have to say about girls' aggression and violence? In chapter 3, we report the findings of in-depth interviews with twenty-seven young women about their experiences in female peer groups. In some ways, young women confirmed common images about mean girls in films, news stories, and popular books by sharing accounts of times that they had been emotionally wounded by mean girls in their lives. This suggests that there are mean girls in the world and the target of their negative behavior is sadly other girls.

That was not all the young women we spoke with had to say, though. Yes, many knew mean girls and some even confessed that they occasionally had been mean. However, almost every girl also reported having close, healthy, and supportive relationships with girls or young women. While some girls are mean, others are faithful and supportive (see also Griffiths 1995), and we wonder why this story has not been told in popular accounts of mean girls. We also wonder why popular accounts have ignored the ethnographic literature on cliques that suggests that boys as well as girls are mean to one another. The girl-on-girl meanness described during interviews did not, according to most accounts, permanently damage girls. Some interviewees even praised mean girls for teaching them valuable lessons about choosing friends wisely and described having vast personal resources that helped them overcome adolescent challenges.

More importantly, we did not find any evidence of the idea that mean girls severely damage their victims. If Simmons, the author of *Odd Girl Out* (2002, 3), is correct, relational victimization is worse than physical victimization because "girls frequently attack within tightly knit networks of friends, making aggression harder to identify and intensifying the damage to victims." We did not find this, and other statements made in popular books like *Queen Bees and Wannabes* (Wiseman 2002), to be true. While the severity of meanness is questionable, other injuries, including those caused by racism and abuse, were not. Some young women of color discussed racial segregation between white and non-white groups in school and a rampant use of racist stereotypes against girls of color that constrained their future aspirations and opportunities. Other girls spoke of the long-lasting injuries caused by sexual abuse. Our interviews suggest that the media has over-blown the significance of mean girls, ignored the larger context in which girls' friendships form, and, as a consequence, has deflected public attention away from larger problems confronting girls in the new millennium.

Speaking to young women about their adolescent peer groups and learning that some girls received more emotional support from their friends than from their parents, reminds us that despite all the social changes of the last few decades, families are still complicated contexts for girls. In chapter 4, we review the surprisingly limited research on adolescent girls and their families. We document that even in the twenty-first century parents are uneasy about their daughters' sexuality, and anxious about their safety in ways that often produce silence about desire and over-estimation of the risks girls face. Even healthy families tend to worry about their daughter's reputation (often framed as arguments about girls' fashion), and fret about the books documenting the problems of girlhood (Brumberg 1997; Pipher 1994; Snyderman and Streep 2002; Wiseman 2002). Girls, understandably, chafe at the restrictions imposed by even well-meaning parents, often resorting to lying in order to enjoy the freedom routinely granted to boys.

Girls who come from more troubled homes often face these same concerns along with far more daunting challenges. Here, issues of physical and sexual abuse emerge as major reasons why girls might seek to avoid family control. No surprise, then, that many girls run away from home, and that studies of chronic runaway girls show extremely high levels of both physical and sexual abuse. What is even more disturbing, as this chapter will document, is the degree to which girls' attempts to escape abusive homes is increasingly criminalized, and we see girls who may well be the victims of neglect and abuse being arrested for "domestic violence."

Moving from the family to the peer group as a setting of policing girlhood, we consider the impact of new school-based programs that have been introduced to monitor and police interpersonal relationships in adolescence. In chapter 5, we chronicle the emergence and imple-mentation of one of the most popular types of violence prevention programs—the anti-bullying curriculum developed by Norwegian researcher, Dan Olweus.

Intense interest in bullying was fueled by a Secret Service report analyzing school shooting episodes (Vossekuil 2002), which noted that the boys involved in a number of high profile school shooting incidents, including the shootings at Columbine High School, were lashing out against school bullies. As we document, policy makers in a number of states sought passage of anti-bullying legislation, and many turned to Bullying prevention programs.

Ironically, given the initial impetus of the bullying focus (male violence), the Olweus approach to bullying relied, in part, on emerging research in the psychological field of girls' aggression (Bjorkqvist and Niemela 1992; Crick and Gropeter 1995). This literature contends that girls and boys practice different types of "aggression," both of which are conceptualized as equally harmful since both are "behaviors intended to hurt or harm others" (Crick and Grotpeter 1995, 710). Crick and her associates contend that the old focus that only males are aggressive has more recently been replaced by a new perspective: "one that posits males and females to be equally aggressive" (Crick et al. 1998, 76).

Based on this research, the program assumed that boys are more likely than girls to be physically violent, while girls are assumed to practice relational or indirect bullying. More to the point, as this chapter documents, these anti-bullying programs have, in the name of being gender responsive, equated the largely nonviolent behavior of girls as somehow equivalent to the physical violence boys tend to commit.

Recall that the national concern about "bullying" emerged out of horrific incidents of violence, like Columbine, virtually all of which involved boys. In addition, girls, and not boys, are often the victims, not the perpetrators of sexual violence at school. But by conflating relational aggression with physical violence, bullying prevention programs not only gloss over the fact that school shootings have been primarily perpetrated by boys, but they have degendered sexual harassment problems in school (see also Brown, Chesney-Lind, and Stein 2005). Finally, this chapter documents that these costly programs waste valuable resources "treating" girls for their relational aggression when, as our interviews with girls clearly show, girls confront much more serious problems in school than the meanness of their female peers.

We further explore the issue of girls' "aggression" in chapter 6, which focuses specifically on the concept of relational aggression and research that takes a more critical look at this phenomenon. We note that in an effort to "treat" girls for their relational aggression, all that girls receive from the bullying prevention criteria is encouragement to be "nice" to one another. In essence, this is a clumsy repackaging of the feminine script Brown has labeled "the tyranny of nice and kind" (Brown 1992, 53). Handed down to girls for generations, this mandate has limited girls' ability to compete in masculine worlds and encouraged them to take out their understandable anger at this system on other girls.

This chapter, in short, offers a feminist perspective of girls' aggression suggesting that girls are actively discouraged from directing their valid frustrations against powerful groups and systems. As a result, girls have a tendency to be frustrated with powerless individuals (i.e., other girls) and simultaneously seek to be "one of the guys" as a way out. By this logic, relational aggression is a reflection of girls' powerlessness, not their inherent meanness. Finally, and most importantly, this chapter reviews a growing body of literature which suggests that the relational aggression literature, with its simplistic gendered notions of aggression, may be in need of a critical feminist reassessment. Rather than being convinced of the parity model of "aggression," we document reasons to be very skeptical about the framing of this whole area of behavior, and particularly the policing of these nonviolent acts. In fact, as this chapter will document, there is growing evidence that boys close the gap in this behavior by late adolescence, that relational aggression is *not* predictive of physical violence, and most importantly, may be a sign of higher, not lower social intelligence.

We argue that the solution to girls' aggression is to offer girls real opportunities to succeed in a variety of ways and to be praised and rewarded for their many skills and talents. Setting up programs based on negative images of girls' nature, like Simmon's assertion early in *Odd Girl Out* about "inherent duplicity of females" (Simmons 2002, 18) blame girls for virtually all the problems of girlhood, while simultaneously failing to offer girls anything other than traditional feminine scripts about being nice and kind as a solution.

Chapter 7 considers the role of schools in the controlling of girlhood, and the ways in which the traditional "hidden curriculum" that has historically constrained girls now interacts with a far more overt system of social controls. Largely as a consequence of soaring rates of male youth violence in the eighties and nineties, schools began to establish "law and order" approaches through increased surveillance over students and rigid "zero-tolerance codes" that promised suspension, transfer, or expulsion for rule violators. These law-and-order responses were based, in part, on the idea that the violence epidemic was due to the emergence of an increasingly homicidal type of violent youth—a "super-predator"—who lacks self control and possesses no remorse for his crimes. We argue that the image that youth are violent because they lack "self control" opened the door for strict "no-nonsense" and no-exception punishments that, in the end, maximized state control over youth via a series of school policies that were easy to establish and enforce.

Not surprisingly, the schools that are most likely to use surveillance and zero tolerance like the Olweus Bullying Prevention Program are those serving poor youth of color. In particular, zero-tolerance policies, we contend, have been disproportionately leveled against African-American students, including girls, and are contributing to the "schools-to-jails track" for youth of color.

Certainly, when we review trends in the juvenile justice system, we see ample evidence of this "track." Girls' arrests, detentions, and incarcerations are soaring, and the trend is clearly related to girls' arrests for "assault." During the period from 1991 to 2003, the nation saw a 98 percent increase in the detentions of girls (compared to a 29 percent increase in boys' detentions), a 92 percent increase in girls' referrals to juvenile courts (compared to 29 percent among boys), and finally an 88 percent increase in girls' commitments (compared to only 23 percent increase in boys' commitments). Most significantly, more girls in court populations were there for "person" or violent offenses than boys (Snyder and Sickmund 2006). The role of race is clear in these patterns as well; take girls' detentions where African-American girls comprised nearly half of those in juvenile jails, despite being only

15 percent of those in the youth population (American Bar Association 2001, 21).

Sadly, as this chapter will document, these trends represent an abandonment of the juvenile justice system's commitment to "de-institutionalization" and "diversion" that characterized juvenile justice in the latter half of the last century. In its place, and with very ominous implications for all girls, we see an increased societal willingness to formally control, police, and punish girls for resisting and challenging the constraints of girlhood.

Again, we hope this book can provide those who care about America's girls with a clearer understanding about the facts and myths about girls' aggression and violence, and most particularly, the toxic role that the media have played in creating the impression that America's girls were going wild. We feel that it is important to challenge this myth, a product, we feel, of a misogynic impulse to publish only bad news about girls and women. We also hope that our work will help document the ways in which this media hype, in most cases aided and abetted by best-selling trade books, has set the stage for increasingly formal and punitive control of American girlhood.

2

THE NEW BAD GIRL: CONSTRUCTING MEAN AND VIOLENT GIRLS

It is Monday morning and you decide to wear jeans to school instead of a skirt. The consequence of this seemingly innocuous decision? You are kicked out of the clique and forced to eat lunch alone. Welcome to "girl world," where, we are told, the rules of popularity are rigidly enforced by a group of "queen bees" and "wannabes" (Wiseman 2002). The manipulative and damaging characteristics of girls' social worlds have been the subject of a spate of popular books (notably *Odd Girl Out* and *Queen Bees and Wannabes*), and their publication prompted innumerable newspaper articles on the topic of girls' aggression.

In a *New York Times Magazine* article titled "Girls Just Want to Be Mean," journalist Margaret Talbot (2002, 24) wrote that "it is not just boys who can bully" and delineated, through interviews with girls, the workings among popular girls. Jessica, a popular girl quoted by Talbot, described what happened to the clique member who broke the rule of wearing jeans only on Fridays. "She wasn't allowed to sit with us at lunch. On that first Monday, she didn't even try; she didn't even catch my eye—she knew better. But eventually she came back to us, and was like, 'I know, I deserved it.'" (Talbot 2002, 24).

It is not just ostracism that girls practice against one another, according to these popular books and articles. They also spread rumors about, leave incriminating phone messages for the parents of, and hurl insults at their victims. According to psychologists, such as Nikki Crick (Crick et al. 1999), if you include these types of behaviors in measures of adolescent aggression, girls emerge just as "aggressive" as boys. Crick and others contend that where boys are more likely to physically victimize other boys, girls practice what has become popularly known as "relationship aggression." "Girls fight with body language and relationships instead of fists and knives," according to Simmons' summary of this literature in *Odd Girl Out* and "now is the time to end the silence" (Simmons 2002, 3).

It is important to place these stories and constructions in a historic context. We have always had "bad" girls and a collection of media eager to showcase their waywardness. In the 1960s and 1970s, we had female revolutionary figures such as Patti Hearst, Friederike Krabbe, and Angela Davis who carried guns and fought alongside male revolutionaries (Klemesrud 1978). In the 1990s, U.S. news reports featured female gang members who, like their male counterparts, carried guns, killed people, and practiced brutal initiation rituals (Chesney-Lind 1997). Given this history, it would seem that queen bees, with their occasional forays into violence, are just the bad girl flavor of the month.

While mean girls appear to be quite different than girl gang members or female revolutionaries, what is common among these many bad girl constructions is that they usually do not reflect the complexity of girls' and young women's behaviors. Often they imply that girls' violence is simply a byproduct of girls becoming more like boys and implying that this "masculinization" is an unfortunate by-product of girls and women seeking equality with boys and men. Similarly, in many ways, the "discovery" of girls' meanness is simply a revisiting of a centuries-old pattern of stressing women's duplicitous nature—appearing superficially "innocent" and "nice" while actually being manipulative, devious, and occasionally evil. As a result, these constructions tend to distort and misrepresent the context of girls' aggression and violence, and more importantly, ignore girls' and women's place in a larger social structure, particularly their relative powerlessness compared to boys and men.

In this chapter, we will explore the "bad," "mean," and "violent" girl hype of the last few decades. We will also consider the evidence for widely accepted notions that girls' violence is increasing. Finally, we will begin to consider the impact these constructions have had on girls' lives, with a focus on the ways these girl images and their consequences are racialized.

Popular Constructions of Bad Girls

In her bestselling book, *Backlash*, Susan Faludi (1991) documented some of the ways in which the detractors of feminism used the media to attack and dismiss a wide array of feminist goals. Faludi (1991, 80) specifically chronicled journalism's efforts to frame "female trends" of the eighties as a litany of female shortcomings including "the failure to get husbands, get pregnant, or properly bond with their children." In the context of that discussion, Faludi noted that "NBC, for instance, devoted an entire evening news special to the pseudo trend of 'bad girls' yet ignored the real trends of bad boys: the crime rate among boys was climbing twice as fast as for girls."

By focusing, even briefly, on the media love affair with "bad girls," Faludi was prescient. At its core, the "bad girl" hypothesis is that the women's movement has a "dark" side, encouraging girls and women to seek equality in the illicit world of crime as well as the licit labor market (see Chesney-Lind and Eliason 2006, for a full discussion of this issue). Freda Adler, for example, in her book, *Sisters in Crime* (1975) wrote "the movement for full equality has a darker side which has been slighted even by the scientific community ... In the same way that women are demanding equal opportunity in the fields of legitimate endeavor, a similar number of determined women are forcing their way into the world of major crimes" (Adler 1975, 3).

While this argument sounds relatively recent, it is actually about a century old. Ever since the first wave of feminism, there have been no shortage of scholars and political commentators issuing dire warnings that women's demand for equality would result in a dramatic change in the character and frequency of women's crime (Pollak 1950; Smart 1976). Here's W. I. Thomas (1923): "The modern age of girls and young men is intensely immoral and immoral seemingly without the pressure of circumstances ... [I]s it the result of what we call 'the emancipation of women,' with its concomitant freedom from chaperonage, increased intimacy between the sexes in adolescence and a more tolerant viewpoint towards all things unclear in life?" (Thomas, cited in Pollock 1999).

Implicit in this "masculinization" theory of women's violence is the companion notion that contemporary theories of violence (and crime, more broadly) need not attend to gender, but can simply "add women and stir." The theory assumes that the same forces that propel men into violence will increasingly produce violence in girls and women once they are freed from the constraints of their gender. Moreover, the masculinization framework lays the foundation for simplistic notions of "good" and "bad" femininity, standards that will permit the demonization of some girls and women if they stray from the path of "true" (passive) womanhood (Chesney-Lind and Eliason 2006).

Media treatments of girl violence routinely stress the equity or masculinization hypothesis; girls are increasingly behaving like boys, we are told. They are carrying guns, joining gangs, and engaging in violence as often as boys. For example, on August 2, 1993, a *Newsweek* feature spread on teen violence included a box entitled "Girls will be Girls" and claimed that "some girls now carry guns. Others hide razor blades in their mouths" (Leslie et al. 1993, 44). Explaining this trend, the article noted that "The plague of teen violence is an equal-opportunity scourge. Crime by girls is on the rise, or so various jurisdictions report" (Leslie et al. 1993, 44). Exactly a year earlier, a CBS program featured a short subject called "Street Stories: Girls in the Hood," which was a rebroadcast of a story that first appeared in January 1992. It opened with this voice-over:

> Some of the politicians like to call this the Year of the Woman. The women you are about to meet probably aren't what they had in mind. These women are active, they're independent, and they're exercising power in a field dominated by men. In January, Harold Dowe first took us to the streets of Los Angeles to meet two uncommon women who are members of street gangs. (CBS 1992)

Years later, the theme was still quite popular. On November 5, 1997, ABC *Primetime Live* aired two segments on Chicanas involved in gangs, also called "Girls in the Hood" (ABC 1997) that followed two young women around their barrio for four months. The series opened with Sam Donaldson announcing that "There are over six hundred thousand gang members in the United States. What might surprise you is that many of them are young women." Warning viewers that "some of the scenes you may see are quite graphic and violent," the segment featured dramatic shots of young women with large tattoos on their stomachs, girls carrying weapons and making gang signs, young women selling dope and talking about being violent, and distant shots of the covered bodies of victims of drive-by shootings.

These stories were but three examples of many media accounts on violent girls to have appeared in the 1990s. Where did this come from? Perhaps the start was an article entitled "You've Come a Long Way, Moll" which appeared in the *Wall Street Journal*, January 25, 1990. This article noted that "between 1978–1988 the number of women arrested for violent crimes went up 41.5 percent, vs. 23.1 for men. The trend is even starker for teenagers" (Crittenden 1990, A14). Immediately following the publication of this story, the media was enraptured by the theme that the women's movement for equality had a "dark" side that included equal opportunity crime sprees. "For Gold Earrings and Protection, More Girls Take the Road to Violence," announced the front page of the *New York Times* a year later. This story, which profiled a girl robber (Aleysha), included the assertion that "[t]here are more and more girls like Aleysha in troubled neighborhoods in the New York metropolitan areas, people who work with children say. There are more girls in gangs, more girls in the drug trade, more girls carrying guns and knives, more girls in trouble" (Lee 1991, A1).

Whatever the original source, at this point a phenomenon known as "pack journalism" took over. The *Philadelphia Inquirer*, for example, ran a story subtitled, "Troubled Girls, Troubling Violence." The *Washington Post* ran a similar story called "Delinquent Girls Achieving a Violent Equality in D.C." (Lewis 1992). And the pattern continued through most of the decade, although in later years it moved from a specific concern about the "girl gangsta" to a more general moral panic about girls' violence. As an example, the *Boston Globe Magazine* ran an article that proclaimed on its cover, over huge red letters that said BAD GIRLS, "Girls are moving into the world of violence that once belonged to boys" (Ford 1998). From the *San Jose Mercury* (Guido 1998) came a story titled "In a new twist on equality, girls' crime resembles boys'," which featured an opening paragraph that argues:

Juvenile crime experts have spotted a disturbing nationwide pattern of teenage girls becoming more sophisticated and independent criminals.

In the past, girls would almost always commit crimes with boys or men. But now, more than ever, they're calling the shots. (Guido 1998, 1B)

In virtually all the print stories on this topic, the issue is framed in a similar fashion. Generally, a specific and egregious example of female violence is described, usually with considerable, graphic detail about the injury suffered by the victim. In the *Mercury* article, for example, the reader learns that a seventeen-year-old girl, Linna Adams, "lured" the victim into a car where her boyfriend "pointed a .357 magnum revolver at him, and the gun went off. Rodrigues was shot in the cheek, and according to coroner's reports, the bullet exited the back of his head" (Guido 1998, 1B).

These details are then followed by a quick review of the Federal Bureau of Investigation's arrest statistics showing what appear to be large increases in the number of girls arrested for violent offenses. Finally, there are quotes from "experts," usually police officers, teachers, or other social service workers, but occasionally criminologists, interpreting the events.

Television stories generally follow these print media stories, and the number of articles and television shows focused specifically on girls in gangs proliferated. Popular talk shows such as *Oprah* (November 1992), *Geraldo* (January 1993), and *Larry King Live* (March 1993) did programs on the subject, and NBC had a story broadcast on its nightly news which opened with the same link between women's "equality" and girls' participation in gangs.

The later ABC *Primetime* segment discussed earlier, "Girls in the Hood," featured many of the sensationalistic aspects of the NBC story. However, it was especially notable for its use of a white woman reporter, Cynthia McFadden, who reacted to the two young Chicanas' accounts of their complex and violent lives with outrage and moralistic hectoring. As an example, the reporter asked one of the young women "Are you a bad person?" The young woman began to answer, "I don't think so. Some people may not agree with what I say but ... " at which point the reporter interrupted and said, "I don't think it's what you say so much as what you do. You sell drugs, you participate in gang violence, you participate in shootings, in robbings, in stabbings." Later in the same interview, in response to her expression of pride over having stolen and kept a coffee maker during the LA riots, the reporter blurted out: "You realize that most of the people watching you want to slap you when you say that" (ABC 1997). ABC's story not only showcased the "bad" girls for their viewers, they also foreshadowed the coming societal response—one that is clearly not good news for these and other young women of color.

Girls, Gangs, Guns, and Emancipation?

The 1990s media hype about girls and gangs primarily focused on gender and crime, namely that girls were breaking into boys' domains. Interestingly, media constructions also told a story about race, class, and crime as well. The imagery of the gun toting, tattooed, African-American boy heavily clad in gold jewelry and gang colors was eventually followed by an African-American girl or Latina who was also tattooed, dressed in gang colors, and sported firearms. With this parallel imagery of the violent boys and girls came an explanatory parallel as well. The media was correct in noting that the youth violence epidemic was located in poor, inner-city neighborhoods and seemed to affect black and Latino youths more often than white juveniles. On the surface, the media imagery suggested that the forces driving African-American boys and Latinos to be violent were also driving girls' violence. The pro-violence forces, therefore, seemed to dissolve the gender gap in crime for particular communities.

What these constructions ignored was that the alternative street-based cultures were not gender blind and certainly did not offer equal opportunities for girls. As ethnographers looking at underground, inner-city economies have illustrated (Bourgois 1996), men who are left with few legitimate means to establish masculine identities often use partner abuse and rape to establish powerful personas. Gang researchers consistently reveal that girls have very limited power vis-à-vis male gang members (Joe and Chesney-Lind 1995; Portillos 1999; Miller 2001), and, although they are more violent than girls who are not in gangs, they are less violent than male gang members (Miller 2001; Hagedorn and Devitt 1999; Deschanes and Esbensen 1999). Gang research also reveals that male gang members sometimes used rape or the threat of rape to control female gang members (Miller 2001). Drug researchers also consistently note that drug markets, even the exploding crack market with seemingly limited sales opportunities in the 1980s and early 1990s (Bourgois 1989), tended to be male dominated domains in which women had a difficult time gaining an equal footing (Koester and Schwartz 1993; Maher and Daly 1996; Murphy et al. 1991). Thus, although the media portrayed an image of the liberated female gang banger, research showed a different image in which girls and women have a very tenacious foothold in alternative street cultures, gangs, and underground drug markets.

Thus, the world of crime and especially the underground crack markets, were far from being locations in which women and girls achieved emancipation. In fact, as gang and drug researchers often indicated, large-scale social problems such as the migration of jobs out of, and a lack of services within, inner cities in the 1980s and early 1990s (Wilson 1996), left many men of color without jobs or legitimate avenues for success. These changes left men of color scrambling for ways to achieve positive identities in many U.S. urban centers. Alternately, the hyper-masculine norms established as a response to the lack of jobs and legitimate avenues for respect and status (Anderson 1999; Bourgois 2001), placed women of color in difficult positions as well as making them targets for men's efforts to take control and earn respect through violence.

Queen Bees as Bad Girls

By the mid-nineties, gang violence stories slipped out of the public spotlight, as national youth homicide rates began to decline. Attention to the subject of youth violence, however, did not abate. A collection of sensationalized and horrific school shootings, the most notorious being the Columbine High School massacre in April of 1999, caught the media's attention. The gangs, guns, and drugs story of the late eighties and early nineties was replaced with images of white suburban teens seeking revenge against their classmates. While virtually all school shooters were boys, the media repeatedly neglected that theme, in favor of framing the issue as "kids killing kids" (Garvey 1999). Then, when research conducted by the U.S. Secret Service appeared that suggested that many school shooters had been the victims of bullying (Vossekuil 2002), policy makers, in particular, took notice. As we shall see in chapter 5, several states, including Colorado, passed laws mandating that schools implement violence prevention programs, many of which promised to increase school safety by changing the social dynamics in school. Specifically, bullying prevention programs began to emerge, without much media fanfare until the discovery of the mean girl.

As we will document, one of the staples of bullying prevention programming is the notion that both boys and girls "bully." These claims are loosely based on the psychological literature on adolescent aggression (Bjorkqvist and Niemela 1992; Crick and Grotpeter 1995). Specifically, psychologists define aggression as "behaviors that are intended to hurt or harm others" (Crick et al. 1999), and Crick, among others, argued that indirect or relationship "aggression" is more typical of girls' aggression while boys tended to specialize in direct aggression (including violence).

The discovery of girls' aggression in the psychological literature was, as we have noted, popularized in books such as *Odd Girl Out* and *Queen Bees and Wannabes*. The best-selling *Odd Girl Out* suggested that mean girls destroyed their victims' self esteem and made going to school a painful event for many girls. These claims came, in part, as a backlash against years of feminist research arguing that women are more nurturing, caring, and relationship-oriented than men (Gilligan 1982; Taylor, Gilligan, and Sullivan 1995).

Virtually all popular treatments of the new girl bully open with the personal experiences of the authors. *Odd Girl Out*, as an example, opens with Rachel Simmons telling us that when she was 8, a "popular" friend whispered to Rachel's "best" friend that they should run away from Rachel and they did, on the way to dance class at a local community theatre. Simmons spent much of that year trying to make sense of their desertion. As she put it: "The sorrow is overwhelming." She concludes that it is time to tell this story and expose the "… hidden culture of girls' aggression in which bullying is epidemic, distinctive, and destructive" (Simmons 2002, 3).

Television and print news media further diffused the images of mean girls found in popular books on girls' aggression. Rosalind Wiseman, author of *Queen Bees and Wannabes* made a guest appearance on *Oprah*, Rachel Simmons' work became the focus of a *Dateline* story titled "Fighting with Friends." In addition, the mean girl story was told in a series of newspaper and magazine articles with titles such as "Girls Just Want to Be Mean" (Talbot 2002), "Girl Bullies Don't Leave Black Eyes, Just Agony" (Elizabeth 2002), "She Devils" (Metcalf 2002), and "Just Between Us Girls: Not Enough Sugar, Too Much Spite" (*Pittsburgh Post-Gazette* 2002). The central idea communicated in these news stories was that girls are socially competitive creatures and that, in their efforts to be popular and powerful, they inflict lifelong damages on their female victims.

In addition, the connection between girls' mean and manipulative natures was often linked in these reports to the larger social problem of bullying. In an article titled "Outcast no More," reporter Slayer notes that "up to 20 percent of American students are chronic targets of bullying at school. Six out of ten teenagers witness bullying at least once a day." Kristi, a once-popular, blonde-haired middle school girl, provided the human interest example of the extent of bullying problems in school. According to the reports "a group of girls at North Lake Middle School who had once been her friends suddenly turned against her."

Not all researchers studying girls' aggression took this girl-blaming stance. Brown, in her book, *Girlfighting*, analyzed over four hundred interviews, many of them conducted at the Harvard Project on Women's Psychology and Girls' Development. Using the voices of girls, Brown does document that girls enlist in the "perfect police," enforce the "tyranny of nice," and engage in covert aggressions—by being catty, nasty, and mean to other girls. She, though, links "girlfighting" to the context of girls' lives, arguing that girls are growing up in a misogynistic world where girls succeed only if they please boys and men, often at the expense of their sisters (Brown 2003). Merten's research on a clique of "mean girls" noted that "meanness" is, in fact, linked to a "taboo" among women and girls towards "open competition," especially among friends (Merten 1997, 189).

Sibylla Artz also links girls' aggressions (and their violence) to, among other things, "internalized notions of being female that assign low general worth to women, hold that women achieve their greatest importance when they command the attention of males, and support of the sexual double standard" (Artz 1998, 195). Finally, Osler and Vincent (2003) explore girls' exclusion from schools and also link this phenomenon to problematic contemporary stereotypes about girls that punctuate media images as well as school-disciplinary policies that uniquely disadvantage girls[1].

Mean Girls Take Center Stage

In 2004, Rosalind Wiseman's *Queen Bees and Wannabes* was adapted for the big screen; the result was the Hollywood blockbuster *Mean Girls*, which offered a comic portrayal of girls' incivility to other girls. The theme of girls' bullying also made it to the stage in Joan MacLeod's play *The Shape of a Girl*, which has toured through Canada and received the Betty Mitchell Award for outstanding original script. Even at the height of the youth violence epidemic, the story of girl gangsters did not make it to best-selling popular books, profitable Hollywood films, or acclaimed plays. Relatively speaking, girl gangsters who were demonized, masculinized, and denounced were more physically threatening and dangerous than mean girls. Why, then, would the mean girls become a best selling topic?

The answer is because the mean girl story is a new twist on a very old and damaging construction of women. As we noted earlier, traditionally women have been viewed as nice on the outside but venomous and manipulative on the inside. That girls are mean to other girls is not a new popular or Hollywood theme in the slightest. In fact, films have consistently portrayed girls as mean to one another. *Jawbreakers* (1999), *Heathers* (1989), *Carrie* (1976), *Peyton Place* (1957), *All About Eve* (1950), *Mildred Pierce* (1945), and *Rebecca* (1940) depict vivid and often deadly images of women's incivility to other women. So the popular culture discovery of relationally aggressive girls was really not a new discovery at all. It was rooted in historic messages about girls' and women's subversive and even evil natures.

Are Mean Girls Becoming Violent?

What happens when cliques' relationship violence becomes physical? An incident at Glenbrook High School on May 4, 2003 gave new life and a new spin to the mean girl hype. On May 4, 2003, the annual powderpuff football game began as a regular hazing ritual with senior girls smearing muck all over a band of girls from the junior class. According to witness Nick Babb, quoted in the newspaper *Glenview Announcements* (Leavitt 2003, 2), the event turned violent when "a few individuals in the senior class decided they hated some of the juniors. Certain people decided they wanted to turn this whole thing into something personal." The violence reported included placing buckets over the heads of girls and beating the buckets with bats as well as pushing and kicking. Girls were seen smearing feces, pig guts, fish guts, paint, and coffee grounds on girls. A collection of students, including boys, looked on, cheered, and drank beer. After the event, five girls required medical attention, one had a concussion, one had a broken ankle, and another needed stitches on a head wound.

When the videotape revealing the mayhem was aired, the incident received national attention and became another example of "girls gone bad." Except this time, the bad girls used violence against their victims rather than simply ostracism, rumors, and manipulation, thus illustrating that under the right circumstances (alcohol, hazing traditions, lack of adult supervision), girls can be physically violent. And, as noted earlier, the notion that even white girls were becoming more aggressive and violent was later solidified in *Newsweek*'s article on this widely viewed fight entitled "Girl Fight: Savagery in the Suburbs" which breathlessly reported the details of the incident.

"Savagery in the Suburbs?"

The idea that these newly discovered aggressive girls could turn to violence came with the publication of two mass market books that essentially contending girls' aggression is now becoming increasingly violent. Harvard professor Deborah Prothrow-Stith and pediatrician Howard Spivak published *Sugar and Spice and No Longer Nice: How We Can Stop Girls' Violence* in 2005, and a year later, psychologist James Garbarino published *See Jane Hit: Why Girls are Growing More Violent and What We Can Do About It*. Somewhat predictably, their appearance prompted yet another round of articles including *Newsweek*'s "Bad Girls Go Wild," which noted that "a rise in girl-on-girl violence is making headlines nationwide and prompting scientists to ask why" (Scelfo 2005). *Time* followed suit with "Taming Wild Girls" (which opened with "never mind the gentler gender. Girls, too can be brawlers" (Kluger 2006, 54).

Both these books, unlike earlier depictions of violent girls, feature Caucasian girls looking somewhat menacing on their covers, and both also rely heavily on arrest statistics to support their contention that girls are becoming more violent. Prothrow-Stith and Spivak do note that self-report data do not confirm their contention, which they justify ignoring, "considering the numerous stories we have been told for over a decade" (Protherow-Stith and Spivak 2005, 51). Apparently, anecdotal evidence trumps data in this instance. In Garbarino's case, there is even evidence that he misstates the arrest data. In a critical review of this book, Males comments: "'Twenty-five years ago, almost ten boys were arrested for assault for every one girl,' Garbarino writes, misstating numbers from Prothrow-Stith. 'Now, the ratio is four to one.' Wrong. FBI figures show that 25 years ago, five boys were arrested for assault per girl, not 10" (Males 2006, 34). Garbarino certainly shops carefully among even the arrest data (sometimes stopping well short of the most up-to-date statistics); he has, for example, an entire chapter on girls who kill despite the fact that girls' arrests for lethal violence actually declined by 36.9 percent between 1995–2004 (FBI 2006, 285).

Books hyping girl problems, in this instance, with aggression and violence, share many common problems with other contemporary works on girlhood. As we shall see, many seem to psychologize and pathologize girlhood and, in some instances, even blame girls for their own problems; attention to boys' violence against girls or sexist and racist institutions that control girlhood are often absent from these analyses (though to be fair, Prothrow-Stith does pay attention to community factors in youth violence).

These newest books on girls' aggression and violence showcase scary arrest statistics about girls' violence, supply lots of powerful anecdotes and media accounts of girls' "brawls," and then proceed to round up the usual suspects (as well as a few unusual ones) to blame. Both books hit the media, particularly "the feminization of the superhero" (Prothrow-Stith and Spivak 2005, 80), television viewing, video games, abuse, and the "intensity" of girls' meanness. In Gabarino's case, feminism ("female liberation and equalization is nearly complete when it comes to aggression") (113), and girls' sports participation are added to the list, along with a "toxic" culture. Sports, he argues, produce girls getting more "physical" and "assertive." He also contends that it produces "elevated levels of aggression" (2006, 4).

Significantly, both books spend a considerable amount of time with advice to parents and others who work with girls to address girls' "new" problems, again stressing the relevance of "bullying" prevention programs and other efforts to make gender prevention and intervention programs more girl relevant. Given both books' focus on white girls, the emphasis on programming, as opposed to justice responses, is significant and noteworthy, suggesting that since youth violence is now the province of white girls, we should seek to prevent rather than punish.

Trends in Girls' Violence: Is the Gender Gap Closing?

Why the media fascination with youth violence, and particularly girls' violence? To put this into perspective, it is important to review the crime trends that drew media attention to youth violence in general. Although the United States had experienced relatively stable crime rates from the early 1980s to the mid 1990s, violent crime rates for juveniles soared during this period. By the mid 1990s, the grim statistics regarding adolescent violence gained national attention. Among the more sobering statistics was an approximately 70 percent increase in youth arrest rates for violent offenses and a nearly 300 percent growth in youth homicide arrest rates from 1983 to 1994 (Snyder and Sickmund 1999). Soon the attention of the media was drawn to what some were calling an "epidemic of youth violence" (Cook and Laub 1998).

Criminologists explained that the epidemic was caused by a combination of the introduction of new crack markets to inner cities, increased distribution of guns among juveniles, and the involvement of gangs in the crack and underground gun markets (all far more relevant to boys' but not girls' violence) (Blumstein 1995; Blumstein and Cork 1996; Blumstein and Wallman 2000). Initially, the media chronicled this trend with alarmist messages about the savage nature of the coming generation of boys—often called "super-predators" (DiIulio 1995). But the boy "super-predator" failed to appear, and by

1994, the violence epidemic among boys, according to most accounts, began to abate as youth homicide rates dropped steadily. Instead of reporting the end of the epidemic of violence—a mostly male phenomenon—the media and the public latched onto the fact that girls were making up a larger percentage of juvenile arrests since the 1980s, and that many of these new arrests of girls were for violent offenses.

Indeed, a review of ten-year juvenile arrest trends revealed rising rates of girls' arrests. Between 1985 and 1996, boys' arrests increased by 24.4 percent, while girls' rates increased 50.1 percent (FBI 1995) and from 1991 to 2000, boys' arrests declined (by 3.2 percent), while girls' arrests climbed by 25.5 percent. Eventually, as shown in Table 2.1, girls' arrest rates also began to decline. Despite these declines, the fact that girls were outpacing boys in arrests meant that girls were making up a larger portion of juvenile arrests. In 1991, girls made up 23 percent of all juvenile arrestees, and by 2004 they made up 30.5 percent (FBI 1997, 215; FBI 2005, 285).

What makes this surge most noteworthy is that girls are increasingly being arrested for violent offenses, not traditional status offenses (non-criminal offenses like running away from home). Over the last two decades, increases in girls' arrests rates for a number of violent

Table 2.1   Juvenile Arrest Trends by Gender

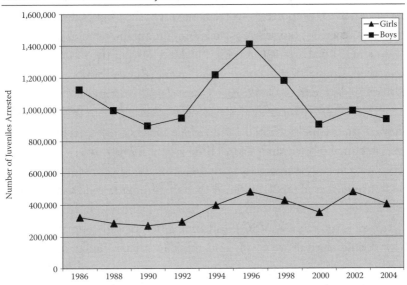

offenses have clearly outpaced boys' arrest rates. Between 1980 and 2000, for example, girls' arrests for aggravated assault, simple assault, and weapons law violations increased by 121 percent, 257 percent, and 134 percent, respectively. Boys' arrests also increased in these categories, but by far less (28 percent, 109 percent, and 20 percent). And the trend continues. Between 1995 and 2004, girls' arrests for simple assault increased by 31.4 percent while boys' arrests decreased by 1.4 percent. Arrests of girls for aggravated assault did drop (by 2.9 percent), but boys' arrests for this offense dropped by 27.6 percent (FBI 2006, 285).

These data certainly caught the attention of media already focused on "youth violence" and, as we have documented, the first media explanation was that girls were changing. They were becoming increasingly like boys, and thus were being arrested for violations that were historically viewed as boys' domain. Despite the intuitive popularity of the claims that girls were achieving a violent brand of equality, there are good reasons to be skeptical.

The first indication that something more complex was occurring came when several self-report data sources failed to corroborate this "surge" in girls' arrests for violence. In fact, self-report studies often found that girls were becoming less violent throughout the 1990s. In the Centers for Disease Control and Prevention's biennial Youth Risk Behavior Survey, girls' self-reported involvement in physical fights decreased. In 1991, 34.2 percent of girls reported being in a fight versus 28.1 percent of girls in 2005. Boys' self-reported violence during the same time also decreased, from 50.2 percent to 43.4 percent (Brener, Simon, Krug, and Lowry 1999; Centers for Disease Control and Prevention 1992–2006) (see Table 2.2). A meta-analysis of data collected from 1991 to 1997 showed that while both male and female violence rates declined, girls' rates declined more dramatically (Brener et al. 1999, 444).

Comparing multiple data sources over several consecutive years, Steffensmeier et al. (2005) found that the dramatic increases in girls' arrest rates for violent offenses were significantly out of step with victim reports (the NCVSO) and two different self-report data (the Monitoring the Future Study and the Youth Risk Behavior Survey). And in a matched sample of "high-risk" youth surveyed in the 1997 National Youth Survey and the 1989 Denver Youth Survey, Huizinga

Table 2.2 Self-Reported Delinquency

GIRLS	1991	1993	1995	1997	1999	2001	2003	2005
In a Physical Fight	34.2	31.7	30.6	26.0	27.3	23.9	25.1	28.1
Carried a Weapon	10.9	9.2	8.3	7.0	6.0	6.2	6.7	7.1
Carried a Gun	--	1.8	2.5	1.4	0.8	1.3	1.6	0.09
BOYS	1991	1993	1995	1997	1999	2001	2003	2005
In a Physical Fight	50.2	51.2	46.1	45.5	44.0	43.1	40.5	43.4
Carried a Weapon	40.6	34.3	31.1	27.7	28.6	29.3	26.9	29.8
Carried a Gun	--	13.7	12.3	9.6	9.0	10.3	10.2	9.9

Source: Youth Risk Surveillance data (CDC 1992, 1994, 1998, 2000, 2002, 2004, 2006).

(1997) found significant decreases in girls' involvement in felony and minor assaults.

Finally, there are the trends in girls' lethal violence. While girls' arrests for all forms of assault have skyrocketed, girls' arrests for murder dropped by 36.9 percent between 1995 and 2004 and girls' arrests for robbery also dropped by 37.2 percent. If girls were in fact closing the gap between their behavior and that of boys, one would expect to see the same effect across all the violent offenses (including the *most* violent offense). That simply is not happening.

Regional data also cast doubt on the "surge" in girls' violence. Males and Shorter's (2001) analyses of vital statistics maintained by health officials (rather than arrest data) conclude that there has been a 63 percent drop in San Francisco teen-girl fatalities between the 1960s and the 1990s, and they also report that hospital injury data show that girls are dramatically underrepresented among those reporting injury (including assaults). Girls are 3.7 percent of the population but were only 0.9 percent of those seeking treatment for violent injuries (Males and Shorter 2001, 1–2). They conclude, "Compared to her counterpart of the Baby Boom generation growing up in the 1960s and 1970s, a San Francisco teenage girl today is 50 percent less likely to be murdered, ... 45 percent less likely to die by guns, ... and 60 percent less likely to commit murder ... " (Males and Shorter 2001, 1). If girls were becoming more violent in San Francisco and elsewhere, one would expect other systems (like hospitals and health departments) to also notice this trend, but that was not seen.

Data from Canada, which has also seen a barrage of media coverage of girls' violence, also indicate that violent female delinquency is rare, even among incarcerated girls. A report on delinquent girls incarcerated in British Columbia notes that "despite isolated incidents of violence, the majority of offending by female youth in custody is relatively minor" (Corrado, Odgers, and Cohen 2000, 189). Surprisingly, a recent study of girls tried and convicted as adults in the U.S. also found the majority of the girls had committed relatively minor offenses (Gaarder and Belknap 2002).

If girls' violence was not increasing, then what accounts for their increasing arrest rates during the past two decades? A collection of researchers (Chesney-Lind 2002, 2004; Males 1996; Steffensmeier et al. 2005) have offered an alternative to the masculinization or parity hypothesis by arguing that the surge in girls' violence arrests reflects an intensified policing of youthful misbehaviors, rather than a dramatic change in girls' behaviors. The reason that girls' violence arrest rates are increasing faster than boys' rates is threefold. First, the policing of youth has become especially vigilant in intimate settings (home and peer groups at school)—the contexts in which girls are likely to offend (although most of their offenses are minor). Second, girls have been particularly denounced in popular venues, which has led to increased scrutiny of them, and increased the likelihood that their misbehaviors will be treated seriously. And third, as a result of national concerns about youth violence and school safety in the post-Columbine years, there has been a widespread recrafting of definitions of violence to include behaviors that would never have been considered violent decades ago.

Although the "hyper policing" hypothesis has been accepted by some as a viable alternative to the idea that girls are becoming more violent, to date there has been very little evidence offered regarding how girls are treated and policed in settings other than the juvenile justice system. This book aims to fill this gap in our knowledge. Where most research hypothesizes that the policing of youth has increased in intimate settings, we look at the available information tracing the intensified control of girls in family, peer, and school settings. Moreover, we link changes in popular culture, family, peer, and school contexts to the increased likelihood that girls' minor misbehaviors will be viewed as serious offenses deserving police attention.

In the chapters that follow, we will explore exactly how the policies of the last decade have impacted patterns of girls' arrests. But briefly, we feel that there are actually three related forces likely at work: "relabeling" (sometimes called "bootstrapping") of girls' status offense behavior into violent offenses like assault often at the instigation of girls' parents, rediscovery of girls' violence, particularly by school officials in the nineties (recall that self-report data show that girls are more violent than their "passive" stereotype indicates), and "upcriming" or responding more seriously to minor forms of youthful violence (including girls' fighting) by all schools and police as a result of the Columbine shootings.

Youth Violence, Bad Girl Hype, and Real Consequences

This century has opened with numerous news stories warning of increasing violence among girls; this on the heels of several decades of negative stories showcasing various "bad" girl epidemics. We have argued, however, that even a careful reading of arrest data fails to support this notion (particularly if you consider lethal or predatory violence like murder or robbery). Other data sources such as self-report and victimization studies should show increases in girls' violence, but they do not. There is very little corroborating evidence to suggest that girls are closing the gender gap in violence.

Despite the fact that multiple data sources tell us that girls are not becoming more violent, popular constructions of violent and aggressive girls are alarming and, in fact, are complicating the trend in girls' arrests. Clearly, the rise in girls' violence arrest rates began before the popular press ran the first stories of gang banging girls. After all, it was girls' arrest statistics that piqued the presses' interest and lent credibility to the violent girl story. Therefore, media constructions certainly did not, at first, cause increases in girls' arrests, but they have probably complicated the problem. In some cases, the media constructions have helped justify the high rates of girls' arrests after the fact (Chesney-Lind and Eliason 2006). And, in other cases, the media hype has persuaded those who have traditionally controlled girlhood to increase the policing of girls in ways that seriously disadvantage all girls and most particularly girls of color.

This difference between the way that violent girls and youth of color are constructed and treated can be clearly seen when examining two different publicized episodes of youth violence. In the Glenbrook High School hazing incident on May 4, 2003, 32 students were suspended and 12 girls and 3 boys faced misdemeanor battery charges. If they were found guilty, these youths could have been sentenced to 364 days in jail and $2,000 in fines. The students, however, secured lawyers and fought these charges. Two students even filed a federal lawsuit to lift their suspensions and recover monetary damages from the school, though this was later denied. The parents, who provided the resources for these lawyers, stood by their children and claimed repeatedly to reporters that their daughters or sons were good kids and had been only marginally involved in the event. In the end, the school offered the students the chance to graduate on time if they agreed in writing to forgo movie, book, and television deals.

Contrast this case with a similar high profile set of suspensions in a Decatur, Illinois neighborhood. There a seventeen-second fight among seven boys attending a high school football game resulted in the boys being expelled from school for two years—despite the fact that the fight involved no weapons and injured no one. Until the intervention of Jesse Jackson, none of these youths were allowed counsel and the two seniors, with less than four credits to go to graduation, would have lost the chance to graduate (Wing and Keleher 2000, 1). While zero-tolerance antiviolence policies in the Decatur school kept students from returning to school, Jackson coaxed the school district into allowing two of the boys to transfer to a reform school in the area and graduate on time.

These two cases clearly highlight the ways that class and race privilege can blunt the force of the official intervention into the "youth violence" problem. Despite the intense media focus on the Glenbrook case, the relatively serious nature of the girls' violence was overshadowed by the "girls gone wild' media construction, and the parents' quick insistence on re-labeling the incident as "hazing." The Decatur incident initially failed to receive the same fanfare and only made it into the national press when Jackson became involved. Without his celebrity status, the press might not have taken notice of the absurd punishments leveled against a group of African-Americans as a result of a short scuffle which resulted in no injuries.

The media-driven "gangsta girl" hype of the eighties and nineties, the millennium mean girl, and "bad girls go wild" of the new century have all served to justify increased formal control of girlhood. Girls' increased arrests came, we argue, not because they were becoming more like boys, but instead because girls would bear the brunt of an intensified system of social control. As we will show in the chapters that follow, girls who were "acting out" in the home, in their peer groups, or in the school are now being punished formally, and often labeled as violent criminals in the process.

In short, it appears that while public fear of the "super-predator" male youth has waned, the public is still very concerned about its female version—the new bad girl, largely because of an unrelenting media hype showcasing images of mean, bad, and violent girls. We are very concerned about the consequences of this hype for girls, particularly girls of color (whose families and communities do not necessarily have the resources to challenge the increasing control of minor forms of youthful misbehavior). In the next chapters, we will examine how these toxic media constructions of girls' "badness," "meanness," and "wildness," untethered from reality, have resulted in the increased surveillance and policing of girlhood. Controlling girlhood in the new century involves not only the official system of social control (the juvenile justice system), but also increased formal scrutiny of girls' peer groups, girls' family relationships, and girls' lives in schools—all in ways that punish and constrain girls while often blaming them for their own problems.

3

SPEAKING OF GIRLS

Acknowledging Meanness

Sadly, one of the most disturbing aspects of the "mean girl" media hype is that aspects of it resonated with many girls' and young women's experiences. Girls, despite their many strengths, are not always "sugar and spice and everything nice" in their dealings with other girls. Many girls and women can remember being deeply hurt by other girls during childhood and adolescence, and there is no denying that on occasion "girlworld" can be a frightening and difficult terrain to traverse. As noted previously, while boys fear physical altercations and challenges, girls often fear interpersonal and relationship conflicts and, ultimately, being unwanted and unaccepted by their peers. Indeed, such threats are potent particularly because relationships tend to matter so much to girls. Beyond that, these betrayals come at a developmental stage when, according to psychologists, life events take on grandiose drama and self-confidence is easily shaken. It is precisely these dramas and emotional extremes that create identification with aspects of the mean girl narratives.

Perhaps even extreme constructions of female bullies seem plausible because so many of us remember our own adolescence complete with the pain and anguish of trying to fit in, only to fail. We can all recall those times that we were rejected, let down, and excluded as well as how hurt we were each time this happened. Because of this, many of us find it easy to believe the claim that it must be the same for girls today. In fact if you feel that adolescence is more difficult today than it was ten, twenty, or thirty years ago, it is almost plausible to assume that today's meanness is more venomous and damaging than it was during our own adolescence. With this logic in mind, it makes sense that today's girls might inflict terrible damage on one another and that their behavior might even constitute a type of aggression almost as damaging as physical violence.

Talking About Meanness

Given the negative popular attention dedicated to the topic of mean girls in the twenty-first century, and especially the proposed relationship between relational aggression and violence for girls, we were interested in knowing what young women had to say about the increasingly pervasive claims made about girl-on-girl aggression. We felt that a thorough examination of these popular constructions would be incomplete without letting girls and young women speak for themselves. Early in this project, therefore, we decided to conduct interviews, allowing individuals to "speak out about girls," and focusing closely on girls' friendships. Between 2003 and 2005, we conducted face-to-face interviews and three focus groups with a total of twenty-seven young women (see Appendix) and, in the following, we describe the design and purpose of the study, as well as our data collection and analysis methods.

The design and purpose of this study was, first and foremost, feminist in nature. In fact, our interest in avoiding exploiting girls and women during the research process often set specific parameters around our research choices that may raise questions from some. We feel strongly, however, that our decisions to avoid exploiting and grant control to study participants actually enhanced the quality of our data, rather than detracted from it.

Regarding the study design, we were interested in giving young women a forum to "talk back" to the popular claims made about them in the media, especially the claims about girls' relationships. Moreover, we wanted to give young women the opportunity to place their friendship experiences in a larger context and to discuss what, in their own perspectives, helped or hindered their ability to become successful young women, with each participant defining what success meant in her own terms. To do this, we loosely structured our in-depth interviews and focus groups around a set of conversational topics and our interviews and focus groups flowed in an informal format that allowed study participants to tell us about their experiences using their own terms and symbols (see Blumer 1969). We also used the same interview guide for focus groups, with the primary difference being that focus groups tended to elicit a group conversation and group "meaning making" among the young women in our sample. As Wilkinson (2004) argues, focus groups can be an advantage for feminist researchers who strive to make their research more natural and want to shift the balance of power toward research subjects by outnumbering themselves during interviews.

The interview guide included questions about the challenges individuals confronted during adolescence, including their relationships with girls, boys, their parents, and their teachers. In this way, our interviews were not solely focused on girl-on-girl aggression, but viewed girls' interactions with their peers as being influenced and shaped by institutional structures that often seek to control youth (e.g., families, schools, and even the justice system). We also utilized feminist interview methods by viewing research participants as collaborators in the research process. More specifically, this meant conforming to a tradition that Fine (1994, 75) called "uppity voice" research in which researchers allow study participants to be their own "constructors and agents of knowledge."

The age range of the sample population was another aspect of the study design that was influenced more by feminist than by traditional scientific protocols. While we understood that a study about girls' meanness should include girls' voices, we wanted our interviews to take on a particular tone, one in which research participants had as much control as possible during the interviews. We are both aware that adults have considerably more power in society than adolescents, and for this reason, we were convinced that we had a better chance of avoiding the exploitation of subjects by interviewing young adults rather than adolescents. To strike a balance between interviewee recall and non-exploitation, we initially set our age parameters between 18 and 22.[1] Midway through the participant recruitment, however, we decided to extend our age range to include individuals up to the age of 26.[2] As we embarked upon recruitment, it turned out that 18- to 22-year-olds were the least likely individuals to express interest in participating in our study, whereas those in their mid-20s were often eager to talk, with several 25- and 26-year-olds explicitly saying that they were looking forward to giving us detailed accounts of girls' meanness. Initially, we relaxed our maximum age limit because we did not want to turn away young women who wanted to talk with us. In hindsight, including these women granted us an important, critical perspective.

Implicit in many of the popular and scientific claims about girls' aggression, is the idea that girls' meanness and aggression leave long-lasting scars. Simmons (2002), for example, opens *Odd Girl Out* with her memories of being bullied by her friend Abby at the age of eight. "Sixteen years later …," Simmons (2002, 2) writes, "… I rode my bike to the library in search of answers about what had happened with Abby … The anguish of being abandoned by all of my friends and of losing my closest at Abby's hand felt real and raw. It was something that never receded gently with the rest of my childhood memories." Like Simmons, some of the young women in our study did not easily forget the emotional ups and downs of their adolescent friendships. Their stories—especially their descriptions of what it means to be a successful adult—allowed us, along with the participants, to put some of the developmental claims about mean girls into a larger perspective.

Another important component of our project was to recruit young women from a variety of ethnic, race, and class backgrounds and to render, as much as possible, the breadth of young women's friendship experiences. We allowed participants to self-identify and disclose as much or as little about their backgrounds as they wanted, again granting them control in sharing personal information with us. Hawaii's ethnic diversity came to our assistance in recruiting a broad spectrum of participants. Summarizing briefly, ten of the study members are Asian-American, eleven are European-American, two are Latina (one self-identifying as Puerto Rican and the other as Mexican), one is Native Hawaiian, and another is African-American. Two of the study participants call themselves "mixed-race" or "multi-ethnic," with one saying that she is Japanese and Caucasian and the other claiming to be Native American and Irish.

The class background of young women in our sample is slightly more difficult than ethnicity to assess, as socioeconomic status in Hawaii tends to be a sensitive topic of discussion.[3] We asked interviewees and focus group participants to describe their socio-economic or class status and their parents' occupation. From the responses we received, which ranged from extremely detailed to vague, we can estimate that six of the young women in the study were from working-class backgrounds, nineteen were middle class, and two young women volunteered that they came from privileged families.

Although we conducted many of our interviews in Hawaii, a location known for its unique geography and lifestyle, we wanted to include young women from many different areas of the country. This would allow us to derive a narrative that was not only true of the local Hawaiian experience, but was also inclusive of as many young women's experiences in the country as possible. Interviewees were from California (6), New York (2), Illinois (1), Texas (2), Montana (1), as well as Hawaii (9). Six participants moved during childhood, with two young women moving more than once. Combined, interviewees represent experiences in eleven different U.S. states.

To recruit interviewees, we used convenience and snowball sampling techniques. Out of convenience, we invited young women that we knew fairly well to participate in the study and then, relying on snowball sampling methods, asked interviewees to refer their friends to us. All of our recruitment procedures were approved by the University of Hawaii's Committee on Human Subjects. As university professors who regularly discussed gender and adolescence in our classes, we had developed considerable rapport with many young women who had taken our classes and with whom we kept in regular contact.[4] Despite the fact that we believed we had "good relationships" with many women from the campus as well as outside of the university, we had some concerns about recruiting current and ex-students. Our primary fear was that our professor status would make young women feel obligated to participate in the study or awkward when making personal disclosures. Although we perceived the young women in our lives to be very outspoken and open with us, we did not want to run the risk of creating an atmosphere of coercion. We took several steps to mitigate this.

We drafted written and verbal descriptions of the study that informed young women that their participation in the study was completely voluntary. Moreover, we described exactly what voluntary participation meant. We gave them written and verbal statements that they were free to not participate in the study for any reason. We explained that their refusal to participate would not change our opinion of them and that we would completely respect their decision. For those who did agree to be interviewed, we let them know (verbally and in writing) that they could refuse to answer any question or end the interview at any time. They could also contact us after the interview and ask us to delete any part or all of the information for any reason. This was their right, and, once again, we stated that we would respect their decision. The University of Hawaii's Committee on Human Subjects was also concerned about coercion during interviews and wanted us to inform students (verbally and in writing) that participation in the study could not count as extra credit for our classes. We were happy to oblige the committee in this regard. Our efforts to protect human subjects, however, went beyond satisfying the concerns of our institutional review board (IRB). We informed study participants that we wanted research participants to feel empowered enough to say "no" to any aspect of the research and that we wanted them to be in control of how much they wanted us to know about them and their lives. In fact, this is what prompted us to interview young adults rather than adolescents. We feared that youths too often feel that they do not have privacy when interacting with adults.

Despite these efforts, we remained reluctant to include current students in the sample. We waited until the end of the semester to ask students to participate in the study, and, on the few occasions that we contacted current students, we took advantage of the fact that there were two investigators on this study. Meda referred her current students to be interviewed by Katherine, and Katherine sent her students to Meda to conduct interviews. In addition, there were several women in the study who were not current or even ex-students, but who were recruited from our friendship networks with young women outside of the university or from referrals from friends at the university.

Interviews lasted between an hour and ninety minutes, depending upon how much time interviewees were willing to spend with us, and were conducted in a location of interviewees' choice. A few interviews were conducted in public locations and a few were conducted in interviewees' homes. Some participants preferred to conduct interviews at an office or an empty classroom on the University of Hawaii campus, probably for its central location and privacy. Focus groups, like one-on-one interviews, were conducted in a location of interviewees' choice. Focus groups, however, were longer and lasted ninety minutes, on average. Two focus groups were conducted in an empty classroom on the UH campus, and another was conducted in the home of one participant who invited two friends to join our discussion. Interviews and focus groups were tape recorded and later transcribed. We read the transcripts of each interview and focus group several times (a minimum of five times and as many as twenty times) and developed a coding scheme to capture the emerging common themes across interviews. We utilized the constant comparative, grounded theory approach (Glaser and Strauss 1967), which allowed us to identify common trends and to go back into the data to locate whether and how each participant in the study related to each of the core emerging themes. All identifying information was removed from the interviews when they were transcribed, and every member of the study was given a pseudonym. Although we use the real names for states and cities where interviewees were raised, all other places and people mentioned during interviews were given pseudonyms to protect participants' privacy.

Meanness as Experience and Hype

Most of the young women we interviewed agreed with the idea that mean girls are dangerous and damaging. It didn't take much coaxing or convincing to open the young women in our sample to the idea that girls are mean to other girls. Many, but certainly not all the girls we interviewed were quick to recount painful stories of female bullies. On the surface, the sheer number of these stories and the vivid memories they evoke seems to suggest that the mean girl phenomenon and all of the claims about it in the media is correct. There are mean girls in the world, their primary targets are other girls, and the pain and disappointment they inflicted have lingered even as young women enter adulthood.

It is important to note here that the identification of girls' aggression or "meanness" in the new millennium is, in actuality, not a revelation. Although the media appears to have "discovered" female bullying, the truth is that social scientists, working within what might be called the female competition paradigm, have documented for decades girls' emotional ruthlessness with their peers. Despite the prior existence of the female competition literature, young women in our study did not allude to these scientific works. They did not discuss their friendship heartbreaks in terms of cycles of popularity (Eder 1985), status maneuvers within cliques (Adler and Adler 1998, 1995; Adler, Kless, and Adler 1992), the transformation of popularity into power (Merten 1997), or even relational aggression (Bjorkvist 1994; Crick and Grotpeter 1995). Instead, they borrowed heavily from popular and contemporary images of "mean girls" promoted in books, movies, and news stories. For example, Violet,[5] an Italian-American in her junior year of college, said that she remains friends with the "Queen Bee" from her adolescence. Others called themselves the "odd girl out," or reported that their middle and high school experiences unfolded like a scene from *"Heathers,"* with their lives being run and ruined by very socially powerful girls. Their stories were usually punctuated with dramatic and almost teenage outbursts describing brushes with mean girls as "a living hell," "catastrophic," or "the end of the world." Violet recalled her experiences:

> I went to a Catholic school for 3 years. I came in as a 6th grader and everyone had gone from kindergarten to 8th grade together. I was like this taller, fully-developed girl. And everyone else hated me. They hated me for anything in the world. But then I was still friends with the popular girls but it was a different friendship. It's like they made your life a living hell.

Violet later describes these events:

> You couldn't just be friends with the guys in junior high. That was not allowed. I always had guy friends because I had brothers and a lot of guy cousins. And they would always say things about me like "She's probably hooking up with him." I had never kissed a boy or anything. They were always like suspicious and they would know right away that I was friends with boys … It was like I was the brunt of the jokes for the rest of the day. I think excluding girls is a really big thing that other girls did to each other. Excluding is the worst like the silent treatment, you know, she's over there by herself.

Katelin, a French-Portuguese college sophomore, born and raised in Hawaii, recalled a similar drama surrounding social exclusion at school and being horrified. In Katelin's case, it was one socially powerful girl who tortured her. She explains:

Well one day, she had a few people she didn't like. I don't remember what she did to them; but to me, she already had it all planned out. There was a table where we all sat at lunch. There weren't enough seats for all the girls. And so one girl had to sit with the boys and usually two would sit with the boys. On this day she had it all planned out so all the girls would sit at the [all-girl] table before I could get to it. So I had to sit with the boys. So it was just known that only one girl is sitting with the boys. Something was wrong with her. Now, it wouldn't be such a big deal, but back then it was HUGE. It was like such an event—Catastrophic.

Linda, a 26-year-old who was born and raised in southern California, described several incidents that were very similar to claims made in newspaper articles and books about mean girls, where wearing the wrong clothes to school leads to bitter social isolation. She said:

In high school, I was with this group of 8 to 10 girls. If you weren't friends with them then you were a loser. They wore the best clothes, had the coolest things at their houses, and everyone wanted to be their friend. And when you were their friend, they were so mean to you. Off and on, you would be completely torn down. One time, in my junior year of high school, I wore the same outfit as one of them. She was supposed to be my best friend. She went home crying that I wore the same thing as her and wanted me to go home to change. For the first time, I said "No, I'm not going home to change." So she ended up going home and changing. It was such a mistake that I made. I was like "I just woke up and got dressed. I didn't even think about it." But they used to go out to dinner and not invite me. And they used to just shut you out and ignore you. There would be a group standing there talking and you would walk up to them and they wouldn't even acknowledge that you were there.

These are just a few stories about girls' meanness. When asked about mean girls, interviewees came up with numerous such accounts although there were also important variations in the story. One young woman, for example, remembered how wearing the wrong type of shoes with her Catholic school uniform resulted in being taunted and ridiculed all day. In another more serious event, Ally, a 26-year-old who was born and raised in San Francisco, announced that her car was vandalized with the word "slut" written in lipstick on the car door panels—a sign warning her not to date a friend's ex-boyfriend.

In one case, meanness became violent. Vivian, a South Asian college senior, was a minority in her high school, which served an equal mix of African-American, Asian-American, and Latino students. She also experienced rather dramatic episodes of female bullying in high school. Because she had moved frequently in her young life—from New York to Louisiana, finally settling in California—she described feeling like a perpetual outsider wherever she and her parents lived. By high school, Vivian had embraced and cherished her outsider identity and found herself gravitating towards the "punk-rock" subculture in San Francisco. For $200, she purchased a friend's fifteen-year-old car, adorned with dozens of stickers of punk bands and which she described affectionately as a "barely legal" but roadworthy vehicle that would "get you where you needed to go." Although she loved the car, a group of older high school students, who also frequented punk shows, decided that Vivian and her friends were "invading" their punk rock scene. She reported that they ganged up together and yelled out names like "poser" and "bitch" at Vivian and Vivian's best friend, Susan. One of the girls in the rival peer group occasionally wore a T-shirt emblazoned with the slogan "Vivian Sucks" and these girls vandalized Vivian's cherished car. One night the tension between Vivian and this pack of female bullies mounted to a violent crescendo. In the following quote, she described what transpired after a show in downtown San Francisco:

> I was walking to my car, and usually I walk by myself. Luckily, it was me and two of my other friends and my friend's older brother. All of a sudden I get this big shove in my back, and I'm like "Oh my god, what is going on?" and then [names the mean girls] shoved me again. And one of the girls is just cussing and rambling on at me. I was at a loss. I didn't know what it was about. I was up against a fence and they were yelling at me. And out of nowhere, one of the girls swings and punches me. Someone grabbed her and pulled her away. Then they walked away. I was so mad. First, that hurt, and second, I didn't deserve that!

As Vivian's experiences illustrate, despite the "sugar and spice" mythology about girls, girls are capable of violence. Female bullying can, and occasionally does, erupt into physical altercations. The Glenbrook High School incident certainly attests to this fact, but it is important to note that such violent incidents are more common among boys than they are among girls (Federal Bureau of Investigation 2003). In fact, Vivian was the only person we interviewed who described mean girl bullying that turned into violence, but other research suggests that while girls' "meanness" does not necessarily predict physical aggression, most of girls' violence has a relational aggression component (Morash and Chesney-Lind 2006).

Like many of the young women we interviewed, Vivian described being deeply hurt by her experiences. The most difficult challenge for her was that she felt that she was physically and socially punished for "just being herself." Most of the interviewees who reported bullying experiences also described being wounded by these episodes. Many suggested that the pain continues to stay with them into their adult lives. For example, Ally argued that she was, eight years later, still haunted by the rejection of her high school best friends. She argued:

> These girls, I know where they all are now. Not to make judgments about their lives and the path that they have chosen, but according to the traditional "hallmarks" for a successful life, I graduated valedictorian of my high school. I went to an amazing law school. They all went to community colleges and are now working one step up from service industry jobs. You think that I could walk into my high school reunion with some confidence, but they haunt me. They have this power over me. There is not a week that goes by that they do not show up in my dreams. It is not about them anymore, it is about whatever they represent—somebody being able to just shun you and treat you terribly.

Erica, a 25-year-old who was born and raised on a small farm in Texas, also felt forever bruised by her best friend's rejection. She recalls her experiences:

> I encountered mean girls in fifth and sixth grade. Not so much in high school. I think that had more to do with me as a person. I stopped really making close connections with girls after a while. When I was in 5th and 6th grade often your biggest enemies are your best friends. One day

you'll be best friends and you would make a diary with them telling why they were your best friends and blah, blah, blah. And the next day, it would be different. I had this one friend, I went to stay at her house one night, the next day she held up this chalk board that said "I'm no longer your best friend." After that, I didn't really have any best friends.

According to Erica, the pain and anguish that she felt by a girlfriend's betrayal soured her towards female friendships. After this event, Erica preferred to spend time by herself and befriended boys instead of girls at school. Young women in the study frequently said that they mistrusted and kept their distance from other girls. Some girls were very critical of other girls' character and felt that many girls lacked the necessary traits to be "faithful friends." Hauʻoliʻipo, a Native Hawaiian and college sophomore, had more male friends than female friends during middle and most of high school. She explained that many of the girls in school were "too concerned about looks, body, and petty issues." In the following quote, she described what she liked about her male friends.

I actually hung out with all the boys. Because they were a little more chill. And it seems like the girls were more like, "Oh, look at me I'm so pretty." [The boys], you know, they are just up for anything. Just willing to not care about other people's expectations … It just helped me out because it gives me someone else's viewpoint. Understanding that it's not all about glitzy-glamour, the way you look, the makeup you wear, the type of shampoo you use. You know, that some guys, maybe not all guys, appreciate the inner side of the person too. It's not the way you walk and what you look like. It's what you have to say like how well you listen to them. And I guess I was able to see that they appreciate it.

Katelin agreed with Hauʻoliʻipo's assessments by noting that the popular girls in her school were too "into being 'pretty-pretty'." Red, a Mexican-American sophomore in college, called girls' peer groups "tiny traps" because girls focused on very minor issues in life. Similarly, Shane, a white college sophomore, said that all of the popular girls in school were overly obsessed with "hair and makeup issues." The theme echoed in these comments was that some girls, especially the socially powerful ones, were focused on superficial concerns and, thus, could not be trusted. Boys, on the other hand, were not petty, and, thus, were worthy friendship candidates.

By discussing the way that girls emotionally wound one another or their preference to be "one of the guys"[6] (see also, Macpherson and Fine 1995; Leblanc 1999; Miller 2001) rather than one of the girls, we are certainly not setting out to "discover" or even corroborate emotional aggression within and among children's and adolescents' peer groups. This has been more thoroughly investigated in the ethnographic peer group literature (see for example, Adler and Adler 1998, 1995; Adler, Kless, and Adler 1992; Best 1983; Canaan 1987; Corsaro 1985; Eder 1985; Fine 1987; Goodwin 2002; Kinney 1993; Merten 1997). Instead, our goal has been to allow young women to "talk back" to contemporary, popular constructions of girls' friendships, drawing particularly from their own experiences. What is interesting is the idea that young women borrowed heavily from popular culture discourse when discussing their earlier friendships, retrospectively applying current terminology and symbols to frame and interpret their past emotional lives. Here young women, many of whom considered themselves to be, if not "feminists," at least strong and independent women, seemed to collude with the contemporary negative press about girls. They were quick to berate girls, pathologize girl-culture by claiming long-term damage from their brushes with girlish bullying, and even to prefer the company of boys to girls.

Although this initially surprised us, maybe it should not have. The "girl bashing" sentiments expressed during our interviews cut to the heart of conventional beliefs that girls and women are untrustworthy. Being mean, nasty, petty, and entirely incapable of meaningful friendship is just one more mainstream message announcing how "bad" girls and women are. As Leblanc (1999) noted in her study, girls use several coping strategies to maintain positive self images in a world filled with derogatory messages about girls and young women. They make bargains with patriarchy (see also Kandiyoti 1998) by attempting to be "one of the guys" instead of a typical girl. Young women buy into the dominant negative generalizations precisely to exempt themselves from them. They announce to the world that they are trustworthy, capable, deep, wonderful people—completely unlike all those petty and shallow girls out there. Identifying and vociferously denouncing the mean girls in their lives is part of this bargain with patriarchy. They confirm negative stereotypes as a way of individually escaping them.

Supporting Girls

Although many of the girls in our study were quick to point out the inherent flaws in other girls, especially socially powerful ones, they also described having deep, supportive female friendships. While interviewees often protested that mean girls were "the worst" and "wrecked their lives," in reality, female bullies did not put them off from other girls forever. The majority of the young women in our study admitted that they had at least one, and often more than one, close and faithful female friend in their young lives. These girls were often described as being "true" or "real" friends. Although they were extremely critical of traditional female traits like preoccupation with appearance and popularity, the young women in our study noted that their best female friends were not at all like the typical mean girl. Here, young women not only separated themselves from the negative traits associated with mean girls, they also defended their girlfriends.

For example, during her junior and senior years of high school, Hauʻoliʻipo decided that girls were not so bad. She explained the events leading up to this realization:

> Yeah, it got a little different 'cause the boys that I hung out with actually liked the [popular] girls. So the group kind of broke down a little. But it was okay because that's how you'll know who your real friends are, who actually sticks with you through all these kinds of problems. Then I actually learned that some girls were cool. Some girls are fun to hang out with.

Erica, who preferred to spend time with boys rather than girls in school, had female family members with whom she spent much of her time. Ally never repaired the friendships she lost in high school, but she remained very close to her childhood girlfriends and went on to form close bonds with four women in college. At the time of our interview, Ally was helping her best friend of twenty-five years plan her wedding. After being hit by one mean girl, Vivian turned her attention away from the social politics at school and spent most of her time with her best friend, Susan. Vivian's friendship with Susan illustrates the important role that other girls played in interviewees' lives. Vivian's school experiences were stressful. Her parents had divorced, and, although her mother took the role of primary caretaker, Vivian did not feel that she could turn to her mom for help with her school problems. She explained:

> I didn't really interact with my mom a lot. I'm not really the type of girl who is best friends with her mother. I didn't tell her because she would try to get involved and come to the school and do something weird. After my car was vandalized, though, she was like "what is going on?" I tried to down-play it a lot. "Oh, it wasn't a big deal. These girls at school are really mad at me." I would try to tell my mom a lot of good things. "Oh, I still have a lot of friends. It's just this group of girls who don't like me." She was like a little concerned about that. She didn't know how serious it really was.

Susan became Vivian's primary support through this stressful stage in Vivian's life and, according to Vivian's accounts, Susan never let her down. Many young women described having similar unconditional support from girlfriends. For example, Jasmine, a Puerto Rican-American college sophomore, completely ignored the popular crowd in school. While they were embroiled in obeying the "rules" of popularity, including having to "dress right, talk right, walk right, date lots of guys," she took a different tack. She said, "I didn't really care. I just made it with a couple of friends that I had. They kept me grounded." While she was not at the top of the social hierarchy at school, Jasmine had close girlfriends who supported her. Because of their friendships, she didn't need or desire popularity.

A few girls in our study never experienced rejection or betrayal from friends. For a variety of reasons, they simply did not encounter any of the relational aggression described in the popular narratives about mean girls. Mia, a college junior and first generation Filipina, has remained close with a group of eight girlfriends from middle and high school. She recalled:

> They were open-minded as far as like trying to put themselves in the other people's shoes. Like if I had a boyfriend, I would want to spend time with him. Or if someone was having a bad day, we didn't take it so personally. It was not as if "she's not talking to us" or that kind of thing. We were a bit different. They weren't two faced. I guess each school has

like that category of girls who would just study and go home and the other girls who were the "scrubs" [the popular kids]. It's funny because we saw that [girls in the other groups] would turn their backs on each other. We were thankful that we were not in that kind of group.

As a first generation Filipina, Mia felt caught between her parents' cultural expectations, which they acquired while growing up in a small rural community in the Philippines, and mainstream American youth culture, which Mia experienced at school. Her girlfriends helped her cope with this "acculturative stress" (Soriano et al. 2004) and manage her complicated feelings about her family. She described how her girlfriends supported her:

> I remember back in elementary school I was kind of ashamed of my parents because they were different. So it was pretty tough. As I got older, I saw that I can be open with people. It's just that I couldn't really be open with my mom. I guess we are from different generations, different things going on so there was no middle ground. Open as far as like just being comfortable talking about girls' stuff. [My girlfriends played this role] and became family.

In their junior year of high school, two of her close friends, Angela and Nadine, began to drink heavily. Members of the group continued to support the two girls. They did not judge or exclude them, but they also did not abuse alcohol with them. Eventually, Angela and Nadine, in Mia's words, "worked through their issues" and stopped drinking. The group weathered that challenge as well as others, and at the time of our interviews they were still in contact with one another. Mia explained, "we always make a point to do something. A lot of the times just talking and like shopping ... have a dinner of all of us at one place. So that works out."

Susie, a 26-year-old African-American who was born and raised in Chicago, also belonged to a very tight-knit and supportive friendship group during adolescence. When asked if she had confronted any meanness or pettiness in high school, Susie explained that she had not. Her friends were very supportive of one another, they did not backstab, or gossip, or practice any of the mean girl maneuvers. Susie's friends, however, drank alcohol and smoked marijuana. They were also not interested in school. These girls made Susie feel special and gave her considerable attention. They listened to her problems and shared stories of their own lives at a time when she especially needed validation. Eventually, the group's drug use and lack of interest in school began to bother Susie, who had always wanted to go to college. She found that she could not prepare for college *and* remain friends with these girls. By her sophomore year in high school, she had dropped out of the group and, soon afterward, most of her former girlfriends dropped out of high school. Susie found herself alone at school and sad to have lost those friendships, but she filled her time with studying, hanging out with her best friend from the neighborhood, or with her extended family. Susie's narrative illustrates that adolescence can be complicated and challenging for a number of reasons that have nothing to do with the social politics of mean girls.

Large networks of female friends like Mia's and Susie's were relatively rare. Most of the young women in our study had just a few close girlfriends. Regardless of the size of friendship groups, there is an important message to take away from these stories of supportive and nurturing girlfriends. Female adolescent friendships are not always wrought with pettiness and meanness. While there were several examples of girls being mean to other girls, there were just as many stories of close female friends who provided the support necessary for girls to overcome multiple adolescent challenges. As Mia's and Vivian's accounts illustrate, girlfriends often became like "family," offering unconditional support and guidance in the face of very difficult challenges. Girls like Ally and Erica who had painful experiences with mean girls, also had one or two close female friends who buffered the effects of relational aggression.

In terms of existing research, the finding that girls can be nice lacks as much empirical novelty as the idea that girls can be mean. Long before researchers documented the competitive side of girls' friendships, there was what might be called the girls' connection tradition, in which researchers tended to focus on the conflict avoidance (Lever 1976; Miller, Danaher, and Forbes 1986) and the emotionally intimate, reciprocal, or connected relations among girls (Eder and Parker 1987; Gilligan 1982; Goodwin 1990; Griffiths 1987; Lambart 1976; McRobbie 1978; Nilan 1991; Taylor, Gilligan, and Sullivan 1995; Thorne 1994, 1986; Thorne and Luria 1986).

What is interesting about our findings is that, while interviewees had a common girl bashing language mirroring the media's mean girl hype, they lacked a discourse to describe the positive aspects of girlhood. More importantly, although they did not speak in terms of a "sisterhood" (see Lambart 1976), they claimed that their friends, like themselves, were different from typical girls. As we noted before, taking part in girl bashing, even by berating "mean girls," was a way for interviewees to distance themselves from the "taint" of femininity (see also Macpherson and Fine 1995). It seems that young women did more than save themselves from negative stereotypes of girlhood. They also attempted to rescue their friends from a feminine stigma and, therefore, they made collective bargains with patriarchy that reflected their emotional connections with particular girls.

Not the End of the World

Another emerging finding from our study is the fact that, despite the popular culture claims, girls' relational aggression does not destroy young women for life. True, young women frequently claimed that girls' meanness was "the worst," "hell on earth," or "catastrophic." And a few, like Ally, claimed that they continued to be haunted by their rejection by female peers. Women were sometimes quick to argue that other girls ruined their lives. This sentiment has contributed to a growing claim that girls' meanness is "intensely" destructive and is as destructive as boys' physical violence.

Although we do not want to diminish or dismiss young women's accounts, we do want to place girls' experiences in a larger context, one that looks at all of the problems that young women face as they navigate their way through adolescence. In the name of offering a holistic image of girls' experiences, we spent quite a bit of time probing beneath our interviewees' claims that mean girls were "the worst" and that female bullies "ruined their lives." What we found when we asked how they dealt with rejection and condemnation from female peers was that, in reality, female bullies did not destroy girls. Meanness did not drive girls into horrible risk-taking behaviors, nor did it propel them into the depths of depression.

Take Ally's case, for example. Although the mean girls she knew in high school still haunt her dreams, they have never been obstacles to her success. Ally was never wrecked, despite the gossip, the loss of close friends, and the vandalism to her car. She was named valedictorian of her high school, won numerous debate awards, gained admission to a top-ranked college, and went on to graduate from a prestigious law school. The summer before our interview, Ally had worked with a team of lawyers attempting to repeal death sentences given to juvenile offenders in Alabama. Ally was at the legal front lines of a national movement that, two years after her work in Alabama, ended in the 2005 *Roper v. Simmons* Supreme Court decision declaring the death penalty of juveniles to be cruel and unusual punishment. In addition to being academically and professionally accomplished, Ally was a vivacious, glowing, energetic, and very balanced young woman who was as passionate about her law career as she was about practicing yoga, eating healthily, and maintaining loving friendships. While girls' meanness did not help Ally on her road to dynamic womanhood, they certainly did not hold her back.

There are many such stories among young women we interviewed. Linda, who was rejected by the popular girls for showing up at school wearing the same outfit as a close friend, was, at the time of our interview, embarking on a filmmaking career and gaining considerable support and critical acclaim in Hollywood's independent film circuit. Erica, who shied away from female best friends after being rejected in the 5th grade, had just been admitted to a highly reputable fine art school. Vivian, who was physically victimized by high school girls, was finishing her undergraduate degree in Women's Studies and had just completed a senior honors thesis analyzing the perceived credibility of male and female news anchors. She described her long-term goals as follows: "I hope to get my PhD, but getting life experience, that is very important too. Making a difference and going into a non-profit organization. That would be the stuff that I am into. If I traveled the world, furthered my education, and made a difference in something, not just making myself more money, but volunteering or helping others."

Although some interviewees claimed to have been devastated by relational aggression, the majority of young women in the study expressed thankfulness for their experiences. Mean girls taught these young women important "life lessons." Katelin explained how she learned to choose friends carefully:

> I never felt like I could be one of the popular girls in elementary and middle school so when high school came, [I thought] so maybe I can. But it didn't work. [Why not?] Just you can feel the vibes. Like most of them were pretty nice. There was a few, there was one I was good friends with. She was actually pretty mean. But I finally got sick of it. It wasn't worth it anymore to try and be friends with somebody who wasn't going to be nice to me when there was a whole group of people that wanted to be my friend and wanted to hang out with me.

Katelin attended an elite, private high school in Hawaii that was generally believed to be highly "socially competitive," meaning that there was a strict hierarchy of cliques and a rigid line dividing the "in" from the "out" groups (see Adler and Adler's 1998 analysis of this dynamic). When she realized that the popular crowd was not going to appreciate her, she left the group and joined another group of girls who treated her very well. Not only do Katelin's experiences attest to the fact that mean girls do not "ruin" their victims—in fact, Katelin seemed to be hardly affected by her high school experiences—but they also show that girls have healthy and supportive peer groups available to them.

Simone, a fourth-generation Japanese-American college junior, was one of the popular girls in school. Her busy schedule of playing soccer, hanging out with her sister, and studying did not allow her much time to become embroiled in the politics in the popular crowd—who she admitted would gossip about and do mean things to other girls. She explained what she learned from her high school experiences:

> Yeah, people will lie and people will put you down to get ahead of you. And if you deal with that when you are younger, I think it would be easier for a person. If you get through it when you are younger, you can definitely get through when you are older because you don't need them as much as you think you needed them back then. To get through school, you needed to be a part of that group. When you are older, you can be a loner. So, it just teaches you that you don't need a lot of people

in your life. You just need the people who will keep you safe. And that was like the biggest thing. You know, I need people to keep me sane.

She kept the interpersonal dynamics in her clique at a distance and, looking back, feels that it taught her an important lesson about who to trust as an adult. An equally important lesson that Simone expresses is that not everyone will "lie and put you down to get ahead of you." There will be people, men and women, who are "safe."

Vivian, who experienced the most dramatic form of female aggression in our sample, explained why she was not deeply wounded by her experiences:

> I guess it depends on how much you let it affect you. I just try to push it aside and it was like a 3 or something. But, like, for people in a society where high school is everything, it might have been a 10. It might have really scarred me for life. But where I grew up, it didn't really matter. There was no popular crowd. Everyone had something to do outside of school. So, who cares! I was happy with my one friend in school. If I was in a setting where there wasn't as much to do, maybe in a small town with not much to do and where high school is everything, it would have been a lot harder. It hasn't scarred me that badly. Yeah, that sucked, but now I can laugh about it and talk about it and be like "yeah, I got through that. I had a tough time in high school, but I learned so much."

Later in the interview, she suggested that her experiences strengthened her character:

> You just have to rise above that. I feel that I'm a strong person. What if I wasn't such a strong person? What if I had let this get to me? What if I dropped out of high school? What if I was one of those emotionally unbalanced girls who tried to commit suicide, or cut myself, or starve myself? Luckily, I was more independent and strong minded. Had this happened to a weaker person, they could have bent the other way and let it ruin their lives. I never even thought about that. I have friends who were suicidal and I have emotionally unbalanced friends. The littlest things happen and they are so upset. I'm like "get over it. Life is unfair. Bad stuff is going to happen." I feel that I can get over it a lot easier having gone through that. I don't feel that I needed all that, but it definitely made me a stronger person and made me think about being nicer to others.

These accounts give a vivid image of girls' resilience and highlight some of the forces that help girls become strong and happy young women. As Ally's, Vivian's, and Simone's experiences illustrate, being popular was not the only game in town for many girls. All three were extremely active and had diverse interests. Simone was an outstanding athlete in high school and college and had a very dynamic and rewarding family life. Vivian, who did not spend much time with her family, had many interests outside of school, including music and cultural events in San Francisco. When confronted with friendship challenges, these young women had many other social opportunities and activities in which to participate. Vivian's comment that she might have been seriously wounded by her experiences if "she was in a setting where there wasn't much to do" speaks volumes about gender specific challenges for girls. If being "popular" is the only opportunity for achievement in young women's lives, then meanness might in fact ruin girls' lives forever. The problem, however, is not girlish cruelty. The problem is that all too often popularity is held up as the pinnacle of success for girls. The solution is not to "fix" girls and make them less mean. The solution is to offer girls the opportunity to achieve success in a variety of activities. It is important to note here that activities for girls should reach beyond traditionally feminine extracurricular pursuits such as cheerleading or pompom (see Merten 1997), which set girls up in a semi-sexualized spectacle (Bettis and Adams 2006) at the periphery of boys' athletics. Moreover, activities and extracurricular pursuits for girls should not reinforce traditional feminine double-standards, where girls are encouraged to be what Schwartz and Merten (1980) call "seductive virgins" who receive attention and empowerment in ways that ultimately reinforce girls' status as the subordinate sex (see also Orenstein 1994; Thorne 1994).

Placing the problem of mean girls within the larger context of girlhood, as these interviews did, reveals that girls' meanness towards other girls does not destroy young women. Indeed, despite the lack of diverse opportunities for them to achieve (relative to the number available to young men), girls did find important ways to develop unique skills and stand out. Our sample included young women who excelled in debate, academics, sports, writing, dance, and fine art. They were active in religious groups, school clubs, family networks, and community and grassroots organizations. Because of these involvements when our respondents were snubbed, insulted, or lost their best friends, it was hardly the end of the world. It was painful, yes, but they had a variety of other activities (and friendships) from which they gained rewards, satisfaction, and meaning (see also Kinney 1993).

The mean girl narrative is not only blind to the real issues behind female bullying, but it is also, frankly, derogatory to girls. It suggests that being "liked" is the lynchpin of every young woman's existence. It assumes that girls who experience rejection lose all self-esteem and become completely unraveled. It subscribes to images like those Vivian described: the weak victim who might have "dropped out of school," "tried to commit suicide," or "cut" or "starved herself" as a result of female bullying. What the mean girl claims are really saying is that we have a nation of girls who are so imbalanced that they will engage in any number of self-destructive behaviors if they lose close friends or find themselves to be unpopular. This was certainly not the case in our study. Some girls were deeply hurt, but their phenomenal personal resources helped them recover. Instead of ending their lives, these events were often viewed as learning experiences and helped girls hone their ability to choose supportive girlfriends. To say that meanness ruins girls does not give enough credit to girls' very good sense and their ability to confront and rise above challenges.

It is common to find numerous underestimates of girls' resilience. It has also become common to overestimate the power of female bullies. Girls disproportionately experience the self-destructive behaviors that Vivian described (cutting, starving, and depression). The blame for these behaviors, however, lies more with the limitations of a society that privileges maleness than with the betrayals and meanness of female peers. The cause of some girls' depression and self-destructive behaviors is not the betrayal of female peers. It is the betrayal of society that places numerous limitations on girls. In chapters 4 and 5, we explore these limitations as well as the societal tendency, aided and abetted by the media, to blame the problems of girlhood on girls themselves.

The media's concern with mean girls diverts attention away from more fundamental problems in and surrounding girlworld. It focuses on the micro dynamics within peer groups and ignores the larger gender expectations structuring girls' lives and relationships. Moreover, it is entirely uncritical of "popularity" and "niceness" as expectations placed on girls (see also Merten 1997). The problem is not meanness, nastiness, and pettiness among girls. As many of the young women in our sample described, people can be mean. This is one of life's many lessons. The ethnographic literature on peer groups demonstrates that boys as well as girls exclude, negatively label, gossip about, insult, or are otherwise "mean" to their peers (Adler and Adler 1995; Best 1983; Eder and Enke 1991; Fine 1987; Kinney 1993). Why, then, should girls' meanness and not boys' raise so many eyebrows and become the focus of so much negative popular attention? Why are books about mean girls so popular? Similarly, why is the discovery that girls can be aggressive and occasionally violent (Crick et al. 1999; Prothrow-Stith and Spivak 2005), as opposed to kind and nurturing be so newsworthy?

It is because the rules of the game seriously disadvantage girls. If they conform to feminine ideals such as being kind to everyone and attractive, they are negatively labeled as shallow creatures who are overly concerned with popularity and appearance. And if they reject or challenge these impossible feminine goals, they are "fat cows," "bitches," or "mean girls." Even covert social skills, like the ability to recognize and deploy indirect aggression, is demonized in girls while in the adult male world, it is seen as an extremely clever political strategy (think Karl Rove). In a world where people are regularly nasty to one another, it is girls who become the focus of our attention and the subject of books, television shows, and newspaper articles. For girls, it shows clearly and poignantly that the game is rigged against them.

Bigger Problems in Girl-World: Sexual Victimization, Racism, and Exclusion

While we failed to find any evidence of girls destroying other girls with their meanness, we did discover a devastating story about racism and race-based exclusion within and between peer groups. We also heard one story of serious sexual victimization (despite the fact that the study did not solicit such information).

Candidly, the stories of relational aggression, gossip, and meanness among girls, although painful, paled in comparison to the stories from girls of color who recounted a different type of exclusion, one that centered on racial and ethnic tensions. Casey, a mixed Japanese and white woman described never being accepted by the upper-middle-class, white, popular girls in school. The popular girls referred to her as "Jap." The underlying message that Casey took from this derogatory moniker was that she was Asian and, therefore, different from popular white students. She would always be a target for their ridicule. This was a common story among girls of color who attended schools where European-American students made up half or more of the student body. In such environments, being white was one attribute necessary to enter the popular crowd. Being white, however, was often not enough as Katelin confirmed when she described the popular students in her high school:

> Little white girls ... we actually called the popular girls "the blondes." That was like a requirement. You had to be a blonde to be a part of them ... All the really thin ones. The ones who, to me looking back, were way more mature like physically and just active like wearing makeup. Just a lot sexier when they shouldn't have been.

To be included in the intimate inner workings of the elite crowd in Katelin's high school, you had to fit a particular physical ideal—one, in fact, that would be difficult for all but a very few girls to attain. Here feminine double standards combine with class, race, and ethnic inequalities. As researchers have previously documented, physical attractiveness can determine a girl's place within the female social hierarchy—what Artz (2004) calls the "pretty power hierarchy." Being pretty, however, is not a universal or an objective trait. To some degree, it can be purchased by those with the resources to do so. As Adler and Adler (1998) found among their sample of popular pre-adolescents, wearing designer clothing and using and talking about particular grooming products was a norm among popular girls. Other research has confirmed the idea that grooming issues are salient topics among popular female crowds (Eder and Parker 1987; Thorne 1994), which further illustrates the idea that expensive status symbols can be markers of female beauty in adolescents' world.

Where the purchasing behaviors common among popular girls set clear economic boundaries between in and out groups, physical beauty norms, to some degree, determined the race and ethnic make-up of elite crowds. Some dimensions of beauty can be purchased, others cannot. In many segments of American society, light skin and hair remain enduring beauty standards, and in predominantly white social settings, these beauty standards seemed to dictate who was considered attractive enough to be popular and who was not. Katelin's description of "the blondes" who were thin and sexy demonstrates that, in her school, the popular girls were all fair-skinned and slim. Probably because of two traits (being thin and blonde), they were viewed as physically attractive. Obviously, the blonde norm among the elite social group in Katelin's school made it difficult for girls of color to enter this elite crowd just as the thin norm made it impossible for girls of average or above average body weight to enter the group. The image presented here is that it is a very limited number of girls who had the financial resources and physical features for popularity.

Jasmine, a Puerto Rican-American college sophomore who was born and raised in Queens, New York, illustrated what it was like for girls of color in predominantly white schools. Jasmine attended a middle school made up mostly of African-American and Latino students. She described the social environment as friendly and easygoing, but eventually she transferred to a suburban high school serving a wealthy, white community. Though she had been a vibrant, outgoing girl in middle school, she became quiet and isolated in the nearly all-white high school. She recalled, "In middle school, everybody knew each other. You don't hang out with them, but you always say 'hi' and 'bye' to each other. If we didn't hang out it was okay. In high school, you wouldn't say 'hi' to that person. It's like 'oh, I don't know you.' They were more snobby in high school than in middle school." Jasmine noted that the popular girls in high school were white cheerleaders and homecoming queens. When asked who the unpopular kids were, she said, "they were mostly other ethnicities."

Jasmine didn't necessarily experience the bullying and "meanness" described in popular books. She did not find herself embraced by the popular girls one day, only to become the brunt of jokes and mockery the next day. She and other non-white girls were never accepted into the popular crowd and, according to Adler and Adler's (1998) research on adolescent peer dynamics, comprised one among the many "middle-friendship circles" that existed outside of popularity quests. As the Adlers (1998, 93) noted, though members of middle-friendship circles are not in the popular crowd, "they derived significant security from the loyalty of their friends." Race-based exclusion, like that in Jasmine's case, represents a definitive trend in our data. In schools where whites were a majority, girls of color quickly learned that they did not meet the criteria for high social status.

Of course, many white students also fell short of the standards for popularity. But what made Jasmine's experience different was that she and other girls of color were simply "not acknowledged." She was not treated amicably during face-to-face interactions and later ridiculed and derided. None of the popular students would say "hi" or "bye" to Jasmine. They didn't even acknowledge her existence. In contrast, her middle school experiences were characterized by much more interaction among racial and ethnic groups. Members of Puerto Rican or African-American peer groups would acknowledge one another and were "cool" with each other, meaning that they exchanged small expressions of respect for one another even if they did not spend time together. Not so in her predominantly white high school. The popular students were not "cool" with her. It is important to note that Jasmine didn't mind being on the social sidelines. She had her own friends, who were trustworthy and faithful. She spent her time carefully in high school by preparing for college and spending time with her family after school and on the weekends. Looking back, she said that she was glad that she put her energy into her academic rather than her social life at school.

Red, a Mexican-American college freshman who was born and raised in Southern California, attended a high school that was half white and half Mexican-American. She described her high school as being wrought with racial tension between white and Mexican-American students. She explained, "There was a lot of segregation in our school. That was the only bad thing. We had two cities that were brought to this one school. And one city is predominantly white and the other one is predominantly Mexican. So you have a total clash and there was a split down the school." Except for the occasional fight between Latino and white students, students honored the rigid race-line by keeping their distance from one another and not venturing into the other group's territory.

As the only Latina in mostly white, college preparatory and advanced placement classes, Red entered enemy territory every day, making herself unpopular with Latina and white students alike. She said, "I had trouble with my friends who would say 'Oh, look at you, think you are better than us.' And then I'm here with this other group of classmates who were just like, 'You're not as good as us.' So it made high school a little stressful." Later in the interview, Red recounted one event that was more than a little stressful. It made her seriously doubt whether she should go to college. She explained:

> There was one incident that I can remember when we went on a field trip to go and look at universities. And it was for an AP [advanced placement] class that I had. We were walking around and went to this one university that was nearby our high school. The lady giving the tour was saying, "Oh, I'm proud of you guys to come to this school, but as you can see, not many Mexicans make it. It's sad to say, but their culture is all about raising kids." So the other students were laughing. And they were like [to me] "You there, you go and do what you are supposed to do." It was disappointing 'cause you hear these remarks and then you get to think, is that the way it is actually supposed to be? Am I supposed to be like that? Then I began to second-guess myself. What am I supposed to do? I want to go to college, but is that right?

After that, Red decided that she could not apply to any college or university lacking a diverse student body, no matter how prestigious and renowned its education. Happily, she eventually enrolled in a racially heterogeneous university and, although she felt much more comfortable in that environment, she was still haunted by past racism in the classroom. She said, "Even now in college, 'cause in high school I never liked to speak up, because whatever I said it would be shut down. So now in college, I still don't like to speak up. That fear of someone always jumping on what you're going to say. Even if what I had to say was right, they would find some way that made it sound like it was wrong."

This type of exclusion and meanness extends beyond the mean girl phenomenon. It has nothing to do with rallying for popularity points and jockeying for greater social prestige by befriending and then betraying your female peers. It is nothing other than racism and the perpetuation of larger racial inequalities. Although played out through the same mechanisms of mean girls' popularity contests, namely through face-to-face interactions among classmates, it is much more damaging than relational aggression and problematic to students' future success and to school climates. The discovery of female bullying and mean girls diverts attention away from more pressing school-based problems, ones rooted in larger social inequalities, but that are played out, like female aggression, in school yards and classrooms across the nation. The problem in some school climates is not that girls are mean to other girls. The problem is racism and the way it interacts with sexism and classism in our schools to limit the opportunities available for all girls.

While most of the young women we interviewed suggested that the girl-on-girl meanness they experienced was "the worst," "catastrophic," or "life ending," in fact, these exclamations were nothing more than ironic commentary illustrating how important it seemed at the time and, once looking back, how insignificant these events really were. This is not the case, however, among students who experienced race-based social exclusion. Racism was not described as "hell on earth" and discriminatory events were not moments when "life seemed to end." Even Red downplayed the seriousness of her high school experiences when she described the racial tensions in her high school as being "a little stressful." To exclaim in youthful jargon that racism was "the worst" would have betrayed the pervasiveness and severity of racial inequalities in young women's lives.

Racism was a grave problem for some of the girls of color that we interviewed. It did not begin during or end after middle or high school. And it was not confined to school yards, classrooms, or peer groups. As some interviewees explained, the racist treatment by school personnel and students exemplified the attitudes, behaviors, and barriers that they would encounter throughout their lives. In this way, racism at school initiated students to an adult world wrought with race- and ethnically-based segregation, inequality, and negative stereotypes. It made these young women second-guess whether white women and men would ever accept them in the colleges, universities, and occupations that confer prestige in mainstream America. It also made them wonder, as in Red's case, whether they "should," or even wanted to, venture onto white people's "turf."

At the same time that the racism and classism in young women's lives was a salient but largely ignored force in many of their narratives, April's story illustrates how sexual victimization experienced by girls is also overlooked. April, a 25-year-old Native-American and Irish girl from Chicago is still traumatized by her sexual abuse at the hands of her pastor. While stopped at a stoplight, she tried to tell her father, "This guy touches me," when her father interrupted her and said "You shouldn't talk that way." Silenced by his unwillingness to hear her, the molestation went on for "several more years." April's anger at her parents is still very palpable, even though her abuser is now in prison for having "tried to rape his granddaughter." "My parents knew this was happening ... nobody stood up for me." April told us, though, that she went to therapy as a result of her experience, and that "I'm never going to tell my father that I didn't love him." She also has been dogged by years of anger and guilt over the experience, and she still feels "It is hard for me to talk about that stuff ... I didn't get to know myself" as a result of it. Her main wish for other girls is that "they need a place to feel safe, to be listened to." "Being heard is the most important thing ... and girls have a really hard time being taken seriously." While April dealt with the trauma of being abused, it was her family's refusal to believe her that deeply wounded her. Though she has reconciled with her father, the desire to be heard and believed inspired her to seek a degree in Women's Studies because she "liked working in a gender-specific environment."

Conclusion

Are girls really mean and competitive in their relationships? Do they alternate between building up and tearing down their peers as they try to survive the cycles of popularity (Eder 1985)? Conversely, are girls supportive, kind, and nurturing to one another, extending their allegiance and intimate trust to their friends? Our answer is that both perspectives of girlhood are accurate. In fact, popular culture images of mean girls, as well as the literature on girls' peer groups, reveals a false dichotomy in how we have imagined and theorized girlhood. The truth is that girls are sometimes competitive, manipulative, and unkind and sometimes cooperative, supportive, and deeply connected. They can also express every trait between the artificial divides of meanness/kindness, competition/cooperation, and independence/interconnection. It is time for our research and popular discourse to embrace the complexity of girls' lives and represent girls within a holistic, dynamic, and multidimensional vision. We draw from Barnett and Rivers' *Same Difference* (2004) thesis to suggest that we need a science that understands girls and boys, not in terms of false dichotomies ratifying gender differences, but in terms of a complex and fully human repertoire of experiences and possibilities.

This research is our modest attempt to represent girls in a complex light, as capable of deep connection with, as well as contempt for, other girls. By borrowing the concept of making bargains with patriarchy (Kandiyoti 1998; LeBlanc 1999), we found that young women did not experience a "sisterhood" per se. They did not see all other girls as allies and "sisters" in the struggle against male domination. In fact, they were quick to berate girls who were too feminine as well as those who broke the rules of femininity. Underlying their dislike for girls and preference to be "one of the guys," however, were deep bonds with girls and their efforts to save their girlfriends, and not just themselves, from the stigma associated with being a traditional "girl." This analysis goes beyond stating that girls gain connection with specific girlfriends by ganging up on female outsiders (see Canaan 1987; Campbell 1984; Griffiths 1995). It suggests that girls are interconnected and collective, although on a small scale, in their efforts to resist the constraints of femininity (see also Currie, Kelly, and Pomerantz 2006).

More important than arguing for multidimensional representations of girls, however, we suggest that the popular discourse about mean girls has trickled into and connected with young women's vilification of girls and girlhood. Society's hatred of girls, as evidenced in numerous derogatory images of femininity, did not begin with the mean and aggressive girl hype (see Macpherson and Fine 1995; Griffiths 1995). However, it is important to note that this hype has provided young women with a specific and negative discourse to vent their frustrations and conflicting feelings about girls. The idea that girls are untrustworthy, manipulative, and underhanded in their competition with other girls is summed up in a powerful popular concept: girls' meanness. Sadly, in the dominant mean girl imagery, young women lack an alternative, but equally relevant language, to discuss the many positive aspects of girlhood. They do not have a language to understand that girls can be trustworthy and supportive friends, or that boys as well as girls can be mean. As Adler and Adler (1995, 159) note, compared with girls in their sample, "… boys are no less skilled at intricate emotional woundings and manipulations." Though this finding breaks the myth about boys' poor verbal and emotional interpersonal skills, it is not big news and has failed to generate a hype about mean boys. Given the pervasive disparagement of girls, it makes sense that girls and young women say that they would like to be "one of the guys," although few of the young women in our study sought emotional refuge in boys' company. And those few who did seek it, sadly, did not find it.

The media focuses on a limited aspect of female behavior (meanness and aggression), but ignores the larger societal context within which girls operate. This larger context would become clear once researchers, journalists, and practitioners gaze not just at girls' meanness, but the socio-cultural and institutional conditions surrounding the rules of popularity for girls (for an example, see Merten 1997; Brown 2003). Certainly our interviews document that girls' relational aggression is a real part of growing up female. We would suggest that anyone seeking to document girls' meanness towards other girls will certainly find corroborating evidence. What we argue here is that failing to look at girls' behaviors as well as the context in which these behaviors emerge not only pathologizes girls, but produces a discourse that ratifies the tendency for girls and society to hate girls and girlhood.

In addition, while investigators can find girls' meanness and relational aggression if they look for it (they can also find boys' meanness if they look), we argue that girls' relational aggression, while hurtful, is not the only or even the most significant harm a girl can experience. Young women of color told us about how institutional racism at school, which seemed to aid and abet a rigid race line between peer groups, kept them alienated from the educational opportunities afforded to white students. Combining the story of institutional racism with the one unsolicited narrative of sexual abuse offers a vivid reminder that girl-world is a complex terrain. Given the many pitfalls, especially those presented to girls of color, we wonder whether girl-on-girl aggression merits the attention that it has been given. Moreover, we wonder why the institutional arrangements and structures within and around the schools remain uninterrogated and unexamined in popular discourse. We especially lament the fact that girls' aggression continues to sell movie tickets and books, when the informal and formal education system regularly limits the availability of a wide range of extracurricular activities for girls, reinforces the idea that girls of color are better suited to raise children than to attend college, does nothing to alleviate obvious racial tensions at school, or fails to act when college prep classes are filled with white students, while students of color find themselves on an alternate path. Given these many problems in girls' lives, we wonder why we currently have a nation obsessed with fixing girls' aggression and relational bullying.

4

GROWING UP FEMALE: FAMILIES AND THE REGULATION OF GIRLHOOD

Girlhood, once largely an ignored and certainly under-researched social category (Lynn 1979), was suddenly the subject of avid public and academic discussion as we left the old and entered the new millennium (Inness 1998; Leadbeater and Way 1996; Brown 2003). Virtually all of the media attention during this period focused on negative attributes of girls, such as their alleged "meanness" and "badness," as we noted in chapter 2. Fortunately, though, that is not necessarily the case with the academic and policy literature which actually began to both focus on the unique aspects of growing up female and also began talking to and, more importantly, listening to, girls.

Research on girls' development and girls' lives, while still sparse, is finally developing into a body of work worth discussing. Much of this improvement is due to the appearance of Carol Gilligan's influential book, *In a Different Voice* in the early eighties. In this work, Gilligan (1982) argued powerfully for a different approach to girls' development. Initially, her work was confined to a rather narrow discussion of the evidence that the "moral" reasoning of girls and boys differed when confronted with difficult "scenarios." She argued that in thinking about these moral dilemmas, girls were more likely to use "an ethic of care" and boys to use "an ethic of justice" (Gilligan et al. 1982, 174). More importantly, though, her work stressed the need to listen to girls' voices and to begin to study girls' and women's experiences "in women's own terms" (Gilligan et al. 1982, 173; see also Gilligan et al. 1988).

A decade later, as we will discuss at length in a future chapter, the American Association of University Women undertook a landmark study of the treatment of girls in schoolrooms across the United

States. "Shortchanging Girls, Shortchanging America" (1991), while focusing on school's treatment of girls, also documented a dramatic drop in girls' self-esteem as they leave childhood and enter adolescence. While some of these findings, particularly with regard to the importance of self-esteem, per se, have been in dispute (Mahaffy 2004), the AAUW study itself set the stage for other more qualitative assessments of girls' lives, particularly girls' loss of "voice" in adolescence (Brown and Gilligan 1992), girls' problems with depression and food (Pipher 1994), girls' relationships to their bodies and their sexuality (Brumberg 1997), girls' relationships with aggression and fighting (Brown 2003), girls' experiences in school classrooms and playgrounds (Thorne 1994; Orenstein 1994), and the emergence of girl culture studies (Harris 2004).

These approaches to girlhood were a significant departure from a nearly exclusive focus on girls' sexuality and, particularly, "out of wedlock" births (Males 1996) that characterized much of the discussion of girls, if they appeared at all, in the policy work of the last half of the twentieth century. While this is clearly an important part of growing up female, until Deborah Tolman (1994) the near exclusive focus on girls' reproductive status, coupled with both a silence of any discussion of girls' desire, and the absence of any concern about boys' sexuality and parenthood is striking from a distance. Indeed, a current review of articles on girls and sexuality done for another project (Chesney-Lind, forthcoming) reveals that the bulk of material appearing even now, focuses on girls as potential parents, not a very long walk from Napoleon's old adage that women were simply "machines for producing children."

Within criminology, the focus on gender and crime has finally escaped its narrow confines and has begun to integrate literature on girls' development, particularly girls of different ethnic groups as well as girls from different social classes and the relationship between those experiences and girls' problems with the law. Initially the literature was trapped in simplistic notions that the second wave of feminism has caused an increase in girls' and women's offending (see Chesney-Lind and Shelden 2004 for a review of this literature), but this interest was refocused by the appearance of ethnographic work on girls in gangs (Chesney-Lind and Hagedorn 1999; Laidler and

Hunt 2001; Miller 2001; Moore 1991). Finally, with the passage of the 1992 reauthorization of the JJDPA Act, monies were set aside to allow states to do planning for gender specific approaches to delinquency in their states (Chesney-Lind 2000). As a result, many states began to construct profiles of the girls in their systems, and also to undertake "gender specific" or "gender responsive" programming (Chesney-Lind and Belknap 2004). But to do good programming for girls, particularly girls on the margins requires that we know what sorts of problems girls encounter as they grow up in a society that tends, particularly in childhood, to celebrate masculinity and control femininity.

Gender in Girlhood

All children are deeply affected by their gender. For example, some theorists suggest that by the age of two, rudimentary psychological gender identity has been formed and children are already perceiving the association of particular behaviors, traits, activities, and occupations with women or men (Money, Hampson, and Mapson 1957; Kuhn, Nash, and Brucken 1978; Cowan and Hoffman 1986). By preschool or first grade, children are well aware of their gender, stereotype one another's gender activities, know which parents they are most like, have a thorough knowledge of gender stereotypes, and know the gender of family members and peers (Fagot 1984; Lott 1987). Obviously, there are developmental stages in the socialization process, and by adolescence, the experience of gender in shaping girls' lives and options may be increasingly external. Katz, for example, has suggested three stages in gender development: learning what is appropriate behavior for a male or female child, acquiring concepts about what is appropriate as a potential male or female adult, and behaving in ways that are deemed appropriate for male and female adults through the life span (Katz 1979, 9).

Distinct things happen in the lives of young people during early and late adolescence, periods that Katz (1979) suggests are preparing youths for adult roles. In early adolescence, these concern adjusting to puberty and sexual feelings, and greater reliance on peers than on teachers or parents as sources of information about the world.

By late adolescence, each sex has acquired an interest in the other, but the effect of the differential futures available to males and females is already being felt. Indeed, even by the end of grade school, girls begin to evaluate themselves more negatively than do boys (Loeb and Horst 1978; Silvern 1978; Katz 1979).

What of girls and their families during the crucial period of adolescence? Perhaps not surprisingly, little is known about this dimension of girls' experiences. Block (1984, 73) notes that "the differential socialization hypothesis has been examined primarily (and for some areas exclusively) in samples of parents whose children were six years old and under." In her review of socialization studies, only 23 percent examined the socialization patterns of parents with older children. She believes this to be a significant omission because parents are likely to be less extreme in their socialization practices in the early years, with their "offspring ... treated more as children than as boys and girls" (Block 1984, 72). Specifically, she thinks that certain areas (notably achievement emphasis, tolerance for sexuality) have not become salient for differential socialization, and other areas' (dependency and aggression) tolerances have not become strained.

Block's now classic and unique studies were designed to rectify this oversight. One was a longitudinal study initiated in 1968. It focused on ego and cognitive development from the preschool period to late adolescence. For example, she examined parental self-reports as well as young adults' perceptions of their parent's child-rearing practices (the 17 independent samples included responses from 696 mothers, 548 fathers, and 1,227 young adults). In general, she found clear evidence of differential socialization of males and females; that the gender-related socialization emphases are appreciably consistent when viewed from differing perspectives; evidence of consistency of parent and sex-of-child effects; and, most important, some evidence that "sex differentiation in socialization emphases appears to increase with the age of the child, reaching a maximum during the high school years." Such a pattern was also suggested by Maccoby (1966), particularly as it touches on the greater restrictiveness imposed on girls.

Looking specifically at the parent-daughter relationship, Block (1984, 88) noted that it is characterized by "greater warmth and physical closeness." Both parents have more confidence in the "trustworthiness and truthfulness" of their daughters than of their sons, and there is a greater expectation by mothers and fathers alike of "ladylike" behavior on the part of daughters. Both parents expressed a reluctance to punish girls, and daughters more than sons were encouraged to "wonder and think about life." Interestingly, mothers' child-rearing practices are more sex differentiated with respect to restrictiveness and supervision of their daughters than their sons. Restrictive parental behavior, according to Block, was associated with "parental anxiety, worry, and concern about the misfortunes that can befall young women as they grow up" (Block 1984, 89).

Sons, by contrast, were encouraged in achievement, competition, and independence. Both parents also encouraged boys to "control the expression of affect," and there was more of a punishment orientation in parents of males. Fathers tended to be more authoritarian with their sons than with their daughters; they reported they were more strict and firm, that they believed in physical punishment, and that they were less tolerant of sons' aggression when it was directed against them. Fathers more than mothers also encouraged the assumption of personal responsibility in their sons. Mothers encourage sons, more than daughters, to conform to external standards (Block 1984, 87).

In a review of her own longitudinal study, plus the work of others, Block found that "boys, more than girls, are reared in ways encouraging curiosity, independence, and exploration of the environment." In contrast, the more restrictive child-rearing practices used by parents of girls (emphasis on physical proximity, expectations of "ladylike" behaviors, close supervision, and provision of help in problem-solving situations) lessen the opportunity for girls to engage in active experimentation with the environment, to encounter discrepancies, and to engage in solution efforts (Block 1984, 275–276).

In one of the most stark examples of this circumstance, Block and her associates videotaped teaching behaviors of parents and found several things. First, fathers "exert greater pressure than mothers for sex-appropriate behaviors." Second, fathers in the teaching situation with sons "set higher standards, attended to the cognitive elements of the tasks and placed repeated emphasis on achievement." With their daughters, fathers focused more on the interpersonal aspects of the teaching situation—encouraging, joking, playing, protecting, and supporting. Mothers with girls, in contrast, provided help in the problem-solving situation even when it was not required, although with sons, they tended to reject bids for help. They also provided girls with more immediate physical comfort after a frustrating experience (Block 1984, 269–270).

Block found that parents "oversocialize" their daughters, with traditional socialization patterns producing girls that are encouraged to "(over)control impulses, to be tractable, obedient, cautious, and self-sacrificing." She notes that while these psychological constructs "may have been functional in yesterday's world of large families, a predominant male work force, and shorter life span, their functionalism in today's world is problematic" (Block 1984, 140).

Others might argue with Block's "oversocialization" hypothesis by pointing to the mounting evidence that girls are given considerable latitude by their parents to be "tomboys." Indeed, one study found that 63 percent of junior high girls said they were tomboys, and 51 percent of an adult sample recalled being tomboys (Hyde 1985, 159). In contrast, boys (particularly in the preteen years) are given less latitude to explore opposite-gender behavior because parents fear the label of "sissy."

Another important modification of the "oversocialization" hypothesis is gleaned from the work of Gilligan on moral development in girls. It is now arguable whether there are pronounced gender differences in the moral reasoning processes of young children; Gilligan's true contribution to the study of gender may lie elsewhere (see Walker 1984 for a review of these studies). Gilligan notes that the inattention to girls' development in the literature has meant that the value of care, connection, and relationships in the moral reasoning process tended to be slighted in favor of approaches that draw upon more traditionally male domains like justice, with its emphasis on fairness, rationality, individuality, abstractions, detachment, and impersonality. Gilligan also suggests that traditional adolescent intimacy with mothers may promote, particularly in girls who are encouraged to stay at home or in closer proximity to mothers, more of a care orientation in day-to-day behavior (Gilligan 1988, xxix). She also speculates that this might in some way be related to girls' lower rates of violent and assaultive crime.

Bursik, Merten, and Schwartz (1985) surveyed adults in a predominantly white-collar suburban community located near a large Midwestern city and add to the discussion of the role of gender in adult views of teenagers. The adults were asked about the age at which teenagers should be allowed to undertake certain activities (including staying out with friends until midnight, riding in a car with other youths, having same-gender friends as guests at one's home without an adult present, going on a date without a chaperon, being left alone in the afternoon, being left alone in the evening, and participating in organized activities). There was a tendency to trust boys with certain activities (notably the last four) at a significantly earlier age than girls; there was still consensus that the first two activities (staying out until midnight and riding in a car with other youths) should be done only by older adolescents and, in these, there was not a significant gender difference. In one instance, being left home alone with a friend of the same sex, girls were trusted at an earlier age.

Upon further examination, Bursik and his colleagues did find that some of this mixed pattern was because males in their sample were likely to feel that boys could be trusted in these activities a year earlier than girls (Bursik et al. 1985, 124); it is important to note that this relationship held up even when one examined the gender of the parent. They concluded both that "girls are considered to be responsible at a much earlier age by female adults than by male adults" and that female adults generally consider girls able to accept this responsibility at the same age as boys; adult males report a very strong differential (126). Their conclusion was that girls receive inconsistent messages about their ability to take on responsibility. They also mention that none of the behaviors they surveyed is explicitly sexual, and consequently, they could not directly measure for the presence or absence of the sexual double standard in parental concern about girls.

Pretty and Popular: Girls, Parents, Beauty, and the Policing of Girls' Sexuality

Wiseman's (2002) work, while problematic in its focus on girls' meanness to other girls, actually provides an interesting perspective on adolescent girls' experiences with their parents. Likely a product of the fact that Wiseman runs groups for adolescent girls, her book provides a candid, though sometimes overly simplistic, assessment of the key themes in girls' lives during mid and late adolescence, particularly with reference to girls chafing at parental monitoring.

Wiseman contends that, at least for middle class girls, girl cliques somewhat ruthlessly determine who is "popular" and who is not; beyond that, particularly in 6th, 7th, and 8th grade, they determine who is to be shunned and excluded (Wiseman 2002, 18-48) In addition to a discussion of how girls' cliques work, Wiseman also focuses on the main areas policed by these girl groups. Here, she stresses the importance of what she calls "beauty," writing that "the pursuit and attainment of the elusive standard of appearance is one of the most critical components of girls' power structure" (Wiseman 2002, 81). Wiseman notes that while the media exerts extreme power with young women, it is the girls themselves that begin to enforce and reinforce certain standards of "beauty," including such mundane matters as what you are "wearing" (Wiseman 2002, 81). It is undeniable that the cultural messages promulgated by the media have a controlling effect in girls' lives. For example, others have speculated on the negative impact of the media on girls' development (see Gilbert et al. 2005; Ward and Harrison 2005), from toy advertisements encouraging girls to focus on looking "pretty" (Sobieraj 1998) to ads that encourage excessive thinness (Hesse-Biber 2007), to the lack of girls and women in television programs and movies (Lamb and Brown 2006; Renzetti and Curran 2003). Our focus here though is on the ways in which girls' parents and peer groups enforce those media supported beauty ideas.[1]

Most parents are largely oblivious to these clique dynamics, Wiseman contends, but they do eventually notice the clique's impact on their daughter's behavior, particularly if the girl is being systematically excluded. Other themes that Wiseman notes include the ways in which school and school structures privilege boys, a theme also noted by Kelly (1998) in her study of two alternative high schools in California, largely because girls competed with each other for boys' approval (a pattern Wiseman calls "pleasing boys, betraying girls") (Wiseman 2002, 234).

As girls age, and as they enter puberty, the constraints of the sex/gender system are foreground, rather than background, in their lives.

First, girls become far more concerned about popularity during the high school years. Consequently, the influence of parents declines as the peer group becomes much more important. This poses special problems for girls, in that parents have traditionally been actively involved in controlling them during this particular period because of the sexual double standard.

To recap, we know from what little research exists on daughters' relationships with parents at this age that, compared with sons, daughters have been allowed less freedom to play away from home, have not been assigned chores that take them out of the home, have been required to return home earlier, and have not been encouraged to choose their own activities (Komorosky 1953; Block 1984). This means that as girls approach puberty, parents begin to exhibit an interest in monitoring them more closely—this precisely when they are becoming less adult oriented. Clashes between daughters and parents may be more likely during late adolescence.

Much of the family disharmony is an outgrowth of the long-standing sexual double standard that tacitly encourages male sexual exploration and punishes female sexuality. Some might expect this traditional orientation to be less relevant today because of changes in the female role, but parental behavior is seemingly more ingrained than many believed it to be. Indeed, Katz (1979) says that there is "no evidence that parental socialization practices are changing drastically" (Katz 1979, 23; for more recent documentation of Katz' claim, see Steinem 1992). She goes on to summarize her own research that suggests that although many parents are concerned about sex-role equality, particularly for their daughters, "there are few who depart significantly from traditional socialization practices" largely because they fear that if they do, their children might become "misfits" (Katz 1979, 24). Certainly, recent research continued to document the role played by the culture of romance and the specter of the "slut" in girls' subculture (Thorne 1992; Alder and Adler 1992).

Another way that the regulation of girls' sexuality has continued is an outgrowth of parental awareness of girls' and women's victimization. Here, parents are concerned about their daughters' safety in a world where "alcohol and drugs are a fact of life in adolescent culture" (Wiseman 2003, 280). This means that girls increasingly are entering a world where parties and being popular with boys matters; in short, it is a world that is arguably unsafe for girls and women. Wiseman also suggests that very frequently girls resort to "lying" and "sneaking out of the house" (70–71). Yet Wiseman does not place this in its context within the sex/gender system which is to say that this behavior likely emerges in reaction to the parents' efforts to control their behavior.

That said, the literature is very clear that parents are uncomfortable talking about their daughter's sexuality (Lamb 2003), instead wanting to talk about "maturity," "commitment," and "real love." Lamb contends that this translates into a "zero tolerance for teen sex" and particularly for girls, a world where "parents typically demand that their daughters postpone their sexual experience" (Lamb 2003, 2). Hence, girls feel compelled to "lie" and "sneak out" on parents who insist that they conform to a clearly unrealistic and unworkable model of modern teen femininity.

Parents are not the only enforcers of the sexual double standard; as we shall see girls themselves grow up in a misogynistic culture and often embrace attitudes that celebrate masculinity, excuse male violence, and blame girls for male infidelity. As an example, Kelly, who spoke to nearly fifty girls in a detention center in Texas, found that the girls had low opinions about other girls, held girls to a higher standard of behavior than boys, expressed "contempt" and disdain for girls' sexual activities, and significantly, "never considered criticism of the males who pressured them into sex" (Kelly 2001, 486). Attitudes that condemn femininity and celebrate masculinity are not found just among girls in detention; take these comments from one of the girls we interviewed:

> Well, I don't know if I ever had anything against the popular girls 'cause I actually hang out with all the boys. [And why was that?] Because they were a little more chill. And it seems like the girls were more like, "Oh, look at me I'm so pretty."

Girls' use of insults like "bitch" and "slut" have, as subsequent chapters will demonstrate, everything to do with enforcement of the sex/gender system which basically means that "while a boy's sexual reputation is enhanced by experience, a girl's is negated" (Lees 1997, 18).

Lees, in her research on teen culture in working-class London observed that there was a "lack of symmetry" between the variety of names to call girls who were sexually active and the absence of words to describe the same behavior in boys. In London, the word was "slag," where in the United States, it's "slut," "ho," or "bitch" but the effect is the same, a "generalized social control along the lies of gender rather than class, steering girls, in terms of both their actions and the aspirations, into existing structures of gender relations" (Lees 1997, 19).

In addition to adolescent subcultures, which are clearly potent in girls' lives, the media also serves as a regulator of girls' sexuality. According to one study of teen magazines, the media construction of girls' sexuality "simultaneously requires them to be sexually alluring *and* devoted to sexual 'responsibility' or even chastity" (Durham 1998, 385). In fact, these media produce the image of physical attractiveness that is defined as sexually desirable: "hetero-eroticized beauty ideals" (Durham 1998, 386), and then actively involve the girls in consuming the products necessary to produce that image: the clothes, the cosmetics, the modeling courses, and the diet products. Of course, these goods are produced by the same industries which provide the advertising base for the magazines (see Hesse-Biber 2007).

What about Class and Culture?

Class and ethnic differences in gender are also marked, and these become more important during the intermediate and high school years. Higher social classes tend to be less rigid in sex distinctions; in working- and lower-class families, there is much more concern about sex segregation. Children from working-class backgrounds tend to differentiate sex roles at earlier ages and to have more traditional standards than do middle-class children (Rabban 1950; Renzetti and Curran 2003).

Adolescence takes on different meanings for girls from working-class backgrounds. Their last years in school represent "the terminal year"—the last chance to find a husband as a way of escaping from an often oppressive family system (Rubin 1976). For these girls, being grown up means being married and having children.

For many low-income girls, as this book shows, even this option is not viable. School life has begun to introduce problems—particularly during intermediate school—as the cost of being poor becomes more explicit. In addition, traditional popularity, with its emphasis on dress, white standards of beauty, academic achievement, and school activities, becomes increasingly elusive. Few low-income girls can achieve traditional marriage because the boys in their lives cannot support them. Adulthood and freedom come through motherhood that until recently was "state supported" (Presser 1980; Campbell 1984a). Lower-class life also means exposure for girls and boys to the "underclass" ways of making money that exist in low-income communities. Miller, in her study of "street women" in Milwaukee, stresses the fact that many low-income females in the ghetto are recruited during adolescence by older males who organize them into pseudo-families and involve them in a variety of criminal activities—chiefly prostitution (Miller 1986).

Because race and class, particularly in the United States, are overlapping systems (Hill and Sprague 1999), it is important to focus on race as well as class in these discussions of growing up female. Important work on the role of race in girls' experiences in school, particularly in intermediate school, comes from Orenstein's qualitative study of two middle schools in California—one that serves a predominantly white community and another that serves a mixed African-American and Latino community. Orenstein's discussion of girls' problems in a predominantly white school more or less parallels the conventional discussions of girls' falling self-esteem and girls' problems with body image. Particularly important in these schools are the pervasive problems of eating disorders as girls strive for an ever more waiflike standard of white beauty (see also Pipher 1994). One young girl explains, while "taking bites," that she "always tries to be a little hungry" (Orenstein 1994, 97).

Different and much more disturbing themes emerge in the lives and classrooms of girls of color across town. African-American girls, while initially praised for their social "maturity," find that their academic needs are ignored (180), and, ultimately, their assertiveness is viewed either as a nuisance or even a menace (see also Fordham 1993). Faced with peer views that define achieving academically as "you talk white, you a schoolgirl, you a nerd, you" (157), and teachers who ignore them in classrooms, many young African-American women simply give up. Resisting pervasive educational neglect (see also Arnold 1995), the girls disconnect from achievement and instead find themselves "attaining a sense of purpose and assuaging loneliness through too early motherhood" (183).

Another key difference in the lives of girls of color in marginalized neighborhoods and schools is their relationships with boys. Whereas the girls at predominantly white schools complain bitterly about sexual harassment and boys belittling them in classrooms (Orenstein 1994, 129), Hispanic and African-American girls must also negotiate the gangs that are omnipresent in their neighborhoods, the violence from other girls, and, finally, male violence. And, as noted above, both African-American girls and Latinas also face early pregnancy and motherhood.

Latinas, though, unlike their African-American counterparts, must face entrenched cultural attitudes that expect them to work at home and to remain sexually pure while deemphasizing academic success (203); language difficulties also make it extremely unlikely that Latinas will be recognized as leaders in school (200). Finally, the machismo that characterizes masculinity in their community, and particularly gang behavior, also has sinister meanings for young Latinas.

Ward (1996) explores the "intergenerational transmission of race-related resistance strategies" in her interviews with black parents and their children. Focusing specifically on girls, Ward documents the role played by black girls' mothers as they teach their daughters how to "sublimate" rage and hostility in pro-social ways (Ward 1996, 91) through the practice of "truth-telling" (Ward 1996, 94). Other researchers (Cauce et al. 1996) note that there's a common saying among African-Americans that "mothers *raise* their daughters and *love* their sons" (Cauce et al. 1996, 100). Specifically, this exploration of African-American girlhood stresses the role played by mothers in teaching their daughters how to confront not only sexism but also racism. Both Latina and African-American girls are taught by their parents to be "biracial" (Taylor 1996, 117), meaning that they are taught to negotiate both their own cultural world as well as the white world.

That said, a number of studies also note that both African-American and Latino girls have predictable arguments with their parents. African-American girls as well as Latinas have conflicts with their mothers, mostly around "mundane" issues like "cleaning around the house" and "going places without parents" (Cauce et al. 1996, 109). Conflicts between African-American daughters and mothers might well escalate precisely because they learned their "resistance" strategies well. African-American mothers defend their attempts to curtail their daughters' "freedom" by pointing to the "often hostile and dangerous environments" that their teens lived in as well as the fact that "they were also less likely to be given a break when they err than white teens" (111).

Latino girls also chafed at the controls exercised over them, saying that their parents were "too concerned" about their safety. (Taylor 1996, 128). And, as noted earlier, Latinas also reported feeling constrained and frustrated by watching their mothers being constrained by a culture that expects them to "do everything for everybody" (124), while also reporting that if the daughters complain about people taking advantage of their mothers, the mothers get angry.

Running Away: Girls Coping with Family Trauma and Abuse

Running away from home and prostitution remain the only two arrest categories where more girls than boys are arrested; moreover, many more girls are arrested for running away than prostitution, despite the public fascination with the latter. In 2003, for example, 43,949 girls were arrested for runaway, while less than a thousand were arrested for prostitution. In 2003, girls constituted more than half (58.9 percent) of those arrested for one status offense—running away from home. This means that despite the intention of the Juvenile Justice and Delinquency Prevention Act in 1974, which, among other things, encouraged jurisdictions to divert and deinstitutionalize youth charged with status offenses (like running away from home), arrests for these offenses remain substantial, particularly for girls. Having said that, it should be noted that the arrest rates for runaway have been decreasing slightly for both girls and boys.

Historically, status offenses like runaway have played, if anything, a more significant historical role in girls' official delinquency. These "uniquely juvenile offenses" include truancy and offenses known variously as "incorrigibility," "unmanageability," and "being beyond parental control." In some states, a child who "is in danger of leading an idle or immoral life," who is a "wayward child," who "endangers the morals of himself or others," or "who associates with vagrant, vicious or immoral persons" can be brought before the juvenile court (Bortner 1988, 98–100).

Current attempts to differentiate between status and delinquent or criminal offenses are somewhat ironic because, as we shall see, the early juvenile justice system developed the concept of delinquency to include status offenses and to avoid the notion that delinquent behavior and criminal behavior were the same (Platt 1969, 138; Sutton 1988, 162–163; Feld 1988, 822–825).

For many years, statistics showing large numbers of girls arrested and referred to court for status offenses were taken as representative of the different types of male and female delinquency. Yet, studies of actual delinquency (not simply arrests) show that girls and boys run away from home in about equal numbers. As an example, Canter (1982) found in a National Youth Survey that there was no evidence of greater female involvement, compared to males, in any category of delinquent behavior. Indeed, in this sample, males were significantly more likely than females to report status offenses.

A major source of the bias in contemporary juvenile courts is undoubtedly parental use (some might say abuse) of the status offense category. Ketchum (1978, 37) reported that 72 percent of status offenders are referred to police or the court by relatives. Recent national data, while slightly less explicit, also show that petitioned status offenses are less likely to be referred to court by police than delinquency offenses. In 1999, 84 percent of youth charged with crimes were referred to juvenile courts by police, but only 40 percent of petitioned status offenders charged with runaway were referred by police (meaning parents, schools, and social service agencies were responsible for the referral) (Puzzanchera, Stahl, Finnegan, Tierney, and Snyder 2003, 31, 64).

That parents are often committed to two standards of adolescent behavior is one explanation for the overrepresentation of girls charged with status offenses in court populations—and the standards should not be discounted as a major source of tension even in modern families, as was noted earlier in this chapter. Contemporary ethnographies of school life echo the validity of these parental perceptions. Orenstein's observations also point to the durability of the sexual double standard; at the schools she observed that sex "ruins girls" but "enhance[s] boys" (Orenstein 1994, 57). In her study of gender in grade school youth, Thorne noted that parents have new reasons to enforce the time-honored sexual double standard. Perhaps correctly concerned about sexual harassment and rape, to say nothing of HIV/AIDS if their daughters are heterosexually active, "parents in gestures that mix protection with punishment, often tighten control of girls when they become adolescents, and sexuality becomes a terrain of struggle between the generations" (Thorne 1994, 156; see also Lamb 2003). Finally, Thorne notes that as girls use sexuality as a proxy for independence, they sadly and ironically reinforce their status as sexual objects seeking male approval—ultimately ratifying their status as the subordinate sex. Whatever the reason, parental attempts to adhere to and enforce the sexual double standard will continue to be a source of conflict between parents and their daughters.

Another reason for different responses to running away from home speaks to differences in the reasons that boys and girls have for running away. Girls are, for example, much more likely than boys to be the victims of child sexual abuse. According to the *Third National Incidence Study*, girls are sexually abused three times more often than boys (Sedlak and Broadhurst 1996). Sexual abuse typically starts at an early age, with both boys and girls being most vulnerable to abuse between the ages of 7 and 13 (Finkelhor 1994). Not surprisingly, the evidence is also suggesting a link between this problem and girls' delinquency—particularly running away from home, since girls (and not boys) are more likely to be the victims of intra-familial abuse (with estimates indicating between one-third and one-half of girls' sexual abuse is of this sort as compared to only between one-tenth and one-fifth of boys' sexual abuse) (Finkehor 1994). Moreover, this sort of abuse lasts longer and has more serious consequences than stranger abuse (Finkelhor 1994).

Studies of girls on the streets or in court populations are showing high rates of both sexual and physical abuse. One study of 372 homeless and runaway youth in Seattle found rates of both childhood sexual abuse and street sexual victimization were reported, with females experiencing much greater rates compared with their male counterparts; specifically, "young women were twice as likely to be the victims of sexual abuse" (30 percent versus 15 percent), and "rates of extremely violent sexual abuse also tended to be higher among females (43 percent) compared with males (31 percent)" (Tyler, Hoyt, Whitbeck, and Cauce 2001, 161). An earlier study of a runaway shelter in Toronto, for example, found that 73 percent of the female runaways and 38 percent of the males had been sexually abused. This same study found that sexually abused female runaways were more likely than their non-abused counterparts to engage in delinquent or criminal activities such as substance abuse, petty theft, and prostitution. No such pattern was found among the male runaways (McCormack, Janus, and Burgess 1986).

Widom found that victims of child sexual abuse are 27.7 times more likely to be arrested for prostitution as adults than nonvictims (Widom 1995), with the speculation being that some victims become prostitutes (if female) or abusers (if male) because they have a difficult time relating to others except on sexual terms. Not all studies find a link between sexual abuse, runaway, and prostitution, however. Nadon, Koverola, and Schludeermann (1998) found that in a comparison of prostitute and nonprostitute (but runaway) youth, prostitute youth were not significantly more likely than an appropriate comparison group to report sexual abuse. However, adolescent prostitutes ran away from home significantly more often than adolescent nonprostitutes. State the authors, "It was determined prostitution may be a particular survival strategy for girls in very difficult circumstances" (Nadon, Koverola, and Schludeermann 1998, 206).

Early sexual victimization and runaway leads to a pattern called, "risk amplification" (Chen, Tyler, Whitbeck, and Hoyt 2004, 1). Chen and associates interviewed 361 homeless and runaway girls in four Midwestern states, and found that early sexual abuse "indirectly" affected drug use on the streets since youth who were abused ran at an early age, spent more time on the streets, and used deviant strategies to survive (including trading sex and affiliation with deviant peers).

Another study that tracked the gendered consequences of running away for girls and boys (Tyler, Hoyt, Whitbeck, and Cause 2004), found that for females, running away from home for the first time at an earlier age was associated with engaging in deviant subsistence strategies, survival sex, and victimization by a "friend or acquaintance." For boys, survival sex (if engaged in) was associated with stranger victimization; for homosexual boys, though, the victimization came at the hands of an acquaintance or friend (Tyler, Hoyt, Whitbeck, and Cause 2004, 503).

Not surprisingly, a higher rate of suicidal behavior has been found to exist among girls who run away. Rotheram-Borus, in a study of predominantly African-American and Hispanic runaways in a New York City runaway shelter (1993), found that girls, more often than boys, had attempted suicide and were also classified as depressed. Specifically, 44 percent of the girls but only 29 percent of the boys had attempted suicide. Almost two-thirds of the girls (62 percent) were classified as depressed, in contrast to 44 percent of the boys.

Most girl runaways have fled homes where abuse, including sexual abuse, was a prominent theme in their lives. Yet, ironically and tragically, their lives on the streets are almost always even more abusive in nature because, like all other aspects of life, the streets are gendered. Once on the streets, girls quickly discover both the dangers involved in street life and the narrow range of survival options available to them as girls. They also discover that they are in possession of a form of "sexual capital" that they can access, while boys tend to engage, as we have seen, in a wider variety of survival strategies.

Boyer and James (1982) in their research on female prostitution in Seattle developed a clear insight into the direct relationship between sexual abuse of girls and their subsequent involvement in prostitution. "The imposition of adult sexuality on children disrupts psychosexual development," and among its effects are promiscuity, rebellion, feelings of shame and guilt, and a loss of self-esteem. Once girls reach puberty, they often come to the realization that their experiences are different from those of their peers and they begin to withdraw. Many "hold a distorted image of their own bodies," which may "lead them to expect that their worth will only be acknowledged when they permit sexual access" (Boyer and James 1982, 79–80). Further, the girls may learn "that the most effective way to communicate with adults is through sex" (Campagna and Poffenberger 1988, 66) and view themselves as "salable commodities" (Boyer and James 1982, 80).

The tragedy here is that a girl who runs from physical and sexual abuse is forced to confront terrible choices since she does not want to return to an intolerable home, yet she cannot legally go to school, get employment, or find housing without risking return; in short, her legal options are criminalized by a system that has traditionally encouraged her to return home and obey her parents (never mind how abusive). Even systems that want to explore other sorts of placement possibilities face numerous challenges, not the least of which is a shortage of programs for girls (Freitas and Chesney-Lind 2001). Faced with terrible choices, some girls turn to survival sex (trading sex for food or a place to stay) which they may not even recognize as sexual exploitation (Beyette 1988), or some other form of sex work like prostitution. For some but not necessarily all girl runaways, then, survival sex and then possibly prostitution becomes a way to survive in the absence of few other earning skills (Campagna and Poffenberger 1988; Miller 1986, 139).

Girls' Assaults and Domestic Violence

Ironically, family disputes and disagreements might also be responsible for the dramatic increases in arrests of girls for "other assaults." As noted above, while girls have long been arrested and referred to court for running away from home (and other non-criminal behavior for which only youth can be arrested), the deinstitutionalization of these "status" offenses in the seventies made it more difficult for parents to have their defiant daughters taken into custody. In essence, federal initiatives aimed at diverting non-criminal youth, like runaway and incorrigible girls, from the juvenile justice system made their arrest and detention difficult. Perhaps as a consequence, family members (sometimes encouraged by the police) have been relabeling behaviors that were once categorized as status offenses (noncriminal offenses like "runaway" and "person in need of supervision") into violent offenses so that their daughters can be taken into custody (see Chesney-Lind and Belknap 2004).

Certainly, available evidence on the types of "assaults" involved in girls' cases suggests this pattern directly. A review of over two thousand cases of girls referred to Maryland's juvenile justice system for "person-to-person" offenses revealed that virtually all of these offenses (97.9 percent) involved "assault." A further examination of these records revealed that about half were "family centered" and involved such activities as "a girl hitting her mother and her mother subsequently pressing charges" (Mayer 1994).

More recently, Acoca's study of nearly one thousand girls' files from four California counties found that while a "high percentage" of these girls were charged with "person offenses," a majority of these involved assault. Further, "a close reading of the case files of girls charged with assault revealed that most of these charges were the result of non-serious, mutual combat situations with parents." Acoca details cases that she regards as typical including: "father lunged at her while she was calling the police about a domestic dispute. She (girl) hit him." Finally, she reports that some cases were quite trivial in nature including a girl arrested "for throwing cookies at her mother" (Acoca 1999, 7–8). In another study, a girl reported that she was arrested for "assault" for throwing a Barbie doll at her mother (Belknap, Winter, and Cady 2001).

Changes in police practices with reference to domestic violence might also have played a role. A recent California study found that the female share of these arrests increased from 6 percent in 1988 to 16.5 percent in 1998 (Bureau of Criminal Information and Analysis 1999). African-American girls and women had arrest rates roughly three times that of white girls and women in 1998: 149.6 compared to 46.4 (Bureau of Criminal Information and Analysis 1999).

More recently, Buzawa and Hotaling (2006) undertook a careful study of police data involving 320 incidents of domestic violence in five Massachusetts jurisdictions operating under a "pro-arrest statute" during a four-month period in 1999. The authors found that only 47 percent of the cases involved "standard intimate partner" violence. Instead, many incidents (over one-third), including quite serious violence, involved family and household members, disputes between parents and children.

With specific reference to domestic violence involving juveniles, the authors found that these youth were "often less likely to receive statutorily required police actions," with authorities often minimizing the violence if youth were victims and making arrests of juveniles even if it was clear that parents had also engaged in violence. As examples, the researchers reported that two cases involved daughters who were slapped by their mothers and retaliated by slapping or pushing their mothers back. In neither case, they noted, was the parent arrested. Instead, parents, as the complainant, were treated by the police as the "injured parties," and the girls were arrested (Buzawa and Hotaling 2006, 29).

In addition to a bias against youth, the authors also found evidence of gender bias. Both women and juveniles (particularly daughters), if suspects, were more likely to be arrested. In fact, the authors found "higher odds of arrest of females existed across all major household relationships." Whether the incident involved adult partners, daters, siblings, or parents and children, the odds of female arrest were always higher. For example, when a daughter assaulted a parent, the odds were almost certain that she would be arrested (91.7 percent of incidents) whereas arrests occurred in 75 percent of incidents in which a son assaulted a parent.

The researchers expressed considerable concern about these patterns, particularly since the data showed that "sons and daughters were more likely to experience injury in disputes with parents and were much more likely to be threatened with harm" (Buzawa and Hotaling 2006, 29). Their research found both the minimization of youth victimization (at the hands of parents) coupled with a willingness to arrest youths, particularly daughters, even when the parents had also engaged in violence. They concluded "from their perspective, it would appear that certain family members can use threats and violence and others cannot" (Buzawa and Hotaling 2006, 29).

Relabeling of girls' arguments with parents from status offenses (like "incorrigible" or "person in need of supervision") to assault is a form of "bootstrapping" that has been particularly pronounced in the official delinquency of African-American girls (Robinson 1990; Bartollas 1993). This practice also facilitates the incarceration of girls in detention facilities and training schools—something that would not be possible if the girls were arrested for non-criminal status offenses. Similarly, some parents admit to using detention as a "time out" from conflict with their daughters, including some mothers who would rather have their daughters in detention than at home with the mothers and their boyfriends, when it is often the mothers' boyfriends who caused the girls' running away (Lederman and Brown 2000).

Conclusion

For centuries, families have treated their daughters differently than their sons and sought to control their daughters' behaviors while allowing their sons to "sow wild oats." The evidence is that this insistence on girls' obedience to parental authority has long involved the juvenile justice system, indirectly, in the policing of girls' sexuality through "status offenses" like running away from home.

In more recent years, though, the evidence is mounting that the family has been using a more serious kind of intervention to control girlhood—arrests of their daughters for "assault." Certainly, the relabeling of girls' defiance from a noncriminal status offense to a criminal offense, could not be coming at a worst time for girls. As we will document in future chapters, the juvenile justice system is increasingly a site of punitive control and detention rather than the rehabilitative system that focused on the "best interests of the child."

5

POLICING GIRLS' PEER GROUPS: COLUMBINE AND THE HUNT FOR GIRL BULLIES

While it took time for the second wave of feminism to pay attention to girls' problems as well as the problems of adult women, researchers in subsequent decades slowly began asking "What about the girls?" Concomitant with that, there was a growing dissatisfaction with "youth" research that was focused exclusively on boys. What came to be known as girls' studies has thrived in and out of the academy during the last two decades (see Brown 1998; Gilligan 1982; Gilligan and Brown 1992; Harris 2004; Inness 1998; Leadbetter and Way 1996). Increasingly, youth researchers who do not specifically consider girls in their research are often viewed as offering incomplete or gender "biased" analyses. Moreover, programs which do take gender into account in general, and girls' and women's experiences in particular, are praised for offering "gender balanced" approaches.

This is not to say that the focus on girls did not meet with resistance and even backlash. Indeed, years after conservative pundits like Christina Hoff-Sommers (2000) began to warn of a "war against boys," we've started to see mainstream media pick up the argument. *USA Today* warns, "Pay Closer Attention: Boys are Struggling Academically" (Anonymous 2004). *Business Week* calls it "The New Gender Gap" (Conlin 2003) and claims boys are now "The Second Sex." In *Newsweek*, it's "The Trouble with Boys" (Tyre 2006). The issue has even attracted the attention of the White House, where Laura Bush is leading a campaign to help boys improve in school. She told National Public Radio, "I feel like, in the United States, that we've sort of shifted our gaze away from boys for the last several decades, and that we've neglected boys" (Brown, Chesney-Lind, and Stein 2006).

This backlash against girls' programming notwithstanding, the new millennium has been marked by the development of a considerable array of youth programs that contend that they are able to work effectively with both girls and boys and even a number that claim to be gender responsive. This is particularly true in the area of programs attempting to prevent and intervene in youthful aggression and violence in and around schools. Among many practitioners, social scientists, and youth advocates, the implementation of "proven" or "best practices" prevention programs was seen by those who advocated for them as an alternative to punitive law and order strategies.

Unfortunately, as we will show, major gaps in scientific literature and problematic conceptualizations of girls' violence and aggression encouraged the creation of programs that did more to hype and exaggerate girls' offending than to combat and mitigate the many gender-specific challenges in girls' lives.

Gender Responsive or Gender Blaming?

Public concern about "youth violence" and the many programs created to prevent and intervene in the "problem" offers an instructive and cautionary case study of the new gender balanced approach in youth programming. Instead of just implementing programs for boys or taking programs developed for boys and then superficially adapting them for girls, policy makers and program designers in the post-Columbine years drew from the studies about girls and specifically responded to the idea that girls and boys experience and express violence and aggression differently. They have made a specific effort to include these "indirect" or covert aggressions in their definitions of "aggression" that violence prevention programs attempt to address. In this chapter, we will explore the ways this gender balanced strategy went awry—in ways that we feel seriously disadvantaged girls.

The Emergence of "Bullying" as a Social Problem

Linda, aged 12, was allegedly victimized by her classmates because she was "too posh." It appears that Linda had made friends with another girl in the class and they went around together. The alleged ringleader of the small bully group tried to destroy this friendship and eventually succeeded, leaving Linda fairly isolated. Later on, another girl in the bully group persuaded Linda to give a party at home, then made sure no one came. Linda's self confidence was completely destroyed. (Olweus 1993, 8)

Linda's story was one of those chosen by Dan Olweus to open his book *Bullying at School: What We Know and What We Can Do.* When the book first appeared in 1993, bullying was considered a normal aspect of adolescent life both in the United States and Norway. Olweus, a psychology professor at the University of Bergen, Norway, had been up to that point best known in the academic community for his research on aggression among adolescent boys (Olweus 1977, 1978, 1979). His interest remained largely scientific and academic until 1982, when the suicides of three adolescent boys who had been severely bullied shocked Norway. In Olweus' (1993, 2) own words, the triple suicide "triggered a chain of reactions, the end result of which was a nationwide campaign against bully/victim problems in Norwegian's primary and secondary/junior schools." Having spent a decade researching peers and aggression, Olweus found himself taking a leadership position in the northern European anti-bullying movement, lending a scientific and research-based perspective to the design and implementation of national "anti-bullying" strategies and ultimately he would create his own intervention curricula.

The construction of bullying as a social problem in Europe provides an interesting counterpoint to "discoveries" of other youthful problems at the end of the twentieth century (see Males 1996). As this book has documented, often, central to the construction of a youth "problem" is the appearance of a popular or mass market book, in this instance, *Bullying at School.* Intended for teachers, parents, school administrators, and legislators who were eager to do something about bullying at school, the book was actually central to framing the problem as well as offering potential "solutions." In fact, Linda's "story" was gleaned from newspaper accounts and was "slightly adapted" for inclusion in the Olweus' book. Including "Linda's story" before launching into the research and facts about bullying was to imply that the problem of bullying had both a female and a male face (see also Brown 2003; Brown, Chesney-Lind, and Stein 2004).

That Linda's friends were certainly cruel, at least in this constructed account, is undeniable. However, the narrative item immediately following Linda's in Olweus' book, details a far more serious situation.

> Schoolboy Philip C. was driven to his death by playground bullying. He hanged himself after being constantly threatened, pushed around, and humiliated by three of his classmates. Finally, when the shy 16-year-old's examination notes were stolen days before he was due to sit for an important exam, he could take no more. Frightened to tell his parents, Philip chose to die. When he came home from school, he hanged himself by a rope from his bedroom door. (Olweus 1993, 8)

Note that girls' gossip and relational aggression is clearly equated and conflated with boys' violence in the positioning of these two accounts of "bullying." However, none of this would have necessarily been any concern in the U.S., had a critical event not occurred in the late nineties that would propel bullying to the top of every school administrator's "to do list."

Columbine and the Moral Panic about Bullying

As we have noted earlier, by the late 1990s, the crime drop, particularly in the arrests of boys' for violent crimes was well underway; these peaked in 1993–1994 and proceeded to drop steadily through the end of the decade (in fact, they continue to decline in the new millennium). As an example, boys' arrests for serious crimes of violence declined by 34.3 percent between 1995 and 2004 (FBI 2005, 284). To many, it appeared that the job of curbing what had appeared to be a surging youth violence problem was largely accomplished.

That perception was shattered when on April 20, 1999, Eric Harris and Dylan Klebold, armed with two sawed-off shotguns and two 9mm semi-automatic guns, rushed onto a school campus, shooting and killing students along their way. The public immediately concluded that youth violence, and particularly violence in schools, had become a significant problem in the United States. And the fact that the Columbine shooting was not an isolated event made the need for continued anti-violence efforts an easy sell.

In response to Columbine, the U.S. Secret Service and the U.S. Department of Education conducted a study of thirty-seven deadly school attacks, called "targeted events," that occurred between 1974 and June, 2000. Columbine, with the death toll of fourteen students and one teacher, was at the time the most tragic and alarming of all these events and led to a common public perception that school shootings were becoming an intolerable and increasingly brutal national trend in the United States.

Despite the fact that far more students die each year off school grounds than on them,[1] the public's fear of school-based violence would be unshakable for years to come. Beyond their immediate impact, the school shootings of the late 1990s shared another significant feature: none of them occurred in the sorts of communities and settings the public had long associated with youth violence—inner-city, low-income neighborhoods with large minority populations. White boys living in suburban or rural environments were disproportionately the perpetrators of these events (and girls and women often, though not always, their targets). However, this aspect of the problem would be lost, as would be the gender of most of the shooters (Klein 2006).

The Columbine shootings, then, changed at least three aspects of the anti-violence campaign. First, it altered the public image of youth violence by suggesting that the problem cut across race, class, and regional boundaries. It could erupt in the most impoverished neighborhoods riddled with gangs, joblessness, and drug sales or it could emerge in the most tranquil suburban or rural communities. White boys who were emotionally unbalanced and hopelessly unable to fit in among their peers, it seemed, could be just as lethal as the gun-toting, urban gangster of color. Second, it solidified the logical connection between schools and anti-violence initiatives. Youth violence was now perceived as a crisis facing all American schools. Any school district, no matter how safe and peaceful looking from the outside, could harbor dangerous students. Schools in places like Littleton, Colorado, Jonesboro, Arkansas, Pearl, Mississippi, or West Paducah, Kentucky were viewed as needing well-organized safety plans and strict security measures as well as ambitious new violence prevention programs. Third, and more to the point for this chapter, as America digested the media narrative that emerged around the school shooting phenomenon, the country would discover "bullying" as a youth problem.

School Shootings: A Bullying Problem

The Secret Service and the U.S. Department of Education's study and report on school attacks in many ways directed national school-based violence prevention policy in the post-Columbine years. As can be expected from a report authored in part by the U.S. Secret Service, the proposed "safe schools" initiative advocated by these agencies was to engage in surveillance and advance "information"-gathering techniques on campus. Given that "almost all of the attackers [95 percent] planned out the attack in advance of carrying it out" (Vossekuil 2002, 24), the report recommended that schools develop "the capacity to pick up on and evaluate available or knowable information that might indicate that there is a risk of a targeted attack" (Vossekuil 2002, 41).

More to the point, the report also launched the national anti-bullying campaign. According to the report, "almost three quarters of the attackers [n=29] felt persecuted, bullied, threatened, attacked or injured by others prior to the incident" (Vossekuil 2002, 21). The report even suggested that several of the shooting perpetrators were severely bullied for long periods of time, although it did not mention how many such cases it found. It did describe one school shooter whose classmates claimed to regularly tease, trip, and throw things at him, in addition to throwing him against a locker and holding his head under water in the school's pool.

The report strongly asserted that there is no standard profile for a school shooter, and shooters varied in both background and motivation. The statement (which is repeated several times in the report) that "there is no accurate or 'useful' profile of students who engage in targeted school violence" (Vossekuil 2002, 11) suggested that the report was never meant to help identify potential school shooters or to make claims about what caused these shootings. Despite this, journalists, legislators, school districts, and school administrators made note of the fact that so many of the school shooters "felt persecuted, bullied, threatened, attacked, or injured by others" (Vossekuil 2002, 21). The idea also struck a chord with the American media, who increasingly focused on bullying problems in school.

In fact, compared with the perceptions of the typical perpetrator of the youth violence epidemic of the 1980s and early 1990s, school shooters were painted in a much more sympathetic light. The character from the Secret Service and U.S. Department of Education report who was described as "the kid everyone teased" and suffered regularly from being thrown against lockers, pushed, and tripped by almost every student in school (Vossekuil 2002, 21) generated some public concern about bullying victimization. While the Columbine attackers were more difficult to sympathize with, some Americans did at least identify with the two boys' feelings of estrangement and their deep dislike for high school jocks. After all, Klebold and Harris were by no means the first teens to fantasize about getting back at the hyper-masculine and socially powerful athletic crowd (think *Revenge of the Nerds*). What this popular sympathy did was to make the American public sense that the social climate at school, especially the poor treatment of unpopular students, might push some particularly unstable adolescents over the edge and end in disaster. Like the triple suicides in Norway, Columbine gave a public face to bullying as a social problem in the United States.

Perhaps not surprisingly, Colorado set a national precedent by being one of the first states to link bullying and school violence and pass anti-bullying legislation in 2001. While previous legislation addressing school violence had usually focused on zero-tolerance policies, the Colorado anti-bullying legislation mandated that each school district adopt a bullying prevention and education policy, and strongly encouraged schools to adopt anti-bullying programs (see the National Conference of State Legislatures, www.ncsl.gov). Oklahoma followed suit by requiring school safety committees to review bullying prevention programs used by other states and make recommendations to Oklahoma schools.

By May 2003, thirty-two states had introduced anti-bullying legislation, and according to the National Conference of State Legislatures, by 2006, twenty-six states had passed some sort of anti-bullying and harassment legislation. Many of the states, however, did not focus on prevention or education as much as Colorado did. Instead, states such as Washington, West Virginia, Connecticut, and New Jersey passed laws requiring schools to prohibit bullying and respond formally to bullying problems. Illinois went one step further and passed a bill requiring schools to not only report students who were bullies but to report those who were "at risk" for bullying. Schools were required to send official notes to the parents or guardians of these "at risk" bullies informing them that their sons or daughters were behaving aggressively.

Once bullying became a behavior that could result in official reports and formal reporting, it became necessary for states and schools to define what constituted bullying. In some states, like Georgia, bullying was limited to actions that caused or threatened bodily harm. Other states, including New Jersey, adopted broader definitions that also included actions or words meant to insult or demean students or to interfere with the orderly operation of the school. In fact, some states have combined anti-bullying with anti-harassment policies. The merging of bullying and harassment problems created particular problems for girls, which will be discussed in more detail later in the chapter. Once bullying was discovered as a school-wide social problem and linked, however tenuously, to school shootings, we see that school-wide prohibitions of behaviors expanded. In many ways, because of the ranging and often imprecise ways that bullying and harassment were being defined in state codes, school prohibitions and policies were becoming increasingly subjective. As we will see, this increasing subjectivity of school-wide policies will disadvantage girls and students of color.

Despite the attempts of some school districts to respond to the "bullying problem" with the same punitive measures long associated with responding to teen violence (which had been previously coded as behavior engaged in by low-income minority students), there was federal momentum to deal with the problem through education and prevention programs. In January of 2005, Representative John Shimkus from Illinois introduced legislation to include bullying and harassment in the Safe and Drug Free Schools and Communities initiative. In addition to defining bullying and harassment as violent behaviors, this amendment also provided districts with financial support for the implementation of bullying prevention programs.

It seems that the focus on bullying problems, in part, opened a door for violence prevention programs (see Stein 2003).

Indeed, the link between bullying and youth violence in general turned out to be serendipitous for proponents of violence prevention programs. As noted earlier, Norway had already discovered the bullying problem in the 1980s and had designed, implemented, and evaluated anti-bullying programs in the decades that followed. More to the point, some of these, Dan Olweus' program prominent among them, had already been replicated in American schools, and the outcome evaluations of the program implemented in America appeared promising. For example, in a South Carolina study of 6,388 4th through 6th grade boys and girls, researchers found that Olweus' bullying prevention program significantly reduced self-reported rates of bullying as well as delinquency (Melton et al. 1998).

Suddenly, it appeared that there were bullying prevention programs complete with curricula, training packages, and early intervention strategies ready and waiting for implementation. The discovery of the bullying problem and the identification of tested bullying prevention programs built upon a national movement to identify and implement "proven" programs. The movement gained a significant boost in the early 1990s, with the passage of the 1994 Safe and Drug Free Schools and Communities Act (SDFSCA), which provided formula grants to states to support prevention programs. In 1995, over $600 million in grants were available to develop, evaluate, and replicate drug and violence prevention programs in preschool to grade 12.

Schools also received several benefits for selecting prevention programs. Implementing programs listed by government agencies as "best practices" programs (i.e., those that performed well during research trials, had been rigorously evaluated, and found to be effective in reducing violence) were sometimes seen by schools as a chance to increase their overall funding and develop and enhance existing educational curricula.[2] Although there are clear benefits to violence prevention programs, the programs did have some serious disadvantages, which ultimately compromised their ability to compete with the simpler and more punitive "law-and-order" solutions being advocated by many at roughly the same time.

First, they did not offer quick fixes or "silver bullet" solutions. Prevention programs took enormous amounts of time, effort, and resources to implement.[3] Second, federal sources, such as the Safe and Drug Free Schools initiative and the Office of Juvenile Justice and Delinquency Prevention, provided initial startup funds but often required schools to match these seed funds or find other resources to maintain the program. Thus, schools turned to their own school districts for full- and long-term funding.

In fact, schools could pay as much as $58,000[4] per year to implement a model violence prevention program and the Olweus Bullying Prevention Program does not come cheap, at roughly $20,000 per school (Olweus 2006). In addition, virtually all these programs sell their curricula to schools and, through copyright laws, forbid schools from copying them. Schools are also required to pay for expensive training and technical assistance consultations. Some of these programs even run on a for-profit basis, with the program designers drawing heavily from the corporate "free market" model by claiming the prerogative to profit from any product that they invented. The irony was that prevention program designers developed their products through state and federal grants that they originally received to design, implement, and evaluate their programs. Most importantly, though, the high cost of these "best practice" violence prevention programs means that, in reality, they are an option open only to wealthy school districts.

Girls and Bullying Prevention

Initially, the focus on bullying as conceptualized by Olweus seemed to offer schools an egalitarian approach to youth violence and an alternative to many of the more punitive approaches also being implemented at the time. After all, prevention programs, as opposed to zero-tolerance strategies (school policies that mandated suspension, expulsion, or transfer of rule violators), offer an integrated approach to school behavior problems. Instead of removing bullies from the school, the Olweus program was designed to intervene in bullying and change behaviors at early stages, working with bullies or potential bullies before they became more serious delinquents. The fact that self-reported rates of delinquency also decreased when bullying prevention programs were implemented in research trials (Melton et al. 1998) also seemed to suggest that schools do not need to suspend, transfer, or expel students to solve behavior problems. Moreover, bullying prevention programs consistently tout the idea that bullies should be confronted and face negative consequences, but not be excluded from the school.

So what about gender? For years, researchers had critiqued the fact that delinquency prevention and intervention programs were too often developed using data from studies of boys, then applied in practice to boys and girls (Kersten 1989; Mann 1984; Chesney-Lind and Shelden 2004). Olweus wanted to avoid this problem. Although his primary research focus was boys' aggression, he was aware of emerging research about aggressive girls (Bjorkqvist and Niemela 1992), and made sure to consider these research findings as he created his program. He also tested the program with girls as well as boys, and his guides to implementers thoroughly discussed the ways in which both genders experienced bullying (Olweus 1993).

Olweus' attempts to address girls' aggression with his program emerged at the same time that collections of research findings about girls' developmental outcomes chronicled additional reasons to be concerned about the state of girlhood. Since Gilligan's path-breaking work in the 1980s, a growing literature on girls' development documented that adolescence is a difficult time for girls, but later girl-focused books would increasingly locate the source of the problem not with sexism, ageism, or racism in the settings that girls find themselves, but rather in girlhood itself. This notion, born out of girls' vulnerability to victimization, portrays girlhood as "poisoned" and can be found not only in *Reviving Ophelia* (1994) but also *The Body Project* (1997) and *Girl in the Mirror* (2002). Some of these books even took feminism to task for putting girls under pressure to perform not only to traditional standards of femininity but also to the contemporary standards dictating women's achievement:

> [T]he pressure on girls has increased. In addition to the "old" cultural expectations—be pretty, sexually alluring, thin, nurturing, understanding, deferential, and the like—that accompanied puberty, girls are also expected to be strong, athletic, and high-achieving. As he puts it, the

challenge is clear: "Now that you can do all of these things, why aren't you?" (Dr. Peter C. Scales quoted in Snyderman and Streep 2002, 50)

But the arguably misogynistic impact that these books had pales in comparison to that of a spate of popular "mean girl" books which would popularize literature on girls' aggression—literature that Olweus and his colleagues were also reviewing and integrating into their "gender balanced" approach to bullying.

Olweus' efforts to incorporate research regarding girls' aggression into bullying prevention seems on the surface to offer an approach to violence prevention that includes the unique challenges that girls confront on the pathway to adulthood—being the "victim" of other girls' relational aggression. We are fundamentally concerned, though, that this "equity" is misleading, and encouraged both negative attention to and inappropriate interventions with girls.

The program's primary flaw was that it included an overly broad spectrum of behaviors into its definition of bullying. According to Olweus (1993, 9), "a student is being bullied or victimized when he or she is exposed, repeatedly and over time, to negative actions on the part of one or more other students." Furthermore, "such negative actions include intentionally inflicting, or attempting to inflict, injury or discomfort upon another" (Elliott, Olweus, Limber, and Mihalic 2002, 7-8). Bullying was categorized as direct—physical or verbal attacks—or indirect—"making faces or obscene gestures, or intentional exclusion from a group" (Elliott, Olweus, Limber, and Mihalic 2002, 8).

According to the logic of the bullying prevention program, rolling one's eyes at another person is a less extreme form of bullying than hitting or punching them but they are both, at their core, bullying. We argue that this construction of "aggression" is problematic, for a number of reasons. Notably, there is evidence to suggest that non-physical but emotionally hurtful behaviors such as rolling eyes, spreading rumors, or excluding individuals from a group, belong in a different category of behaviors than physical attacks in terms of the dynamics involved, the consequences of the behavior, and the long-term implications of the behavior. Beyond the logical imprecision of conflating indirect or relational aggression with direct bullying (i.e., violence), there are important practical reasons to separate the two behaviors. As we have seen, bullying has been increasingly connected to school violence, particularly lethal school violence, in popular opinion and legislative action. For this reason, we argue that this conflation has encouraged public condemnation of and increasingly harsh punishments against girls, absent any data to indicate that these interventions are either warranted or necessary.

In their attempts to educate the public about the consequences of bullying, the Olweus program contends that bullying is a serious problem and should not be treated as a normal part of growing up for either boys or girls. The data used to advance these claims were usually alarming. For example, in his bullying prevention literature, Olweus argues that long-term studies of bullying victims demonstrated that they were more prone to depression and low self-esteem than non-bullied individuals (Olweus 1993). In addition, it was argued that "in some cases, the victims' devaluation of themselves becomes so overwhelming that they see suicide as the only possible solution" (Elliott, Olweus, Limber, and Mihalic 2002, 12). The bullying prevention program encourages schools to make parents aware of the seriousness of bullying by circulating informational fliers and fact sheets about bullying. Included in one sample brochure is the statement that "60 percent of children who are identified as bullies in middle school go on to have arrest records. We need to address the behavior problems of these children at an early age, before it becomes [sic] even more serious" (Elliott, Olweus, Limber, and Mihalic 2002, 69). Apparently, schools also suffer at the hands of bullies. In "schools with high levels of bullying problems, students tend to feel less safe and are less satisfied with school life" (Elliott, Olweus, Limber, and Mihalic 2002, 13). The message is that bullies are making schools unsafe places. Moreover, if bullying is not stopped, society will have a worse time containing the bullies when they become even bigger menaces.

These arguments about the severity of the bullying problem come from research on the long-term effect of *boys'* direct bullying, not girls' or boys' indirect bullying, and the data that only direct bullies went on to have arrest records comes from research on male bullies. Because the program defines bullying as direct and indirect behaviors, however, the public assumes that it is both types of bullying that lead bullies to become criminals, victims to develop depression and low self-esteem, and students in general to feel less safe and satisfied at school. And because the public perceives girls to be the major culprits of indirect bullying (although, as we shall see, this is not consistently found in the research literature), it is consequently assumed that it is *both* girls and boys who are responsible for these negative outcomes.

Bullying, Depression, and Sexual Harassment

Another significant concern is that bullying prevention programs have begun to imply that their prevention strategies can solve problems disproportionately experienced by girls—e.g., depression, low self-esteem, and sexual harassment. Regarding depression and low self-esteem, these aspects of girls' experience of adolescence have been increasingly linked to the "mean girl" phenomenon in popular books about covert or relational aggression. Simmons' *Odd Girl Out* (2002) thesis, for example, was that girls' indirect bullying leaves long-lasting scars and should be taken as seriously as boys' direct aggression. In fact, when asked whether girl-on-girl meanness is just part of growing up during a *Dateline* interview, Simmons (NBC 2002) replied, "I don't think kids who want to kill themselves because of what their friends are doing constitutes [sic] just something that's part of growing up. I don't think incredible depression at the age of 13 or 14, having to be medicated, should be part of growing up." In fact, in an MSNBC on-line interview conducted the next day (www.msnbc.com Chat 2002), Simmons advocated for bullying prevention programs to address problems unique to girls by arguing that, "Right now, most [school] policies favor physical and direct aggression, which are often the province of boys. We need to make these policies more specific and attend to the indirect, covert acts of girls."

In other words, what Simmons and others suggest is that aggressive girls are to blame for the wide range of negative emotional problems that girls experience in adolescence. While this simplistic notion might have an undeniable allure for the public, there are some serious questions about whether Olweus' program can really offer girls who suffer from "incredible depression at the age of 13 or 14" an effective intervention that targets the root of their problems. In fact, such a construction deflects attention from far more serious societal problems confronting girls, such as media sexualization and trivialization, sexual abuse, and pervasive educational neglect. Instead of focusing on the ways that girls are systematically ignored, silenced, and shortchanged in traditional classrooms and school, for example, the bullying prevention program has targeted female bullies as the primary problem in girl-world. Now, instead of changing the chilly school climate for girls, we are focused on blaming girls for the problems of girlhood.

Even more troubling are efforts to enfold girls' problems with sexual harassment in school into a bullying framework. Sexual harassment is a very serious problem for girls in school, as the results from two reports, *Hostile Hallways: The AAUW Survey on Sexual Harassment in America's Schools* (AAUW 1993) and the 2001 update (AAUW 2001) indicate. America learned that virtually all girls experienced sexual harassment, and the 2001 AAUW study added the fact that girls were much more likely than boys to experience negative effects due to sexual harassment. Finally, while the report also found high rates of sexual harassment against boys, it is important to note that boys were overwhelmingly the perpetrators of sexual harassment against girls and boys.

Based on these reports, it seemed clear that to address girls' needs in schools, the subject of boys' sexual harassment should be considered. Interestingly, anti-bullying policies and programs were often offered as one solution. The effort to link bullying with sexual harassment was evident even in the title of the AAUW report, which by 2001 was *Hostile Hallways, Bullying, Teasing, and Sexual Harassment in School*. While the report claimed to discuss the bullying problem, in actuality it only addressed *sexual* harassment.[5] Bullying was further linked with sexual harassment by the anti-bullying legislation passed after Columbine, in which states like New Jersey and Oregon specifically defined bullying to include harassment (sexual or non-sexual). In the recommendations section of the 2001 report (AAUW 2001, 44), the AAUW was praised for targeting bullying and sexual harassment problems by coordinating "workshops on sexual harassment and bullying. Through activities such as these, girls and boys themselves might transform the culture of fear and harassment to a culture of camaraderie and trust." The de-gendering of girls' experience of sexual harassment is more than simply unfortunate; it also strips girls of very important legal rights and the ability to sue school districts for damages (see Brown, Chesney-Lind, and Stein 2004).

For the same reasons that bullying prevention programs are inappropriate interventions for girls' depression and low self-esteem, bullying prevention is also a poor solution for sexual harassment. By incorporating efforts to combat sexual harassment with bullying control measures, we ignore the fact that it is primarily boys', and *not* girls', behaviors that need to be changed to make schools safer for students. Recall that although boys are the primary perpetrators of sexual harassment and direct bullying, bullying prevention programs aim to change both girls' and boys' behaviors. There are serious questions about whether it is appropriate to "treat" girls for problems that are caused by boys' behaviors. If anyone's behavior needs to be treated or anyone should be implicated in an "intervention" to make schools safe, it should be boys and not girls. Beyond this, girls have very specific civil and legal rights such as sexual harassment established in both court precedent and law, and they risk losing those protections in overly de-gendered approaches to sexual abuse and harassment (Brown, Chesney-Lind, and Stein 2004).

Policing and Punishing Bullies

Attention to indirect or relational bullying has contributed to a general trend where girls are increasingly blamed for their own problems and even their own victimization. Bullying prevention programs, though, may be doing more than contributing to an increasing condemnation of girls. They may increase the punishments leveled against girls, primarily in the specific bullying interventions advocated in the program. For example, the bullying prevention literature promotes the idea that bullying is not a problem confined to face-to-face tussles between students. Instead, it stems from an entire school system. Multiple agents—parents, teachers, administrators, and student bystanders— are implicated in the behavior as much as individual bullies. To stop the emotional and physical assaults, bullying prevention programs aim to change the entire school environment. They launch a school-wide awareness campaign so that every student, teacher, and administrator is aware that the school is taking a stand against bullying (Olweus 1993). In addition, the program defines bullying so that students and teachers are aware of the behavior not to be tolerated. Remember that the definition of bullying being widely distributed is one that includes physical and non-physical transgressions. The program asks schools to create and visibly post a very clear set of anti-bullying rules that include explicit statements that bullying will not be tolerated.

Another key aspect of the program is that it asks students to become the watchdogs for bullying behaviors. This means monitoring and reporting bullying to parents and teachers. Students are encouraged to police their peers' behaviors and take responsibility for their collective role in the problem. In some places, students are encouraged to use anonymous drop boxes to write up reports of any bullying that they see in the hallways or other locations. Students are instructed that it is not "tattling" or "ratting out" their friends, but comprises an important service for their schools and peers (Olweus 1993).

What these programs have done, essentially, is to create an atmosphere of intolerance for physical, verbal, *and* indirect bullying, although the most severe consequences of bullying are really about direct aggression. Also, the most pressing problems for girls seem to be boys' sexual aggression toward them. In addition to creating an environment in which girls and boys are equally to blame for bullying, these programs have also encouraged a policing system whereby behaviors that were previously considered non-serious are now brought to the schools' attention. The reporting and policing of bullying does not distinguish between physical and relational altercations. Thus, boys and girls are apt to end up on the radar for their role in the bullying problem. In addition, this system of reporting creates an infrastructure for a set of behaviors viewed as problematic—and not just bullying—to come to teachers' and administrators' attention.

What we see here is that these prevention programs have expanded schools' surveillance over students' behaviors that a decade earlier would have been completely ignored and gone completely unnoticed. Encouraged by these seemingly "effective" programs, and nervous after Columbine, schools developed even more surveillance techniques by collecting and officially reporting information about violent threats.

When combating bullying became a national priority, schools did more than increase their access to information about violence. They began to collect information, usually from students themselves, about social exclusion and even "meanness" among students.

In summary, programs that conflate girls' nonviolent "aggressions" with boys' violence are problematic for a number of reasons. As this chapter has shown, the hard evidence of the harms of bullying come not from indirect aggression, but rather from youth who were violent or engaged in direct aggression. In the name of being gender responsive, these programs begin to suggest, unfairly in our view, that the problems girls encounter, particularly in early adolescence, are really their own fault. At the same time, the vague and overly inclusive definition of "bullying" runs the risk of depriving girls of important civil rights victories in the areas of sexual harassment. Finally, as we will demonstrate in the next chapter, the inappropriate focus on girls' "meanness" only encourages official enforcement of what Brown and Gilligan have called the "tyranny of nice," where girls are rewarded for silencing themselves (Brown and Gilligan 1998, 62).

6

PATHOLOGIZING GIRLS?: RELATIONAL AGGRESSION AND VIOLENCE PREVENTION

Girl 1: You are a total prostitute.
Angela: Hey, that's how things really are. You just don't know 'cause
you're this pampered little suburban chick.

-American Beauty (1998)

Are girls mean? Are they meaner than boys? If one is watching television, reading the papers, or going to the movies, as we saw in chapter 2, it's impossible to ignore the flood of stories about the "mean" girl. As we noted earlier, a veritable torrent of mass market books on the topic have appeared, and while most of these books are overly simplistic and flawed, they rely on recent psychological research on aggression, particularly what is called "relational" or "indirect" aggressions (Underwood, Galen, and Paquette 2001, 248). A critical assessment of this literature is vital since this research clearly informs current violence prevention and anti-bullying programs and concomitantly, policies attending to girls' needs and developmental challenges.

To understand girls' aggression, it is first important to understand the psychological concept of "aggression," and how this academic definition relates to common-sense understandings of aggression (which is often conflated with fighting and other forms of violence). Psychologists define aggression as "behaviors that are intended to hurt or harm others" (Crick et al. 1999). As noted in the previous chapter, this means that a wide variety of behaviors fall under the category, ranging from rolling one's eyes and deliberating ignoring people to assault, rape, and murder. As we shall see, this area of research has created an interesting set of conversations about the harms of "indirect" or "covert" aggression. But we must also keep in mind that there may be some problems with a concept of "aggression" that is so inclusive that such disparate behaviors are covered by the same concept. While an understanding of all forms of aggression is important, the degree of harm involved in such behavior is important to keep in mind as well. Finally, we need to recall that this concept clearly includes both illegal and, however unpleasant, legal behaviors.

More to the point, there is increasing evidence that this "new" aggression is prompting more formal monitoring of girls' behavior. As an example, the concept of "indirect bullying," as it appears in the Olweus' anti-bullying program, is closely linked with and partly based on the emerging research on girls' aggression. For this reason, it is important to closely and carefully examine this literature, particularly notions of indirect or covert aggression as well as gender differences in these domains.

A Critical Look at Research on Girls' Aggression

Early research on aggression has concluded that as a group, boys exhibit significantly higher levels of aggression than girls (see Crick and Grotpeter 1995 for review). This is consistent with statistics illustrating higher rates of violent crime (i.e., murder, forcible rape, robbery, and aggravated assault) for male versus female youth (FBI 2005). The perception that males are more aggressive, however, might be more of a factor of *how* aggression is defined, which historically tended to reflect more overt manifestations. Increasingly, in both the empirical and popular literature, the concept of girls and "relational aggression" has been discussed.

As noted earlier, the concept of relational or covert aggression relates to a repertoire of passive or indirect behaviors (e.g., rolling eyes, spreading rumors, and ignoring), used with the "intent to hurt or harm others" (Crick and Grotpeter 1995; Crick et al. 1999). As such, the concept of relational aggression expands the range of behaviors that are considered aggressive in nature. On one end of the spectrum are covert, non-physical forms of aggressive behaviors, while on the other end are overt, physical forms of aggressive behaviors that are generally described as violent.

By identifying a "relational," "covert," or "indirect" aggression rather than physical type of aggression, researchers argued that they shattered the myth of the non-aggressive girl (see Bjorkqvist and Niemela 1992). These researchers note that girls are as aggressive as boys when these indirect aggressions are included. In fact, these aggression researchers claimed that they were not only shattering myths, but that they were unraveling years of gender bias in which male researchers tended to only look at male problems. Bjorkqvist and Niemela (1992, 5) argued that researchers, " … the majority being males, … may, for personal reasons, find male aggression easier to understand and a more appealing object of study." Consequently, the "discovery" of female aggression was seen as taking on old "stereotypes." It also seemed to end a long history of male-biased research and lend a more gender-balanced approach to adolescent development.

While this characterization of the "discovery" has been widely accepted, there are reasons to be a bit more skeptical about whether this concept is an innovation. Does this concept of aggression really challenge stereotypes and myths about girls and women? Recall that the behaviors included in relational or indirect aggression include retaliating against or manipulating another person by spreading rumors about them, giving them the silent treatment, or threatening to end a relationship. In essence, this research is arguing that girls and women are manipulative, sneaky, mean spirited, and backstabbing. These ideas are hardly new, which may in fact be one reason that the public and the media embraced them so quickly.

What this area of research is really doing is systematically measuring a set of attributes that have always been associated with girls and women (i.e., their devious and venomous natures), and then intellectually equating these "aggressions" to boys' violence. Consider researchers' contention that the "discovery" of girls' meanness is part of a gender-balanced project and a systematic assessment of problems that are "relevant to both sexes" (Crick et al. 1999). In the name of gender balance and equity, we are actually seeking new ways to devalue and demonize girls while also setting in place the need to police their behavior even more assiduously.

Such a development is all the more ironic since many in the area of relational aggression point the finger at the societal insistence that girls be "nice" as a reason that girls rely on these behaviors in the first place (Brown and Gilligan 1992). As an example, Simmons (2002) contends that girls are socialized into an impossible double bind psychologically. They are told that they must be good, nice, and quiet, and they are also told that they should have and value close and intimate relationships. Of course, with intimacy comes conflict, and again according to Simmons, girls fear that an expression of conflict will damage their relationships. In short, girls experience anger but they are not permitted to express it, because they "fear that even everyday acts of conflict would result in the loss of people they most cared about" (69). Trapped in a constraining, stereotypical gender role, some girls begin to craft ways of expressing their anger covertly.

Implicit in this discovery is also the contention that there is a significant gender difference in this behavior, and that "girls are more likely than boys to engage in relational, as opposed to overt, aggression" (Crick 1996, 2317). We note that while this notion is intuitively appealing since it tracks gender stereotypes, research has been decidedly mixed on this issue. Crick and Grotpeter (1995), for example, found that girls in their sample of 3rd- through 6th-grade students were significantly more relationally aggressive than were boys. Moreover, relationally aggressive youth were significantly more disliked and lonelier than non-aggressive peers. Bjorkqvist and Niemela (1992) found that when types of verbal aggression (e.g., gossiping, spreading rumors, etc.) were included in their overall measurement of aggression, only 5 percent of the variance was explained by gender. This suggests that by using a broader definition of aggression, both boys' and girls' unique forms of aggression were accounted for in their study.

Despite initial claims that girls gravitate toward subtle forms of hurting others, there are a number of psychological studies finding no differences between boys' and girls' perpetration of relational aggression (Prinstein, Boergers, Vernberg 2001; Hart et al. 1998; Putallaz, Kupersmidt et al. 1999). There are a few studies concluding that boys are actually more relationally aggressive than girls (Craig 1998; Hennington, Hughes et al. 1998). According to Olweus' research, for example, boys perpetrate the majority of indirect bullying experienced by girls (see also Whitney and Smith 1993). Note that if

Olweus' findings are correct, girls are indirectly victimized more often by boys than by girls; yet this phenomenon rarely makes it into any of the popular books on the topic,[1] which instead showcase girl-on-girl aggression almost exclusively (Chesney-Lind 2002).

Differences in how aggression is defined and measured may account for the mixed gender findings. For example, Olweus was examining bullying, which is direct or indirect victimization carried out repeatedly over time. In contrast, relational aggression can include, but is not limited to, single hurtful acts. Given this, boys might be more likely than girls to practice indirect aggression repeatedly. These differing findings might also be due to sample size. Olweus' research included large samples ranging from 900 to 130,000 students, and in contrast, the relational aggression research tended to draw from smaller samples with 500 and often even fewer students (sometimes as few as 105; see Storch, Werner, and Storch 2003). In addition, Olweus relied on students' self-reports of victimization to identify bullying problems. Many relational aggression researchers identify aggressors through peer nominations. While there is some debate regarding the efficacy of peer nominations versus victim reports (De Los Reyes and Prinstein 2004), research shows that peers tend to tolerate aggressive boys and reject relationally aggressive girls (Cillessen et al. 2006; Salmivalli et al. 2000). Peer nominations, therefore, may be charting this trend by under-identifying boys' relational aggression, which is normalized, and over-reporting girls' relational aggression, which is condemned (see also Merten 1997). We will explore the implication of this for girls later in the chapter.

Another reason for the conflicting findings regarding the difference between girls' and boys' relational aggression might be due to the practice of indirect aggression at different developmental stages. Girls may be more aggressive than boys in early childhood. By late adolescence, however, girls and boys might be equal in their perpetration of relational aggression (Bjorkvist 1994; Chessler 2001; Paquette and Underwood 1999; Prinstein, Boergers, Vernberg 2001; Roecker-Phelps 2001; Rys and Bear 1997; Storch et al. 2003).

To date, it is not clear whether girls are really more relationally aggressive than boys. What we do know, however, is that a look at the existing literature suggests that the early statements made by Crick and colleagues were preliminary and perhaps overstated (see also Underwood et al. 2001). The truth is that we need studies with larger samples and multiple measurement techniques in order to definitively state, once and for all, that girls dominate this category of hurtful behaviors. Also, it is probably necessary to distinguish between single relationally aggressive acts and relational aggression that is repeated over time as well as including victim reports in aggression measurements.

Does Relational Aggression Harm?

One of the core claims in this literature is that relational aggression is a major problem that has been ignored. These aggressions, we have been told, exist underneath the radar of most parents and virtually all teachers, since teachers and parents have their hands full dealing with the much more obvious physical aggression and violence of boys. As a result, "the day-to-day aggression that persists among girls, a dark underside of their social universe, remains uncharted and explored. We have no language for it" (Simmons 2002, 69). Paying attention to this aggression as both academics and journalists in this area would have us do, means that Simmons is correct. Not only do the behaviors "intend" to harm, they *do* measurable harm arguably to both the victim and the perpetrator. Let's review the evidence to see if this is, in fact, the case.

When finally deriving measures of relational aggression, it appears that it is one of the most common forms of aggression among children (see Crick, Bigbee, and Howes 1996). Here researchers have argued that the commonplace nature of it implies that it should be taken seriously. Specific arguments for the damage caused by relational aggression are that girls report relational aggression to be very hurtful and distressing (Crick 1995; Galen and Underwood 1997), and that victims of relational aggression experience difficulties with peer rejection, depression, isolation, and loneliness (Crick and Bigbee 1998; Crick and Grotpeter 1995, 1996; Nansel et al. 2001; Prinstein, Boergers, and Vernberg 2001; Storch et al. 2003; Werner and Crick 1999). Similar to the findings that girls are more aggressive than boys, the connection between relational aggression victimization and negative outcomes is inconsistent and questionable. In some studies, relational aggression does not lead to isolation (Storch et al. 2003) or depression (Werner and Crick 1999; Storch, Werner, and Storch 2003). Moreover, support from peers may mediate the relationship between relational aggression and loneliness (Storch et al. 2003).

To date, the vast majority of studies in this area have been cross-sectional rather than longitudinal (for an exception, see Xie et al. 2002), meaning that researchers cannot establish the temporal order between the onset of relational aggression and other problems among youth. Of the few longitudinal studies conducted, the time period examined was very short. For example, one study (Crick 1996) looked at 3rd- through 6th-grade students for six months and established relationally aggressive girls persist in their behaviors through most of a school year, but this hardly establishes a temporal order among all the factors under investigation. The research has tended to imply causation when, in fact, they have only established correlations (and inconsistent correlations at that) between relational aggression, victimization, isolation, depression, and peer rejection. This is a significant shortcoming of the current literature.

Turning now to the idea that relational and physical aggression comprise two types of the same underlying behavior, there is reason to question this version of "equality." Certainly, the two behaviors have vastly different consequences. Relational aggression may lead to emotional or psychological anguish for a day, a week, or even years. Although popular books like Simmons' claimed that there were many harms associated with relationship aggression, the truth is that, to date, aggression researchers have failed to identify any long-term negative consequences of this type of aggression.

More importantly, there is some evidence to suggest that some "indirect" or "relational" aggression is actually pro-social, rather than anti-social, for youth (Underwood, Galen et al. 2001; Xie et al. 2002). Specifically, in a narrative study of aggression among 475 7th-grade youth, Xie and colleagues found that "social aggression," which they defined as "concealed social attack," was associated with "higher network centrality" among adolescents (Xie et al. 2002, 205). Expanding on the meaning of this, they speculate that "the majority of socially aggressive children and adolescents may be neither socially incompetent nor suffering from deficits in social cognition" (219); instead, they argue that youth that use indirect aggression might actually have "higher social intelligence" than their counterparts who do not. They assert that "socially aggressive behaviors serve important functions for the individual and social groups" (219).[2]

Finally, and most importantly, is relational aggression predictive of violence? Recall that it is violence prevention that started the whole anti-bullying initiative and supplies the justification for intervention into the lives of young people. There is certainly reason to continue to be concerned about youth violence in the United States. While incidence of youth violence has been dropping in the last decade, the United States still has the highest rate of firearm-related deaths among youths in the industrialized world (U.S. Department of Health and Human Services 2001) and as of 2003, violence was still the second leading cause of death for 15- to 24-year-olds (CDC 2006). This doesn't include the physical injuries that youth sustain and survive on a daily basis as the outcome of physical violence.

In contrast to the failure of scientists to identify any long-term negative consequences of relational aggression, the bullying research has identified several negative outcomes of direct bullying. For example, Olweus (1993a) stated that bullying is part of a repertoire of anti-social and conduct-disordered behavior that starts in adolescence and becomes progressively worse as time goes on. This statement stems from the finding that 60 percent of bullies in grades 6 through 9 were convicted of a crime by age 24 (Olweus 1993). It is important to note that this likelihood of arrest was only true for the perpetrators of direct bullying, not indirect.

Researchers have generally supported the idea that relational and physical aggression are different types of the same underlying behavior because relational and physical aggression are moderately correlated (see Crick and Grotpeter 1995). As Crick and Grotpeter (1995, 715) argued, "the moderate magnitude of this correlation [$r=.54$, $p<.01$] is what one would expect for two constructs that are hypothesized to be *different* forms of the *same* general behavior." If they lacked any correlation, then these behaviors would be seen as completely different, and if they were highly correlated they would be viewed as the same behavior. We, however, argue that establishing a moderate correlation is not sufficient to state that physical and relational aggression are two parts of a whole.

Indeed, other more careful research has failed to confirm a clear relationship between violence and covert or relational aggression. Data from a longitudinal study of 475 youth followed from grade 7 into adulthood showed that while physical aggression "significantly increased a person's risk for school dropout and criminal arrest," and verbal aggression "significantly increased teen parenthood," social or relational aggressions "were not predictive of developmental maladjustment." The authors argued that these results "suggest that subtle aggressive behaviors may be normative in development" (Xie et al. 2002, 219).

Fact and Myth about Relationally Aggressive Girls

So far, we have argued that the science of girls' aggression is incomplete and inconclusive. Despite this, as we've noted, the research made a huge splash in popular culture, and a small cottage industry of proposing interventions to deal with the problem (Chesney-Lind 2002). A close look at these suggests that they oversimplify the science on covert aggression, and then tend to endorse stereotypical thinking about the downsides of girlhood.

The psychological literature is virtually silent on the role of boys' relational aggression. In addition, as we have noted previously, we certainly have no popular culture image of the "mean boy," although we have plenty of images of mean girls. The mean boy story is simply not being told, although there is clearly enough evidence to suggest that boys, especially at later ages, are also relationally aggressive. Best (1983) offers a vivid tale of gender differences in meanness in *We've All Got Scars*. As a group of "winner" boys come to dominate social relations in elementary school, Best observes them ritually taunting other boys for being "cry babies" or otherwise too "feminine." These popular boys also regularly taunt and harass girls in the class, a move that sends a clear message to girls about their second-class status. Even more problematic is that "loser" boys, those who are rejected by the male in-crowd, attempt to avoid harassment and prove their masculinity by putting down girls and reducing them to sexual objects. While it is true that girls can be mean to one another, it is also true that girls are harassed and tormented by both high-status and low-status boys. We wonder why this aspect of youth peer culture has not been addressed in the popular or scientific relational aggression discourse.

Related to this is a second problem with the media construction of relational aggression—that it is a major feature of girls' lives and that many girls engage in the behavior. That is also not correct, and it neglects findings that girls engage in far more pro-social behavior than boys. Finally, there are plenty of reasons to question the dominant idea that relationally aggressive girls are "queen-bees"—the stereotype is that relationally aggressive girls are socially powerful and use their popularity to keep other girls down (see Wiseman 2002 as an example of this construction). In media representations, popular girls rule the school with their gossip and social exclusion rituals. They are seen as self-confident, highly visible, and worshiped by others. Due to their manipulation and relationship "games," they seem to singlehandedly destroy the self-esteem of other girls.

The literature is divided on the issue of popularity and relational aggression. While some popular boys and girls do seem to practice relational aggression (see Andreou 2006; Cillessen and Rose 2005; Cillessen and Borch 2006; Rose et al. 2004; Salmivalli et al. 2000), there is indication that relationally aggressive girls are significantly more depressed and isolated than non-aggressive youths (Crick and Grotpeter 1995, 713). They do not belong to the popular well-liked group, and instead find membership among peers called the "controversial group," which is comprised of youths who are well liked by a few individuals and not at all liked by other individuals. Grotpeter and Crick (1996) found that friendships characterized by relational aggression were very close and intimate, meaning that these friends shared high levels of self-disclosure and emotional closeness. Along with the closeness and intimacy, however, these friendships were also characterized by high levels of conflict. Whether "controversial" youths and those who have very intimate yet stormy relationships are also high status youths is unknown to date.

There is reason to believe that relational aggression is not a component of social power. Despite having a few intimate friends, relationally aggressive girls saw themselves as being poorly liked by others (Crick and Grotpeter 1995). Studies have also found that relationally aggressive youths tend to have what is called a "hostile attribution bias." This means that these youths tend to interpret others as having hostile intentions towards them. In 3rd-grade children, relational aggression was correlated with borderline personality features such as negative affect and dissatisfaction with relationships (Crick, Werner, and Rockhill 1997).

Clearly there are conflicting images of relationally aggressive youths. One image is of a socially marginal youth who sees herself and others in a negative light. She senses her own marginality and feels that others have negative intentions towards her. While she has a few friends, her friendships are intense and filled with conflict. In addition to being manipulative and exclusionary, she also has a host of negative assets, such as depression and borderline personality characteristics. She is not the picture of confidence, coolness, and social desirability. The other image is of a socially central youth who uses relational aggression, or meanness, as a way of turning popularity into power (see Merten 1997). She might not be well liked by her peers, but she is highly visible and is perceived as being popular. The research to date is much too limited to discern which (if any) of these images is accurate.[3]

In addition to questioning some of the popular claims about relational aggression, we also have to seriously question interventions like Wiseman's "Empower Program" that asks relationally aggressive girls to "step down" from their social power (Talbot 2002, 40), since it is still unknown whether relational aggression is an expression of social power. The good news to keep in mind, and that programs to combat relational aggression tend to ignore, is that youth who engage in large amounts of relationally aggressive behaviors are a minority. The vast majority of girls are pro-social and capable friends. Popularity, as we will also show, is not the sole domain of mean girls. There seem to be plenty of popular, well-liked girls who do not practice relational aggression (see also Griffiths 1995).

What about Girl-on-Girl Violence?

If relational aggression is not predictive of girls' violence and direct aggression, what is? It turns out that girls' victimization plays a significant role in girls' violence. In her analysis of self-reported violence in girls in Canada, Artz (1998) noted that girls who reported problems with violence reported significantly greater rates of victimization and abuse than their non-violent counterparts, and that girls who were violent reported greater fear of sexual assault, especially from their boyfriends. Specifically, 20 percent of violent girls stated they were physically abused at home compared to 10 percent of violent males and 6.3 percent of non-violent girls. Patterns for sexual abuse were even more stark; roughly one out of four violent girls had been sexually abused compared to one in ten of non-violent girls (Artz 1998).

Follow-up interviews with a small group of violent girls found that they had learned at home, often from watching abusive male parents, that "might makes right," and they engaged in "horizontal violence" directed at other powerless girls (often with boys as the audience). Certainly, these findings provide little ammunition for those who would contend that the "new" violent girl is a product of any form of "emancipation" (as is often hinted in media accounts). Histories of physical and sexual abuse, then, may be a theme in girls' physical aggression, just as it is in their runaway behavior.

The context of girls' aggression and violence is clearly important. Ironically, aggressive and violent girls are often quite committed to the "ideology of familial patriarchy … supports the abuse of women who violate the ideals of male power and control over women" (DeKeseredy 2000, 46). This ideology is acted out by those males and females who insist upon women being obedient, respectful, loyal, dependent, sexually accessible, and sexually faithful to males. Artz (1998) builds upon that point by suggesting that violent girls more often than not "buy in" to these beliefs and "police" other girls' behaviors, thus serving to preserve the status quo including their own continued oppression.

Sadly, such themes are particularly pronounced among girls who have the most serious problems with delinquency. Artz, Blais, and Nicholson (2000, 31), in their study of girls in custody in British Columbia, Canada, found that the majority of these girls were male-focused, expressed hostility to other girls, and wanted very much to have boyfriends—always making sure that they had at least one, both in and out of jail. One girl strongly identified with the boys and saw herself as "one of the guys," also admitting that she had "always wanted to be a boy." Only one girl spoke little about boys—at 18 years of age she was the oldest girl in the center. All the girls used derogatory terms to describe other girls, and when they spoke about girls, their words reflected views of females as "other." Many girls saw other girls as threats, particularly if they were pretty or "didn't know their place" (i.e., thought they were better than other girls). A "pretty" girl, or a girl that the boys pay attention to, was a primary target for girl-to-girl victimization because she had the potential to unseat those who occupied the top rung on the "pretty power hierarchy" (Artz, Blais, and Nicholson 2000, 124). An "ugly" or "dirty" girl (a girl designated as a slut) was also a primary target for girl-to-girl victimization because she "deserved" to be beaten for her unappealing looks and for her "unacceptable" behavior.

Such a perspective is puzzling, but the reality is that marginalized girls who have been the victims of male power often see that sort of agency as the only source of power available to them. Most of these girls regarded their victims as "responsible" for the violence that they committed, since they were acting as "sluts," "total bitches," or "assholes" (189). Clearly, where these girls live, "you've gotta watch your back" (189) because "the world is a piece of shit" (189).

In short, those girls who have problems with violence suggest that both girls' and women's victimization as well as girls' violence towards other girls are really twin products of a system of sexual inequality and valorizes male violence as agency and has girls growing up "seeing themselves through the eyes of males" (Artz 1998, 204).

What about the Good News? Girls' Friendships

While the relational aggression literature has focused the lion's share of attention on girls who display relationally aggressive traits, it turns out that the developmental literature, and even the aggression literature, found another gender gap, one that has received virtually no attention. When assessing whether youth are relationally or physically aggressive, relational aggression researchers also measured whether students are pro-social. Although ranging from study to study, the pro-social behaviors include whether individuals do nice things for others, cheer others up, help others, and are good leaders (see Grotpeter and Crick 1996). Here they found that girls, more than boys, are consistently found to exhibit these positive traits (Crick and Grotpeter 1995). In addition, girls, more than boys, respond to aggression in pro-social ways; for example, by problem solving (i.e., changing something so that things work out) or by seeking support from others (Roecker-Phelps 2001). In fact, criminologists contend that girls' pro-social nature is contagious. McCarthy et al. (2004) found that membership in female-dominated peer groups had a negative effect on property crimes for both boys and girls. Despite the fact that girls are consistently found to be more pro-social than boys, relational aggression researchers fail to discuss girls' positive attributes.

Then there's the issue of the size of the covert aggression problem in girls. Despite media coverage, which seems to indicate that covert aggression is almost epidemic among girls, the evidence is that relatively few girls are relationally aggressive. For example, in their 1995 study, Crick and Grotpeter included 491 3rd- through 6th-grade children, 235 of whom were girls. Only 17.4 percent, or about 41 girls, were identified as being relationally aggressive. Not only is this a rather small number, but again, the other implication of this figure is that the vast majority of girls (over 80 percent of girls in the early studies) were *not* relationally aggressive.

At the same time that relational aggression research ignored girls' positive features, there is also evidence to suggest that many of the behaviors labeled as "aggressive" in the literature might actually serve positive functions. For example, gossip is often viewed as a manipulative, controlling, and maladaptive behavior by aggression researchers. In the peer culture research, however, gossip is seen as a more complex phenomenon and is neither inherently positive nor negative. For example, as Parker and Gottman (1989) found, gossip helped establish a sense of solidarity among peer groups and also became a central tool through which youth came to evaluate and establish their identities. For girls, gossip often reinforces idealized feminine appearance and demeanor norms (see Eder and Enke 1988). Gossip, however, does not always impose rigid gender frameworks on youths and, in fact, through gossip, youths can change and challenge larger as well as more localized group norms and values (Eder and Enke 1988; Fine 1986). Consistent with Underwood et al. (2001)

and Xie et al. (2002) findings, this suggests that some of the behaviors that we are classifying as relational aggression are not necessarily maladaptive or dysfunctional.

The relational aggression research, therefore, is taking an overly simplified interpretation of a set of behaviors that are, as the peer culture literature tells us, really rather complex and highly nuanced (see for example Adler and Adler 1998, 1995; Adler, Kless, and Adler 1992; Best 1983; Eder 1985; Eder and Parker 1987; Griffiths 1995; Kenny 2000; Lambart 1976; McRobbie 1978; Merten 1997; Nilan 1991; Taylor, Gilligan, and Sullivan 1995; Thorne 1994, 1986; Thorne and Luria 1986). What is really troublesome is the fact that relational aggression researchers have launched an entire research program dedicated to locating the negative aspects of youths' peer interactions without making a single reference to the findings in the peer culture literature. This clearly points to the fact that to date, relational aggression research is unnecessarily narrow in its focus.

The relational aggression literature has also used methods that may overstate the problem and are arguably inaccurate. *Peer nominations* ask students to characterize their classmates' behavior traits. Relationally aggressive students are those who classmates perceive as being exclusionary (i.e., they get even with others by using the silent treatment or not including others in the group). In contrast, *victimization reports* measure whether students have been the target of another student's social exclusion. When using peer nomination scales, as we have noted, you collect assessments of which students are perceived as being relationally aggressive, regardless of whether students being surveyed have been directly victimized by these students.

The difference between the two methods becomes clear when reviewing the data reported by Olweus (1994), which relied on victimization reports and found that boys are responsible for the vast majority of direct and indirect bullying. While this may have to do with the difference in the ways bullying and aggression are defined (as we have noted before, bullying is repeated and aggression can be one-time acts), it probably has something to do with how these studies have identified relationally aggressive students. If it is true that girls are victimized (both relationally and physically) more often by boys than by girls, then the way we measure relational aggression is no small consideration. Moreover, it becomes very important to identify victims and perpetrators in these studies so that we can derive a more comprehensive view of girls' and boys' developmental challenges.

By overstating the gendered aspect of covert or relational aggression while at the same time ignoring the data suggesting a clear gender gap in pro-social behavior, the relational aggression literature has tended to pathologize girls. The literature has argued that girls are particularly prone to relational aggression, and that relational aggression leads to a host of "maladaptive" outcomes for victims and perpetrators. As this chapter has indicated, the evidence for many of these assertions is weak or contradictory. More importantly, the literature has failed to report positive aspects of girls' friendships and glossed over the direct and indirect ways that boys victimize girls at school.

Girls' Friendships in Context

The "discovery" of girls' aggression and the development of the girls' aggression research program demonstrates an inherent flaw in "girl-focused" research; it also offers a cautionary tale to those seeking to use this research as a basis for working on a gender balanced approach to bullying and violence prevention. For years, the tendency to ignore girls and focus exclusively on boys has led to the perception that any research that is focused on girls is "gender balanced." We argue that gender focused is not enough to overcome gender bias in research, as can be seen in the flawed research on girls' aggression. Research on and about girls has to look at the larger social context framing girls' lives and experiences and, specifically, must address girls' relative power vis-à-vis boys and society in general.

As the next chapter will indicate, the schools that girls attend routinely deny equal opportunities for girls while underplaying the harassment girls experience in these settings. This situation certainly has not helped bullying prevention programs that adopt the claims of some researchers on aggression that perpetuate rather than solve the problems that daily confront girls on campus. In fact, they have completely misunderstood and mislabeled the girls' peer group experiences. By ignoring the larger context confronting girls and within which girls establish their peer groups, the research that attempts to combat girls' aggression, in fact, opens the door for girls to be blamed and condemned for poisoning their peer groups and diminishing the safety of schools.

An emancipatory research program for girls would take into account the many ways that boys enter the world as the preferred sex. Simone De Beauvoir (1952) acknowledged this in her classic work *The Second Sex*, and researchers have chronicled the developmental effect of this on girls, who learn early on that boys and men have the power in society (Edlehard 2003). Society's preference for men and the systematic devaluation of girls and women, who are the second and auxiliary sex, is historic and, despite attempts to combat and change this core cultural construction, it emerges in storybooks, media, and even by well-intentioned teachers and parents. Research findings that reinforce the common cultural tale about girls' flawed and pathological natures are anything but revolutionary and beneficial for girls. Indeed, the moral tale remains the same across generations—boys are physical, direct, competitive, and assertive. Girls are weak, indirect, sneaky, and untrustworthy.

Brown and Chesney-Lind (2005)[4] bring our attention to the image of the back-stabbing, two-faced girl and argue that this, and all the other ways that women and girls are publicly denounced, are culturally-mediated forms of othering girls. And, as we have shown in chapter 5, the condemnation of girls by other girls is part of this larger trend. Girls consistently monitor other girls' behaviors. Those who are popular, well liked by boys, or physically attractive, are condemned for being petty, boy crazy, slutty, and stuck up. Conversely, girls who are not popular or obsessed with looks and pleasing boys are ugly, fat, and geeky. Those who speak out too loudly or too forcefully are obnoxious and bitchy. Those who are too quiet or obsequious are mindless airheads. There is clearly no winning for girls.

Girl-on-girl condemnation in a context in which girls and women are generally denounced can be read as a form of "horizontal violence" (Friere 1970/1993, 117) in which similarly situated individuals take out their aggression against one another (see Artz 1995; Brown 2003). Girls might be said to internalize or "appropriate" (Tappan 2002) general oppression by accepting dominant messages about what it means to be a good girl, which are from the start messages that ensure that girls cannot win. Working out their own anxieties about failing to meet the impossible standards governing girlhood, girls lash out at other girls who are also failing in a system rigged against them. It is their only outlet.

Instead of reading relational aggression as a type of pathology plaguing girls, we might reread this concept using an appropriate oppression or horizontal violence framework. This would first require us to note that the relational aggression and mean girl hype of the turn of the century has done very little to liberate girls or offer gender-balanced perspectives and programs. The way that science, media, and programs have utilized and advanced the concept of relational aggression has only generated a new language system to chastise and condemn girls. In short, the discovery of girls' aggression has just handed girls more bad news about themselves and more reasons to blame the problems of misogyny on other girls rather than pervasive institutional sexism.

It is the contours of the larger systems that police and enforce girlhood that our gender-balanced science should attempt to document. Girls' developmental challenges should always be linked to the larger contexts in which girls grow up. This means more than acknowledging the peer, school, family, and community environments in which girls are embedded, but documenting specifically how gender inequalities and male privilege runs through each of these contexts to present challenges to girls at every stage of their lives.

One of the most important tasks facing researchers who want to combat and change the gender-specific challenges confronting girls is to offer girls real opportunities to gain status and prestige. This means offering girls opportunities to achieve success, status, and positive evaluations outside of the confines of feminine rules for success because as we have noted, the rules of femininity govern a no-win game and are filled with double standards. In concrete terms, this would mean offering girls something more than programs that encourage them to be "nice," "kind," "well liked," and "popular," but that encourage them to be great thinkers, athletes, scientists, writers, actors, policy makers, community leaders, family leaders, or public speakers (to name a few). The core of any of these programs would be to celebrate, praise, and value girls. We should be suspicious of any and every program that directly or indirectly disseminates negative messages about girls. And we should be especially leery of any program that denounces girls for all the same reasons that girls have been devalued in history—for being manipulative, untrustworthy, and sneaky. These programs are not going to help girls. They are only going to place further limits on their ability to value themselves and one another.

Summarizing briefly, an emacipatory and non-gender-biased approach to girls' programming would acknowledge the larger structural context in which girls grow up, would praise and value girls instead of blaming them for the challenges they confront. It would remain accountable to the ways that research is used against girls in a general culture that routinely denigrates girls and women, continually combat and change the general cultural condemnation that surrounds girls, and would offer opportunities for girls to achieve success in a variety of ways and to value themselves as multifaceted and multitalented. This, we argue, is the difference between regulatory and emancipatory research on and about girls. By these standards, girls' aggression research and the bullying prevention strategies based on only sketchy understandings of this science fail because they increase the extent to which girls are denounced, devalued, and regulated.

Conclusion

In the first decade of the new century, boys had fallen out of the youth violence spotlight, and girls with their meanness and manipulation had taken their place. The invention of a female form of bullying, as we have noted, "took off" in large part because it resonated with the historic tendency to identify and publicly berate "bad girls." As we explored in chapter 2, the press loved to portray girls who had gone bad in one way or another, and when the gun-toting girl "gangsta" slipped out of public attention, the nasty female bully quickly took her place. In fact, the popular culture book *The Friend Who Got Away* (Offill and Schappell 2005), which claimed that girls' friendships were actually loving and not so mean, was criticized in the *New York Times* review of books for not being polemical enough. Hansen (2005, 8) expressed disappointment that the book did not deliver stories about "cheating lovers, hair pulling or face slapping (or both), friendship necklaces flushed down toilets and perhaps a husband or two ensnared at the neighborhood barbecue." In other words, the public doesn't want to hear stories of kindness and connection among girls. They want the cat fights, the meanness, and high drama. And they got it. Never mind that boys can be just as petty and manipulative, according to the scientific literature. That news story is one you are not likely to read.

Ironically, a concern about "bullying" that originated in horrific male violence gradually swept up girls whose "bullying" quickly overtook the more toxic and violent male form, in part because it dovetailed neatly with a more general anxiety about girlhood vulnerability in a post-feminist age. The problem was not about girl-on-girl "bullying," as the data clearly show. Rather, it is that girls grow up in a culture that denigrates, commodifies, and demoralizes women, and then "gets a kick out of the divide-and-conquer consequences" (Brown and Chesney-Lind 2002, 23).

We suspect that if we give girls legitimate avenues to power and means to value themselves, they'd be less likely to go down those underhanded or hostile roads, less likely to take their legitimate rage out on other girls. Our challenge is to join them in creating different cultural stories, images, and realities that open pathways to opportunity, power, and possibility. Instead of offering girls programs designed to combat boys' problems, or worse, programs that disseminate negative messages about girls, let's implement programs that actually open opportunities for girls to be praised, respected, and to achieve in multiple activities. And certainly, let's stop implementing programs that blame girls for poisoning their own school environment.

There are a number of reasons to avoid programs that focus on curbing girls' "meanness" (see Morash and Chesney-Lind 2006). First, and most importantly, relational aggression does not predict physical aggression or violence; there is evidence that it is normative and desirable for youth (Underwood, Galen et al. 2001; Xie et al. 2002). There is even evidence that aggression makes separation from others, individualization, competition, achievement, and the initiation of new relationships possible (Hadley 2004, 391). Second, as already noted, it is debatable that girls are particularly inclined to use or approve of relational aggression, and if there are gender differences in these forms of aggression, they seem to end by late adolescence. Finally, in contrast to physical aggression and violence, relational aggression is not illegal, and any focus on it would expand the juvenile justice intervention net to a group of people that are not prone to use physical violence.

Even for girls who act violently and who direct relational aggression toward other girls, how relational aggression is handled must be carefully thought through. Many girls are socialized to be conciliatory and to avoid conflict so that they are included in relationships and liked by other people (Brown and Gilligan 1992; Underwood 2003; Zahn-Waxler 2000). Indirect acts are sometimes the only way that girls have for expressing their anger towards, or even their preferences for, friends. Alternatives to physical and direct aggressions are, fundamentally, weapons of the weak, and as such they are as reflective of girls' powerlessness as they are of girls' "meanness." Girls, women, and others in relatively powerless groups historically have not been permitted direct aggression (without terrible consequences). As a result, in certain contexts, and against certain individuals, relational aggressions were ways the powerless punished the bad behavior of the powerful. This was, after all, how slaves and indentured servants—female and male—got back at abusive masters, how women before legal divorce dealt with violent husbands, and how working women today get back at abusive bosses. As one psychologist put it, "There is reason to question any approach that potentially serves to discourage females from expressing anger and aggression and reminds them of their subordinate positions in society" (Zahn-Waxler 1993, 81).

Knowing all this, how do we think about violence prevention and girls? We can recognize the context within which girls' aggression and the societal response to it is lodged. Lyn Mikel Brown (2003) notes that in a society that celebrates anything male, "girls simply find it easier and safer to take out their fears and anxieties and anger on other girls rather than on boys or on a culture that denigrates, idealizes, or eroticizes qualities associated with femininity. Girlfighting is not a biological necessity, a developmental state, or a rite of passage. It is a protective strategy and an avenue to power learned and nurtured in early childhood and perfected over time" (5–6). According to Brown, we can challenge girlfighting by teaching girls to talk candidly about anger, and creating spaces where girls can practice voice and activism.

7

POLICING GIRLHOOD: SEXISM, SCHOOLS, AND THE ANTI-VIOLENCE MOVEMENT

It is widely assumed that schools are settings that provide children and young people with the skills they will need to succeed in the world. That has been their explicit function since the emergence of formal public education. Careful research on gender and education since the 1970s has documented, though, that schools also have a very powerful "hidden curriculum," one that has functioned to ignore, silence, and sexualize girls while empowering boys (Block 1984; Sadker and Sadker 1994). In this chapter, we review evidence suggesting that this hidden curriculum, while still at work, has been augmented during the past two decades with a more overt and punitive system of control.

An examination of the way the hidden system of controlling girls at school has partnered with a more overt system is particularly important since, as we have seen in previous chapters, schools have become integrally involved in the monitoring of youthful behavior both to "prevent" and "intervene in" youth violence. We have examined the ways in which this hypervigilance has in recent years involved school officials in the patrolling of the noncriminal behavior of girls in ways that could clearly be seen as part of a larger project of regulating girls' sexuality, deportment, and obedience to authority. In the first section of this chapter, we examine the research suggesting that schools have always been a place where girls have been socialized into hegemonic femininity. In the last half of the chapter, we will examine how this covert gender curriculum has become more overt and explicit as schools have joined forces with criminal justice agencies to control crime and violence on campus. In this context, girls' minor violations of hegemonic "good girl" femininity are being recast as criminal violations, and this trend is particularly ominous for girls of color. Such an interaction is sadly predictable as schools become closer to formal, legal systems of control, such as the juvenile justice system, which have long histories of patrolling both race and gender boundaries in ways that disadvantage both girls and youth of color (Chesney-Lind and Shelden 2004; Feld 1999).

Historically, the social control of school girls has occurred in two ways: first, through formal classroom practices that celebrate boyhood and silence girls, and second, through peer group relationships and extracurricular activities that reward girls' physical attractiveness and participation in romantic spectacles at the expense of girls' achievement. In the end, these different socializing mechanisms distance them from opportunities for success in the public sphere.

Reproducing Gender at School: The Hidden Curriculum and the Chilly Classroom

In 1972, Congress passed Title IX, which established gender equity as a goal in schools. Its preamble sets this out explicitly, arguing that "No person in the United States shall, on the basis of sex, be excluded from participation in, be denied the benefits of, or be subject to discrimination under any educational programs or activity receiving federal assistance" (Owens, Smothers, and Love 2003, 132). The last decades provide considerable evidence of the success of this historic piece of legislation, particularly in the area of girls' participation in sports. As an example, in 1972, about 300,000 high school girls played sports; in 2001, the comparable figure was 2.78 million (Women's Law Center 2002, 1).

In 1991, the American Association of University Women undertook a landmark study of the treatment of girls in schoolrooms across the United States. *Shortchanging Girls, Shortchanging America* (1991) synthesized the findings of many studies on gender and the classroom, and noted among other things that the average classroom was biased against girls in very specific ways (see also Best 1983; Davies 1989; Delamont 1981; Deem 1980; Stanworth 1983; Thompson 2000). Teachers tended to pay more attention to boys, to ask them more challenging and abstract questions, and generally render girls "invisible," in part because they have been encouraged to obey authority and conform to teacher expectations[1] (Owens, Smothers, and Love 2003, 133). Since children spend more time with their teachers than any other adults except their parents (Skolnick 1982), even subtle forms of bias have huge impacts.

The AAUW study also surveyed over 3,000 children aged 9 to 15 in twelve locations across the country, and found that boys and girls have equally high levels of self-esteem in elementary school, despite classroom bias. As girls and boys age, self-esteem tends to drop, but the researchers found that such a drop was far more dramatic in girls. By high school, only 29 percent of girls are "happy with themselves" compared with 46 percent of boys (AAUW 1992, 24).

The AAUW survey explored ethnic differences in girls' experiences with education and found some important differences. Specifically, the study found that while African-American girls maintain higher levels of self-esteem during high school than do white girls, "the schools do not provide the same supports for academic self-esteem," so the girls maintain their positive outlook by becoming "dissociated from school" (AAUW 1991, 27). Latino girls are less confident than their African-American counterparts,[2] though they still feel only marginally better about themselves in high school than do white girls (30 percent compared to 29 percent agreeing that they are happy with themselves). Their problems arise in "confidence in family relationships, school, talents and importance" (AAUW 1991, 27).

Qualitative research on girls and schooling provide at least one explanation for girls' self-esteem drop (although see Mahaffy 2004 for another perspective on self-esteem). Brown and Gilligan (1992) would focus specifically on what was happening to girls between childhood and adolescence in a two-year dialog with girls at Laurel School. Summing up their complex work, they documented how the "tyranny of nice" (Brown and Gilligan 1992, 53) tended to encourage girls to lose their "voice" as they entered adolescence. The authors were particularly disturbed to see girls doing well on "tests of academic achievement" and "standard measures of social and moral development" and yet they were "favored by their teachers and praised by their parents when they dissociated or dissembled" (Brown and Gilligan 1992, 218).

Indeed, as this research indicates, the impact of gender on girls' lives is perhaps most clearly seen in studies that review girls' experiences in middle and high schools. High school, in particular, is a "unique, eccentric, and insulated social system" obsessed with prestige and popularity, and also about as close to the "core of the American experience" as one can imagine (Sadker and Sadker 1995, 98). It is also a place where the "chilly classroom" (Hall and Sandler 1982) experienced by girls in early years takes on an even more consequential meaning. By the end of high school, girls are developing lower occupational aspirations than boys, even when they possess the same abilities and advantages (Marini 1978). Girls are also dropping out of the math and science classes that would prepare them for the more remunerative jobs (Ehrhart and Sandler 1987). One reason for this might be that girls studying science describe themselves as less feminine, less attractive, and less popular (Project on Equal Education Rights 1984). Also, peer pressure may explain the absence of girls from science classes. Although girls do as well as boys in computer classes, for example, they do not join the boys' after-school computer clubs, in part because the boys admitted deliberately harassing the girls (Project on Equal Education Rights 1984; Ehrhart and Sandler 1987). Girls may also feel pressure in such settings not to compete with boys (Weisfeld 1986).

Sadker and Sadker (1994) note that while girls begin school "looking like the favored sex," that quickly changes as they lose their advantage just as standardized tests begin to be most consequential (138), and the gap in these test scores has remained despite modifications in the test (Fairtest 2006, 1). More recently, Steele (1997) found that both girls and African-Americans tend to do worse on standardized tests because they experience stress when taking the test and know that stereotypically their group does not do as well as whites and males.

What about school failure and gender? While boys' school disengagement is marked by disruptive, delinquent, or criminal acts (see Best 1983)—which ultimately lead to several confrontations with school personnel—girls' disengagement is more subtle and often goes under the radar of school staff (see Osler and Vincent 2003). Diedre Kelly chronicles how this unfolds in her ethnographic study of two "alternative" schools in California she calls Beacon and La Fuente. Kelly was specifically concerned about "examining gender relations within the area of disengagement" since she noted that girls were closing the gender gap in drop-out and push-out (xvii). She specifically focused on the role of peer groups and the fact that these key groups "gave a few the power to challenge gender stereotypes, but more often maintained traditional class and ethnic-shaped gender identities" resulting in "more severely negative consequences for disengagement for girls" (xvii).

Kelly first noted that girls felt less stigmatized at these alternative schools and perceived more choice in these settings (69). That said, Kelly also noted that girls disengage from alternative schools in ways that teachers tended not to notice, since "some of the teachers don't really pay attention to girls, they don't think they would be [out causing trouble]" (97), and while boys clowned around to deal with boredom, girls were more likely to try "sweet talking" their teachers, particularly the male teachers. Kelly also observed "more girls than boys actually coming to blows with one another at school." Although, as we will note later, official responses to girls' fighting would shift in the 1990s and 2000s, Kelly found that girls' fights were trivialized by school staff partly because of the reasons for these fights. According to the girls in her study, girls tended to fight with other girls over boys' infidelities. Dressing provocatively could also get girls in trouble, with both boys and girls willing to gossip about girls whom they saw as "sluts," "hoes," and "players," with girls being much more aware of being judged on "the way they looked" (137).

Kelly noted that girls "disengaged" from school for different reasons than boys, often revealed as domestic responsibilities, including "relationships" that often competed with school for the girls' loyalty and attention (125). Even sports, which worked to make boys popular and encouraged them to stay in school, did not work the same for girls. "The girls are getting more involved in sports, [and] they get praise, too, but not like the guys. The guys—they're our school," one girl told Kelly.

Kelly concludes that "we need more research that closely attends to the power relations between boys and girls rather than simply comparing the two sexes." As an example, girls in her study were more likely to disengage from school because of romantic relationships, and many more girls reported feeling "marginal to, and sometimes subordinate within, largely male dominated subcultures" (223).

Notably, teachers in particular did not seem prepared to help girls challenge "gendered cultural beliefs" that they brought to school or encountered in their peer groups, and in fact sometimes conveyed gender-differentiated expectations themselves. Kelly observed that they quite frequently responded differently to girls' and boys' "cutting" school, and they catered to boys' reluctance to do anything "considered feminine" (Kelly 1993, 179). Finally, and most importantly, teachers frequently failed to notice girls disengaging from school and did little to stop male denigration and harassment of girls inside or outside of the classroom. Harassment of girls and boys who were perceived to be lesbian, gay, or transgender was particularly obvious to Kelly, so that "tough girls" were ridiculed as "dykes," wannabe boys, or sluts (186). Likewise, males who were perceived to be gay dealt with being called "fag" almost daily. Kelly saw that while a teacher might occasionally punish a student for such name calling, they "usually ignored these exchanges" (187).

Racism, Educational Neglect, and White Privilege

In addition to Kelly's work, which focused largely on Latino and Latina youth, other recent research on stress in the lives of African-American girls adds important information about the role of school hassles and racism confronted by African-American girls, and also showcases the role racism has (both within and outside of the class-room) in the lives of girls of color. Specifically, a study of stress in the lives of roughly 100 African-American girls revealed that the most common "hassles" reported by girls were "school-related tension" (Guthrie, Young, Boyd, and Kintner 2002, 149), which was attributed by the authors to a lack of parental education, or negative parental attitude, as well as a lack of fit between the adolescent's own culture and background and school expectations. Significantly, reported "experiences with discrimination" were a strong predictor of school-related hassles, unlike income and "toughness of the neighborhood" (150). Those latter factors, though, were related to "peer-related hassles" (e.g., not being part of the "popular group") and feeling isolated. In another study using the same data set, racial discrimination was strongly related to African-American girls' smoking as a way to reduce the stress this experience produces (Guthrie, Young, Williams, Boyd, and Kintner 2005, 189).

Arnold (1995) amplifies this concern in her interviews with fifty African-American women doing time in a city jail. In their reflections on their past, she reports that these women remembered educational systems that were "alienating" and "oppressive." They recalled "going to school every day and not learning anything" from teachers that seemed to be there just to collect a paycheck. One woman said, "It was hard for me to get along with the teachers. Some were prejudiced, and one had the nerve to tell the whole class that he didn't like black people" (Arnold 1995, 140).

Schools' differential policing of girlhood through dress codes in ways that disadvantage black girls is powerfully documented in Morris' ethnographic study of a middle school serving an economically challenged neighborhood in Texas (Morris 2005). The school in question had instituted a uniform dress code to "decrease gang activity," a move which, while having adult support, created considerable student discontent. One young African-American boy told the researcher that the uniforms cost students extra money while also creating "a prison-like atmosphere in the school" (Morris 2005, 43). More to the point, the wearing of uniforms created a site of resistance, with both boys and girls refusing to tuck in their shirts.

"Tuck in that shirt" became the "most often used phrase" in the ethnographic study, and almost invariably the reprimand was directed to African-American girls (Morris 2005, 34). In fact, Morris never recorded it used against Latina, Asian, or white girls (though they received other reprimands). Teachers seemed particularly concerned with "improving the social skills of black girls" and enforcing a "lady-like" code of demeanor and dress on these young women—admonishing them about how to move, sit, and talk.

It seemed as though black girls could not do anything right. Veteran teachers complained about the "speed of their movements," the way they walked and sat ("Close your legs—ladies don't sit like that"), and even the fact that they run around and laugh "boisterously" between classes (Morris 2005, 34–35). Morris also observed African-American girls being scolded, often by older African-American women, for wearing "hoochie-mama" clothing (Morris

2005, 32). Teachers and administrators were also concerned about things like the "volume" of African-American girls' laughter, and their "loud" and "combative" style of talking. Astonishingly, though, these same teachers remark that African-American girls were their best students: "They're loud, but they're a sharp bunch and do their work" (Morris 2005, 34–35).

Morris noted that school officials also policed behavior of Latino boys closely, seeing these young men as "potentially aggressive." They tended to view Latinas, even those involved in gangs, as in need of protection from gang boys. For African-Americans, however, he notes "blackness" of students seemed to indicate "aggression and forceful-ness" (see also Ferguson 2001). Combining this with gender, "adults viewed the boys as dangerously masculine" and also "viewed black girls as inadequately feminine" (Morris 2005, 44).

In his study of what he described as "cultural capital and body discipline," Morris also observed a small population of white and Asian youth, and he "almost never saw these students disciplined in terms of dress or manners, even when I observed clear violations," a pattern he attributed to "Whiteness" or "Asianness" which "appeared to indicate docility and normative masculinity and femininity" (Morris 2005, 39).

Racial differences in school disciplinary policies also come to the fore in Kenny's *Daughters of Suburbia*—a part ethnography and part autoethnography exploring the "culturelessness" (Kenny 2000, 164) of her white, privileged girlhood in a Long Island suburban neighbor-hood and its middle school, Shoreham-Wading River (SWR). During observations of a cultural exchange program between SWR Middle School and the more racially diverse and working-class Riverside Middle School, Kenny observed how SWR engaged in "unconscious race consciousness" by actively ignoring differences between SWR and Riverside adolescents residing just twenty minutes away (see also Mac Ghaill 1993). Kenny (2000, 190) argued that SWR students, who were allowed to eat and drink during and between classes, speak out of turn during classroom discussions, leave campus during lunch, and engage in independent study projects, "were being disciplined to be individuals, to be their own managers, and to be comfortable with supposedly benign and nearly invisible forms of authority ... ."

Riverside students, 30 percent of whom were black, did not enjoy the same autonomy. Posted rules inside classrooms reminded them that they would be disciplined for a number of infractions including talking out of turn during lessons, swearing, dressing inappropriately, carrying weapons (including water pistols), leaving their assigned seats without permission, or being tardy to class. Between periods, Riverside students rushed along the hallways, keeping to the right of a yellow line on the floor, and during lunches they were watched vigilantly by school staff standing guard at cafeteria exits. In this way, Kenny (2000, 190) argues that Riverside students were "… being taught to stay in line (literally as well as more broadly), to follow orders, and not question authority."

Despite the lip service given to multicultural awareness, SWR teachers never discussed these obvious differences, even when students broached the subject. In this way, Kenny argues that adults in the community socialized students into a system of "white lies" that silenced critical discussions of race, class, and gender. This system of "white lies," in which white middle-classness is constantly constructed as normal culture, has a particular effect on the adolescent girls. In efforts to disrupt the silence and the boredom of privileged "normal" life, which is "supposed to be uneventful, unspeakable, and culture-less," (Kenny, 104), girls rebel by collectively dramatizing stories about their own and other girls' everyday lives (see also Owens et al. 2000). What Kenny calls "big stories" are more than girls' "gossip." They are girls' efforts to cope with the normalized, "unspeakable" femininity imposed on them by adults.

The corrosive effect of racial stereotyping can clearly be seen in groups other than African-Americans, whites, and Latinos and Latinas. Mayeda, Chesney-Lind, and Koo (2001), for example, explored the educational experiences of Samoan and Filipino youth in Hawaii and found that many of the students, particularly those of Samoan ancestry, reported the same difficulties with teachers stereotyping them as "lazy," and even that they "hated" Samoans. One 15-year-old Samoan girl told a focus group:

> Like um, um teachers. Well, I thought that one of my teachers, yeah, like I thought she was against Samoans li'dat. Most of our Samoans in

our class, they all would either fail her class, or they would like barely pass, like D's, you know what I'm saying. That was the highest grade any of the Samoans could get. Like we would ask her for help li'dat and she would ignore us. She would just walk away and she go help, um the other ethnic students li'dat.

The authors speculated that one factor that is likely to cause a disproportionate amount of Polynesian youth to be disinterested in school, which was read as being "lazy," is negative interaction with teachers. Reyes and Jason (1993) investigated success factors associated with academic achievement for Hispanic students, and also found that students who were considered high risk " ... cited teachers' putdowns of them and their abilities as sources of embarrassment and dissatisfaction" (67).

Pretty and Popular

Adolescence is a beauty pageant. Even if your daughter doesn't want to be a contestant, others will look at her as if she is. In Girl World, everyone is automatically entered. How does a girl win? By being the best at appropriating our culture's definition of femininity. (Wiseman 2002, 77)

The peer group is one of the most central socializing forces in school girls' lives, and its power clearly increases with age. Peer group relationships and interactions also function independently from teacher behavior, as Thorne found in her qualitative study of elementary school classrooms and playgrounds. Her work documents the significance of informal playground interactions in which the boundaries between girls and boys are sorted out along with themes of aggression and sexuality (see also Best 1981). These settings revolve around exchanging insults ("girls are dumb;" "boys are stupid") between homosocial groups (Thorne 1994, 5). Particularly salient are boys' displays of "masculine superiority" that involve a "contempt for things feminine" while also setting the stage for "adult male privilege and sexism." She notes that this behavior (often tolerated as "boys will be boys") can quickly permit harassment and verbal putdowns of girls inside and outside of the classroom, causing inhibition of their active participation in classrooms.

While boys are being channeled into sports and away from intellectual activities and other more "feminine" undertakings, girls are being pushed, according to Thorne, into a "heterosexualized" femininity that begins to stress, even in grade school, girls' "attractiveness" to boys. Tied up in this are girls engaging in "'goin' with' rituals" (Thorne 1994, 170) and active efforts to establish couples, behaviors that Thorne links to girls later lowering their ambitions in exchange for boys' approval—since ultimately, as Thorne correctly notes, "the culture of romance perpetuates male privilege" (170).

Thorne's concern is also echoed by research on high school girls, particularly around rituals like "prom," which, while affording girls a space to challenge school norms about the proprieties of dress and desire, ultimately also "solidify their place in culture (a place feminist scholars have long found to be troubling)" (Best 2004, 202). Best, in her research on proms, was particularly impressed that despite the obvious role that race and class play in the lives (and life chances) of girls, these aspects were overwhelmed by the "cultural influence of gender" with its emphasis on things like "the dress" and elaborate and increasingly costly "getting ready" rituals like having makeup and hair done by salon professionals. Again, while offering girls some places to resist the contemporary schools' efforts to challenge school rules which "emphasizes modesty in dress for girls and heavily sanctions violations," they also "secure girls' complicity in maintaining prevailing feminine forms." And, of course, they require that girls affirm the "prevailing gender and (hetero)sexual organization of this school event" (Best 2004, 200–201).

At the same time that girls tend to be put down by boys, while interacting in girls' peer groups they receive another set of messages about girlhood. They are encouraged to participate in a set of norms and values that often set them up to measure their worth in relationship to boys. By middle school, girls' peer groups become preoccupied with romantic relationships with boys, dating rituals, and popularity. Girls' dating rituals encourage girls to lower their ambitions in exchange for boys' approval—since ultimately, the culture of romance places boys in the center of girls' social lives. Popularity for girls is different than it is for boys (Adler, Kless, and Adler 1992; Merten 1997). Elder (1969) noted that physical attractiveness figures prominently in girls' popularity with boys and ultimately in their ability to marry well-to-do, successful men.

Thorne's important observations on the ways in which "going with" rituals in grade school set the stage for intermediate and high school dating add an important dimension to this discussion. Specifically, teenage girls are pushed by hegemonic, heterosexualized femininity into cultivating a "teen" femininity that, while often challenging adult and race-based authority in the classroom, ultimately involves a series of "double binds" and "traps" (1994, 156) for girls. As noted previously, this construction recreates and reinforces the sexual double standard by labeling girls who are too overtly sexual as "sluts." But more ironically, the construction of young girls as the objects of male desire means that girls' self-esteem and prestige are far more tied to externals (and particularly male approval) than are boys' (Thorne 1994, 156).

In fact, in studies of "popularity" among boys' and girls' elementary school cliques in Colorado, Adler, Kless, and Adler (1992) report that while single-sex cliques tend to have many of the same dynamics, boys' popularity and status tend to be tied to their accomplishments, whereas girls' status tends to be determined by externals. Specifically, they found that for this group of middle-class, largely white youth, boys achieved status on the basis of "athletic ability, coolness, toughness, social skills, and success in cross-gender relationships" (169); girls, on the other hand, gained popularity because of "their parents' socioeconomic status and their physical appearance, social skills, and academic success" (169). They also concluded, as did Thorne, that boys prosper to the degree that they internalize and express the "cult of masculinity" (183). Girls tend to become absorbed in a "culture of compliance and conformity" (see also Stanley 1993) as well as a "culture of romance" in which they "fantasize about romantic involvements with boys." Finally, girls care about an "inner space," which reflects an "ideology of domesticity," by living indoor lives, focusing on intimacy and cooperation.

Such a constellation of findings is all the more troubling because adolescent girls rate popularity so highly (Coleman 1961; Keys 1976). In a study of high school seniors, Rosenberg (1965) found that when asked if they would most like to be independent, successful, or well liked, 60 percent of adolescent girls and only 35 percent of boys chose being well liked. In contrast, boys were much more likely than girls to choose successful (46 percent and 29 percent). Apparently, even girls who are strongly committed to feminist ideals become "realistic" during late adolescence as they begin to fear that their attitudes might endanger their ability to attract more traditional males (Katz 1979). Some have labeled this the "double bind" between femininity and achievement that confronts adolescent girls: "the adolescent girl [is] finding it difficult to combine, because of imposed cultural contingencies, being a worthwhile individual and a proper female" (Hyde 1985, 162).

Kehily, in her research on gender and sexuality in secondary schools in the United Kingdom, amplifies this point. She notes the importance of "student sexual cultures" for girls and documents the "meanings ascribed to issues of sexuality by students themselves within peer groups and in social interaction more generally" (Kehily 2004, 208). In her view, schools serve not only to reproduce gender, race, and class identities, they actually serve as sites for the *production* of gendered or sexualized identities (see also Wolpe 1988). In the "adult-free and education-free zones" of the "student sexual culture," students collectively determine "what is acceptable/desirable" and what is "too much" (Kehily 2004, 214). Focusing specifically on girls, Kehily did note much that marked the "persistence of gender polarities" as well as a continued concern for "reputation" and the "naturalization of heterosexuality" (Kehily 2004, 213). With nearly one in ten young high school students identified as "gay, lesbian, bisexual, or questioning," such heteronormativity is particularly problematic (see also Prezbindowski and Prezbindowski 2001).

Crucially, though, Kehily found that a "same-sex friendship group" can provide sites for "autonomy and agency in the confined space of school" (Kehily 2004, 215). The importance of the same-sex peer group as a countervailing force also suggests possible interventions to empower young women, which include such themes as "practicing sisterhood," teaching girls how to "read school culture critically," and not "buying into cultural stories of good girls and bad, mean girls and nice" (see Brown 2003, 199–228).

Class and ethnic differences in gender are also marked, and these become more important during the intermediate and high school years. Higher social classes tend to be less rigid in sex distinctions; in working- and lower-class families, there is much more concern about sex segregation. Children from working-class backgrounds tend to differentiate sex roles at earlier ages and to have more traditional standards than do middle-class children (Rabban 1950). This might be because, as Delamont (1981) and Thompson (2000) note, school systems tend to ignore the underachievement of working-class students in general and working-class girls in particular.

Where popular girls socialize other girls into cultures of compliance and romantic preoccupation, research suggests that girls' interactions with boys at school are even more problematic. When asked what girls' problems are in school, an author of a current book on educating girls put it quite succinctly: "The problem for girls is boys" (O'Reilly 2001, 19). Several studies demonstrate that girls' victimization by boys at school is substantial. The AAUW report on sexual harassment at school, *Hostile Hallways* (AAUW 1993), randomly sampled 1,632 boys and girls (828 boys and 779 girls) in grades 8 through 11 in 79 public schools, and found that 83 percent of the girls and 60 percent of the boys reported experiencing sexual harassment in school. For some of the most serious forms of sexual harassment, the gender gap was particularly notable: take, "touched, grabbed, or pinched in a sexual way," which was reported by 65 percent of the girls and 42 percent of the boys, or "intentionally brushed up against in a sexual way," which was reported by 57 percent of the girls and 36 percent of the boys (Stein 2000). The violence that confronts girls in inner-city schools is considerably more widespread than the victimization endured by white girls in suburban districts.

"Girlworld" and Girl Blaming

In many ways, the increasing attention to the ways that girls have been ignored and marginalized at schools has done much to raise awareness of girls' issues in education. As the AAUW reports, *Shortchanging Girls, Shortchanging America* and *Hostile Hallways* argue girls not only need to become central to the educational curriculum, but they also need protection from victimization by boys on campus.

As we have documented, the development of anti-bullying programs that blur the distinctions between girls' sexual harassment victimization and girls' perpetration of "indirect" bullying have the unfortunate affect of tending to blame girls for the problems of girlhood while also stripping them of important civil and legal protections from sexual harassment (see also Stein 2003).

Since the 1980s, the media has been awash in bad news stories about girls, all in the name of making the public aware of girls' needs. The publication of *Reviving Ophelia* in many ways became a pivotal moment in this era and warned audiences that girls confronted a "poisoned culture" that compromised their development. As we noted in the introduction, by the time of the "mean girl" epidemic at the turn of the century, the poisoned girlhood theme had transformed into a poisoned girls theme. Suddenly, the source of trouble in "girlworld" was no longer rooted in aspects of institutions (like schools), but was located in girls themselves. This negative press has increased the likelihood that girls' minor misbehaviors will be taken seriously by school staff. Where girls who pass notes in class or gossip about who is dating whom might have been ignored decades ago, in today's climate, teachers and administrators are told that these are serious problems that deserve intervention.

Tough on Youth Violence: Punitive Control in Schools

The last decades of the twentieth century saw an ominous shift in U.S. social welfare and penal policy, as the nation embarked on a strategy of "mass incarceration." The U.S. prison population increased by over 600 percent between 1970 and 2003 (Bureau of Justice Statistics 2003), as the nation achieved the dubious distinction of incarcerating more of its citizens than any other nation on earth (Mauer and Chesney-Lind 2002). The reliance on punitive control strategies would not just dramatically influence America's correctional system, but eventually it would affect the U.S. educational system as well. The epidemic of youth violence in the 1980s and early 1990s followed by the spate of school shootings in the late 1990s, gave those eager to embrace this tough-on-youth-crime agenda considerable support to ramp up penalties against youth.

The surge in youth violence and the series of school shootings that would follow it, however, alone do not account for the dramatic shift in public fears of crime as well as a political and popular call for more rigorous policing and punishment of law violators. As many scholars have noted, the increased reliance on what is often called "law and order" strategies to control crime and delinquency runs deep within American culture, economy (see Garland 2001), and race relations, and, in fact, rests within the larger shift in the United States from a "welfare state" to a "penal state" (Wacquant 2001).

Central to this shift are attitudes about race in America, and particularly race and crime. With the rise of a political agenda that encourages the dismantling of social welfare programs in favor of a free market and increasing profits for large corporations, African-Americans have found themselves both displaced in the American labor market and left without critical social services. Wacquant (2001) argues, then, that prisons have taken up the slack of this surplus human capital by containing individuals who are left out of the labor market and who are marked with the "taint" of criminality.

A similar process was at work among school-age African-Americans. The shift away from welfare towards a free market state has dramatically changed the landscape of American schools. Increasingly, education is no longer being viewed as a "universal right" for all children, but a privilege to be bestowed upon hardworking, legal, and deserving citizens. Where segregating lawless adults in jails and prisons has been a popular means of controlling the unemployed criminal class in the United States since the 1980s, segregating offending students through expulsion serves a parallel function. That this mass imprisonment especially disadvantages African-Americans is common knowledge (Mauer 1999; Mauer and Chesney-Lind 2003). Like the race implications of America's imprisonment binge, the race effect of harsh social control practices in schools is becoming more obvious and has led to the assumption that there is a "schools-to-jails track" for African-American students (Advancement Project 2003, 2005; NAACP Legal Defense Fund 2005; Wald and Losen 2003). Demonstrating the link between dropping out of school and prison, Pettit and Western (2004, 151) studied a cohort of men born between 1965 and 1969, and found that among African-Americans "60 percent of high school dropouts went to prison by 1999."

As public crime fears mounted and the youth violence epidemic gained increasing media attention, schools were increasingly co-opted into the larger crime control agenda. This is somewhat ironic, since the surge in youth violence in the 1980s and early 1990s did not have any measurable effect on school crime. By almost every measure, schools were one of the safest places for adolescents before, during, and after the youth violence epidemic. In 1989, 3 percent of students reported being the victims of violent crime at school, and by 1995 this percentage rose to 4 percent—a small and insignificant increase. Of all of the youth homicides occurring between 1992 and 2000, only 0.9 percent occurred either on school grounds or while students were traveling to or from school sessions or school-sponsored events (DeVoe et al. 2004). In 1994, only 7 percent of serious juvenile assaults and 4 percent of juvenile robberies occurred inside of school (Snyder and Sickmund 1995).

Despite this, the public perception at the time was that schools, like inner-city streets, were becoming chaotic, crime-ridden places. Between 1997–1998 and 1998–1999 (years that saw a 40 percent decline in school-associated violent deaths), the number of Americans who were concerned about safety in schools rose 50 percent (Maccalair 2000, 1). And most certainly, if there was any public hesitation about the seriousness of the school violence "problem," this skepticism was silenced by the enormous media attention given to school shooting incidents discussed in the last chapter.

In an effort to respond to the public perception that schools were unsafe, school boards increasingly looked to punitive, law-and-order approaches, including "zero-tolerance" policies. The term "zero-tolerance"—referring to policies that punish all offenses severely, no matter how minor—grew out of state and federal drug enforcement policies in the 1980s (Skiba and Peterson 1999). As these harsh and strict policies spread from the military to civilian environments, they engendered quick controversy—particularly when then-Attorney General Edwin Meese encouraged the U.S. Customs Department to seize any vessel where drugs were found, and as a result, in the adult world, they were quietly phased out (Skiba and Peterson 1999).

The appeal of zero-tolerance with reference to youth misbehavior was undiminished. By the late 1980s, a number of school boards adopted this strategy. In Orange County, California and Louisville, Kentucky, education administrators adopted policies of "zero-tolerance" programs, calling for expulsion of students for "drugs" and "gang-related activity." At the same time, the superintendent of the Yonkers public schools developed a sweeping zero-tolerance program to respond to students who caused "school disruption." The Yonkers approach restricted school access, placed a ban on hats, implemented immediate suspension for any school disruption, and increased use of law enforcement; ultimately, this program contained many of the elements that have come to characterize zero-tolerance approaches in the 1990s (Skiba and Peterson 1999).

Federal involvement and endorsement of a zero-tolerance approach to school violence was signaled by passage of the Clinton administration's Gun-Free Schools Act of 1994. The act required states to pass laws requiring mandatory one-year expulsion for any student caught bringing a weapon to school. Although this act specifically focused on guns and allowed chief education administrators in each state to amend the law on a case-by-case basis, many states expanded this approach by making it less flexible (in many locations the case-by-case clause was deleted). Schools, districts, and states also amended this law by adding a variety of perceived disruptive behaviors to the list of infractions that would result in mandatory removal from campus. Some of the prohibited behaviors, including possessing drugs or drug paraphernalia, or wearing gang attire, were somewhat logically connected to mounting concerns about school safety. Other rules began to be added, sweeping up all sorts of youth deportment issues, including a ban on wearing outrageous hair dye, having too many body piercings (Savoye 2001), or carrying fingernail clippers (Lovekin 1995), Midol (Fisher 1996), cough drops (Stone 1997), or plastic knives to school (Wald 2000).

Unlike the violence prevention programs discussed in a previous chapter, these no-nonsense strategies were seemingly easy to implement and did not take extra grant funds. Nor did they require teachers to receive training and teach curricula. Considering this, they appeared to be simple solutions that were attractive to many, but they were ultimately far more costly than they first appeared. Policing strategies designed to bring offenders to the administrators' attention and zero-tolerance measures that suspended, transferred, or expelled students guaranteed that public schools would lose substantial funds, since schools, in most parts of the country, receive funding based on the number of students enrolled at school. In the 2002–2003 school year, public schools in the United States received on average $8,044 per student per year (U.S. Department of Education Statistics 2005). To put this in concrete terms, according to a school safety survey administered after the 1999–2000 school year (DeVoe et al. 2005), schools surveyed reported permanently transferring or expelling approximately 20,934 students that year. This was a pricey disciplinary action that ultimately cost the schools in this survey $144,695,808 in lost revenues,[3] while also punishing marginalized youth whose futures were made far more bleak by failing to complete school.

By 1997, 79 percent of schools were employing zero-tolerance policies (Kaufman et al. 1998). Of these zero-tolerance schools, over 90 percent had prohibited weapon carrying. Interestingly, less than half of the schools (40 percent) actually expelled, suspended, or transferred students for fighting (U.S. Department of Education 1998). Even fewer schools leveled these punishments for firearm or other weapon carrying (5 percent and 22 percent of schools, respectively, practiced these punishments one or more times during the 1996–1997 school year) (Kaufman et al. 1998).

Reporting school crimes to police also increased. In 1997, 57 percent of schools surveyed reported at least one school crime to the police and 10 percent reported at least one serious violent incident to police (Kaufman et al. 1998). By the 1999–2000 school year, there is no parallel statistic about reporting "school crime," but 14.8 percent of schools surveyed reported at least one serious violent incident to police (DeVoe et al. 2004); a rather steep increase in a short period of time hinting that more U.S. schools were bringing violent incidents to the attention of police.

There is also some evidence to suggest that even relatively minor forms of acting up were now being reported to the police. For example, in the 1996–1997 school year, approximately 187,900 non-serious violent incidents would be reported by schools to the police (Kaufman et al. 2000). Just three years later (during the 1999–2000 school year), the number of non-serious violent incidents reported to the police would reach 222,600; an increase of 18.5 percent.

It also seems that schools were reclassifying less serious incidents into major violence. In 1996–1997, serious violence included sexual assault (including rape), fights with weapons, or robbery. Less-serious violence included fights without a weapon. By the 1999–2000 school year, a *threat* with a weapon was added to the serious violence category and a *threat* without a weapon was included as a less-serious act of violence. In fact, by the 1999–2000 school year, there would be no such category as "non-serious" violence. There was just "serious violence" and "violence" (Kaufman et al. 2004), which signals a symbolic shift in the official school view of minor forms of youthful violence.

A Case Study of "Upcriming" of Youth Violence: Juvenile Robbery in Honolulu

Upcriming refers to policies (like "zero-tolerance policies") that increase the severity of criminal penalties associated with particular offenses. Research on the dynamics of juvenile robbery in Honolulu documents the ways in which shifts in school and police policies can dramatically affect juvenile arrest rates for crimes of violence— including offenses like robbery (see Chesney-Lind, Paramore, Mayeda, and Okamoto 1999; Chesney-Lind and Paramore 2001). Hawaii, like the rest of the nation, saw an increase in the arrests of youth for serious crimes in the mid-1990s including a sharp increase in juvenile arrests for robbery and assault. Between 1994 and 1996, for example, the number of youth arrested for robbery doubled in Honolulu.

These increases prompted a study of the actual dimensions of juvenile robbery in Honolulu. In this study, police files from two time periods (1991 and 1997) were identified that focused on robbery incidents resulting in arrest. According to these data, in 1991, the vast majority of those arrested for robbery in Honolulu were male—114 (95 percent) versus 6 (5 percent) female. However, a shift occurred in 1997—83.3 percent were males. Thus the proportion of robbery arrests involving girls more than tripled, between 1991 and 1997.

The study found evidence that suggested that no major shift in the pattern of juvenile robbery occurred between 1991 and 1997 in Honolulu. Rather, it appears that less serious offenses, including a number committed by girls, are being swept up into the system perhaps as a result of changes in school policy and parental attitudes (many of the robberies occurred as youth were going to and from school). Consistent with this explanation are the following observable patterns in our data: during the two time periods under review, the age of offenders shifted downward, as did the value of items taken. In 1991, the median value of the items stolen was $10.00; by 1997, the median value had dropped to $1.25. Most significantly, the proportion of adult victims declined sharply while the number of juvenile victims increased. Finally, while more of the robberies involved weapons in 1997, those weapons were less likely to be firearms and the incidents were less likely to result in injury to the victim. In short, the data suggest that the problem of juvenile robbery in the city and county of Honolulu was largely characterized by slightly older youth bullying and "hijacking" younger youth for small amounts of cash and occasionally jewelry and that arrests of youth for those forms of robbery accounted for virtually all of the increase observed.

The study also interviewed school personnel and police officers assigned to the robbery detail. These indicated quite clearly that changes in both school and police practices had had an impact on the number of robberies reported. One principal stated, "In the past, many schools handled these offenses within the school, but now more and more principals are leaning towards the help of law enforcement." He went on to say, "Law enforcement personnel are viewed as more qualified to handle violent offenses, not schools."

Law enforcement personnel were candid in their assessment of the increase in juvenile robbery arrests. When asked to explain the increase, an officer from the robbery detail stated, "We cannot make an arrest unless we are called," meaning that juvenile robbery arrests are a function of reporting. The officers suggested that the Department of Education (DOE) had perhaps become more aggressive in its efforts to curb youth violence. One officer who had previously worked within the schools remarked that "schools are requesting the police more than in the past."

Another theme that emerged was the increasing criminalization of youthful confrontations. Specifically, one law enforcement officer noted, "It's not that schools have not been reporting 'hi-jacking' all along; it's that law enforcement personnel have begun to classify schoolyard bullying and thefts as robbery offenses." This officer went on to make it clear that this reclassification was an outgrowth of the shift in the type of items stolen as well as the broader local and national concerns about youth violence and victimization.

Interviews with both education personnel and police in Honolulu seem to indicate that the national "get tough" attitude has clearly affected school reporting of less serious forms of violence. It is also clear that as less serious forms of violence are reported to the police, more girls will be arrested. Significantly, Hawaiian and Samoan girls comprised over two-thirds (67.8 percent) of those arrested in 1997, and many of those girls came from a school that served inner-city youth and had one of Honolulu's first police officers in school programs (Chesney-Lind and Paramore 2001, 148).

Gender-, Race-, Class-, and School-Based Violence Control

By the late 1990s, the most popular law-and-order response to youth violence was zero-tolerance policies, but some schools also paid law enforcement officers to patrol hallways, had metal detectors stationed at school entrances, and conducted random searches of students and lockers. While these practices were relatively rare, it is important to note that they were disproportionately used in schools serving large numbers of minority and poor students (Kaufman et al. 1998).

In the 1996–1997 school year, 6 percent of all public schools had police or other law enforcement representatives stationed at school for thirty or more hours per week. In comparison, more than double that number (13 percent) of schools with a minority enrollment of 50 percent or more practiced this crime control strategy. Schools with 50 percent or more minority enrollment were also more likely than schools in general to conduct random metal detector checks of students (9 percent versus 4 percent) or to force students to pass through metal detectors every day (4 percent versus 1 percent). In addition, while 1 percent of all schools in the 1997 study had students pass through metal detectors each day, 5 percent of the schools serving low-income students used this technique (schools in which 75 percent or more of the students were eligible for free lunches). It appears, then, that the most draconian approaches to school safety were disproportionately implemented in schools serving poor and predominantly minority youth.

In addition, school safety surveys demonstrate that zero-tolerance policies are more likely to exist in ethnically and racially diverse schools than in predominantly white schools (DeVoe et al. 2004), meaning that students of color were more likely than whites to be affected. While school safety surveys do not reveal the gender of students who are expelled, from the U.S. Department of Education (2000) we know the race of suspended students. In 2000, African-American students made up 34 percent of students who were suspended that year; however, they only made up 17.1 percent of the student body (Maccalair et al. 2000). One frequently cited statistic was that suspension rates for African-Americans were two to three times higher than the rates for other students (U.S. Department of Education 2000).

Other research suggests that blacks were more likely than whites to be charged under subjective offense categories. A report from South Carolina Public Schools, for example, showed that black and white students were charged equally with weapons violations, but black students were much more likely than whites to be charged with assault (71 percent versus 27 percent), possessing a pager (59 percent versus 40 percent), disturbing school (69 percent versus 29 percent), and threatening a school official (69 percent versus 29 percent). While assault sounds like a serious infraction, as we will explore later, the simple assault category is a "catch-all" category for minor misbehaviors (Currie 1998). Similarly, possessing a pager is another ambiguous and arbitrary infraction that may or may not indicate that a student is dealing drugs or is involved with gangs. Interestingly, whites were more likely than black students to be charged for drug offenses on campus (65 percent versus 32 percent, respectively), suggesting an extremely tenuous link between drug offenses and pager possession. It is also unclear what constitutes disturbing schools or threatening a school official. These are up to school administrators' interpretations, which as we will see, often change with public fears of school crime.

In addition, as Osler and Vincent (2003) note, the burden of proof is extremely loose in schools, and students lack formal procedures within the school to grieve disciplinary decisions.

While official data rarely present *both* race and gender data, there are some clues about the gendered nature of formal discipline procedures at school that we can glean from newspaper reports. Zero-tolerance strategies, in particular, expanded across the nation, and after Columbine became increasingly common in white suburban schools looking for ways to increase school safety and circumvent school shootings. Once these policies moved from predominantly minority to predominantly white schools, the media stories about the irrational excesses of the zero-tolerance movement clearly document that girls' as well as boys' minor forms of violence and drug use were being swept up in this new "get tough" era.

There was the arrest of an 11-year-old 6th-grade girl in Florida for "possession" of a weapon. The weapon? A butter knife. In this instance, she was handcuffed, "taken to the Hernando County jail and charged with possession of a weapon on school property" (Kruse 2005). Overly vague "drug" bans have also resulted in girls' arrests, like the girl in Dayton, who was expelled from school for giving Midol to a classmate (Fisher 1996), the girl in Houston who was suspended for carrying Advil to school (Horswell 1996), and the 8th-grade honor student who faced five months in a "military-style boot camp" for "bringing to school a 2-ounce bottle of Cherry 7-Up mixed with a few drops of grain alcohol" (Cauchon 1999). Finally, there was the 11-year-old 5th-grade student who was "arrested and removed from Walker Elementary School in handcuffs" after a shoving incident. In this case, the victim's mother was dissatisfied with the school's response of a two-day suspension, so she filed a complaint with the police department (Zerointelligence 2005).

When instances such as these began to surface, zero-tolerance defenders emerged, and their arguments clearly linked zero tolerance to a larger conservative agenda to replace rehabilitative welfare programs with punitive control strategies. As a case in point, one *New Republic* article (*New Republic* 1999) proclaimed that the message of zero tolerance is "that we will not, in the name of educating all children, force the vast majority to live under conditions that make education impossible." Noting that in predominantly black and poor urban areas "teachers were spending enormous amounts of time dealing with drugs, guns, assaults, and brawls," the *New Republic* article contended that it is best to banish unruly students and end their "regimes of terror" over the school. Finally, the article celebrated zero tolerance as a blow to "therapeutic liberalism" that allows the "able-bodied to claim government money absent a day's work."

Note that in a series of rhetorical turns, the debate was moved from the stage of education to welfare policies, and eventually to the domain of punitive control and segregation. Students expelled under zero tolerance are alternatively viewed as either the "undeserving" poor or violent thugs who deserved harsh punishments and segregation in the name of public safety. Since both these images resonate with long-held racial stereotypes of African-Americans, it seems quite clear that the explicit intent of these policies, at least in the minds of some defenders, was and is to control youth of color.

Legal challenges to zero-tolerance policies have also emerged and they highlight the role of race or class in blunting the impact of these penalties. For example, one California couple took their son's school district to court for expelling their 12-year-old for bringing nail clippers to school. The parents won their case, but the school district upheld their ban on this grooming device. In a newspaper report, the director of pupil services was quoted as saying "We are not changing our policy on zero-tolerance of weapons ... Students who bring a nail clipper with a knife blade will be recommended for expulsion with no exceptions" (Lovekin 1995). Apparently, the school district let this one student slide because it wanted to avoid a long legal battle. So, despite the director's protests, there actually were exceptions to this rule.

There are numerous cases across the country with the same results: certain students who went to court were individually exempted from these zero-tolerance penalties, but the penalties and policies often remained. While the media has tended to ignore the class and race implications of zero-tolerance polices, Alex Smith—a student expelled from school after delivering a comic spoof of school administrators, who in turn charged him with verbal assault—spoke to this issue in a news article he published after winning his long legal battle:

> Had I not been a white, upper-middle class teen, with two married parents, each with a postgraduate education, the verbal assault law might never have been struck down. Fortunately, we had the resources to draw attention to our case, hire a lawyer, understand our rights and fight it out. Unfortunately, there is a vast majority of people who do not have such resources. The situation is much worse for low-income, single-parent or minority families, who are more likely to be charged under zero tolerance policies. (Smith 2003)

Ironically, zero-tolerance policies have often been framed as race and gender-blind justice approaches because they are, in theory, unilateral and "unambiguous." But what scant evidence we have suggests that zero-tolerance policies clearly are highly racialized, and that they disproportionately punish low-income students of color, including girls of color.

It is noted that in the 1990s, juvenile arrests, particularly girls' arrests, for crimes such as simple assault increased dramatically. It has long been known that arrests of youth for minor or "other" assaults can range from schoolyard scuffles to relatively serious but not life-threatening assaults (Steffensmeier and Steffensmeier 1980). Currie (1998) adds to this the fact that these "simple assaults without injury" are often "attempted," "threatened," or "not completed." A few decades ago, schoolyard fights and other instances of bullying were largely ignored or handled informally by schools and parents. But at a time when official concern about youth violence is almost unparalleled and zero-tolerance policies proliferate, school principals are increasingly likely to call police onto their campuses. It should come as no surprise that as a consequence, youthful arrests in this area are up—with both race and gender implications, as we shall see in the next chapter.

Paying Attention to and Punishing Girls

This chapter has traced the changing experiences of girls in schools from an era marked by a "hidden curriculum" to an era characterized by a coupling of both hidden and overt systems of punitive control. Girls have always been and continue to be subjected to a hidden gender curriculum where they are socialized away from academic achievement. Studies of girls' experiences at school demonstrate the ways that this occurred through a system that ignores and trivializes girls. In the past, girls who disengaged from school, refused to fall into the feminized depiction of the "model student," or who acted out were likely to be overlooked. Girls are still being steered away from academic success and are encouraged to follow a hegemonic gender script—one that emphasizes compliance and consideration of others (even offering them programs to increase their kindness towards others).

What has changed is that girls' disengagement, resistance, or acting out are no longer simply ignored and trivialized. Decades of research about schoolgirls and, more specifically, the publication of nationally recognized reports on the status of girls in education, have increased the awareness of the challenges that schoolgirls face. Unfortunately, this greater awareness of girls' concerns has occurred during a time of political backlash against women and girls. As a result, the media in particular tends to frame girls' "problems" in ways that increases their culpability for their own situations. Pathologizing girls for their preoccupation with body image, blaming them for the "boy crisis" in educational achievement, and showcasing the hidden, indirect aggression that they express toward other girls are all staples of this backlash journalism. Finally, and most relevant here, is the media hyping of the "rising" rates of girl-on-girl violence, showcasing girls of color looking menacing, and blaming this on girls seeking equality with boys and becoming more "masculine." These constructions clearly ratify the overpolicing of girls both within and outside of school, particularly girls of color.

The partnership between schools and criminal justice agencies was not necessarily designed to punish girls, but we suspect this has been an undeniable consequence of the interaction, coming as it did just as the penal paradigm began to dominate the American political landscape.

We have shown in chapters 4 and 5 that wayward white girls going to privileged schools are largely the dubious "beneficiaries" of high-priced prevention programs which police their "deportment" and conformity to the "tyranny of nice" in the name of bullying prevention. Their African-American and Latina counterparts are being criminalized for minor forms of violence that in previous years would have been ignored, and finally, as the next chapter will show, being jailed for their "offenses."

8

STILL "THE BEST PLACE TO CONQUER GIRLS":[1] GIRLS AND THE JUVENILE JUSTICE SYSTEM

While the stereotype of juvenile delinquency is generally that of a boy delinquent, the juvenile justice system actually has a long but largely unrecognized history of involvement in the policing of girls, particularly in the legal and judicial enforcement of traditional gender roles. Indeed, as the title to this chapter attests, the focus on controlling girls' and women's sexuality was at the center rather than at the periphery of the early history of the juvenile justice system (Rafter 1990). By the middle of that last century, the chief vehicles for gendered control were "status offenses" (noncriminal offenses for which only youth could be arrested like truancy, running away from home, and being "incorrigible") (Chesney-Lind and Shelden 2004). Because these offenses also involved an essentially judicial system in the moral behavior of youth, they had also become controversial by that time.

Thirty years have now passed since the passage of the landmark Juvenile Justice and Delinquency Prevention Act (JJDPA of 1974). This legislation focused national attention on the treatment of status offenders. In addition, over a decade has passed since the 1992 Reauthorization of this same act; a reauthorization that specifically called for more equitable treatment of girls in the juvenile justice system. For both these reasons, it might well be time to take stock of progress made. Is the juvenile justice system now dispensing justice to girls or is it still haunted by its history of differential and unequal treatment?

A Century of Girls' Justice Legislation

In 1974, when the original JJDPA was passed, reformers concerned about judicial abuse of the status offense category by juvenile courts were applying considerable pressure on Congress. Interestingly, although generally concerned about the legal treatment of status offenders, reformers were fairly silent on the status of girls in the system. Based largely on broad constitutional concerns about institutionalization for noncriminal statuses (like mental illness and vagrancy) common during the era, this federal legislation required that states receiving federal delinquency prevention money begin to divert and deinstitutionalize their status offenders. Despite erratic enforcement of this provision and considerable resistance from juvenile court judges, it initially appeared that girls were the clear beneficiaries of the reform. Incarceration of young women in training schools and detention centers across the country fell dramatically in the decades since the JJDPA of 1974, in distinct contrast to patterns found early in the century.

Through the first half of the last century, the juvenile justice system incarcerated increasing numbers of girls. The girls' share of the population in juvenile correctional facilities (both public and private) increased from 19 percent in 1880 to 28 percent in 1923. By 1950, girls had climbed to 34 percent of the total population of youth in custody, and in 1960, they were still 27 percent of those in correctional facilities. By 1980, the impact of the JJDPA was clear, and girls had dropped back down to only 19 percent of those in any type of correctional facility (Calahan 1986).

However, while the impact of deinstitutionalization was gendered in ways that arguably benefited girls, at the time Congress passed the Act, programs for girls in general (and female delinquents, in particular) were an extremely low priority. For example, a report completed in 1975 by the Law Enforcement Assistance Administration revealed that only 5 percent of federally funded juvenile delinquency projects were specifically directed at girls, and that only 6 percent of all local monies for juvenile justice was spent on girls (Female Offender Resource Center 1977, 34). This despite the fact that girls were, at the time of the passage of the JJDPA of 1974, a clear majority of those in institutions for status offenses. One study in Delaware done at the time the law was enacted found that first-time female status offenders were more harshly sanctioned (as measured by the decision to institutionalize) than males charged with felonies; for repeat status offenders, the pattern was more stark: female status offenders were six times more likely than male status offenders to be institutionalized (Datesman and Scarpitt 1977, 70).

Since virtually no programs targeted them and their needs, girls with a history of family dysfunction, physical and sexual abuse, and running away returned to the sometimes violent and predatory streets, often to be victimized. The public, led by juvenile court judges, pointed to this pattern and clamored for a return to the time-honored means of protecting female status offenders: incarceration (see Chesney-Lind and Shelden 2004 for a detailed review of this history).

Crucial ground was lost during the Reagan years, including the passage of legislation on "missing and exploited youth" as well as changes to the JJDPA which permitted the incarceration of status offenders in violation of a "valid court order" (Chesney-Lind and Shelden 2004, 177). Years later, it would be revealed that the national hysteria about missing and abducted children was essentially a moral panic fueled by extensive media coverage of a few high-profile and highly unusual child abductions. The vast majority of "missing" or "abducted" children, it turned out, were actually children caught in custody battles after contentious divorces, or runaway youth (Joe and Chesney-Lind 1996). However, the laws passed during that period did erode the gains of the deinstitutionalization movement by enhancing the abilities of law enforcement and others to track and hold missing children and publish their pictures so as to "reunite" them with their parents (Joe and Chesney-Lind 1996).

The tide turned briefly in girls' favor when the 1992 Reauthorization of the JJDPA was passed. This reauthorization was noteworthy precisely because it provided a forum for practitioners, activists, and scholars, all of whom voiced concerns about the deplorable options for and treatment of girls (see Chesney-Lind and Shelden 2004 for details of these hearings).

A hearing held during the reauthorization of the act provided an important focus on the issues of gender bias that had long haunted the courts' treatment of and programs for girls, and at that hearing, perhaps for the first time, academics and practitioners who had worked with girls in the juvenile justice system had an opportunity to be heard. As a result of this historic hearing, when the Reauthorization was passed, the legislation funded states to begin their own needs assessments for girls in their systems. Specifically, the 1992 Reauthorization of the JJDPA required that each state should:

(1) Assess existing programs for delinquent girls and determine the needs for additional programming,

(2) Develop a plan for providing gender-specific services for girls, and

(3) Provide assurance that all youth were treated equitably, regardless of their sex, race, family income, and mental, physical, and emotional abilities.

Through the "Challenge E" section of this act, over twenty-five states across the United States applied for and received funding to address these goals (Belknap, Dunn, and Holsinger 1997).

The popular "challenge grant" activity created and supported initiatives that had already begun in certain states and rapidly spread to others. While there was optimism, however, that the passage of these new requirements would give birth to a new national focus on girls, to date the results have been somewhat uneven. As an example, the JJDPA required states receiving federal money "to analyze current needs and services for girls and to present a plan for meeting girls' needs" in their state plans. Yet a review of plans completed in 2002 by the Children's Defense Fund (CDF) and Girls, Inc. concluded that "many states had not taken significant steps toward implementing this framework. An overview of current state approaches finds that (1) a significant percentage of states acknowledge the need for gender-specific services; and (2) the majority of current state plans are lacking and inappropriate pertaining to gender issues" (Children's Defense Fund and Girls, Inc. 2002, 3). Beyond this, federal efforts to fund grants on girls' issues (both research and practitioner oriented) were initially issued by the Clinton Administration and subsequently cancelled by the Bush Administration on the heels of the September 11 attacks (Ray 2002). A scaled-back version of the initiative was issued by the Bush Administration's OJJJDPAP in 2003, and in 2004 the for-profit Research Triangle Institute was funded to convene the Girls' Study Group. To date, the group, of which one of the authors is a member, has produced a manuscript of edited academic papers on female delinquency. The project's principal investigator has presented a Power Point presentation based on the book's content to mixed reviews by academic and practitioner groups.

Research and Girls in the System

A federal focus on girls' issues and programs is clearly long overdue. One of the chief concerns raised at the time of the 1992 legislation was the general lack of information, research, and theories available about the causes and correlates of girls' offending that in turn left girls with a set of programs and interventions that were at best sorely lacking, and at worst damaging and counterproductive. Commenting on the state of the field at the time the states were beginning their work, Reitsma-Street and Offord (1991, 12) argued that there existed "a collection of policies and services for female offenders ... propelled, as well as legitimated, by truncated theories and incorrect assumptions." While some programs were based on incomplete theories, others were just plain inappropriate. For example, some services did nothing more than reinforce derogatory and limiting gender stereotypes (like modeling and makeup classes) (Gelsthorpe 1989; Kempf-Leonard and Sample 2000; Kersten 1989; Smart 1976). Even more problematic than enacting policies based on faulty information and archaic assumptions, a common practice was to fit girls into programs designed for boys. The philosophy was that if it worked for boys, then it might work for girls, too. More often than not, these programs, especially the sports activities, were considerably limited compared to what boys received (Kersten 1989; Mann 1984). Marian Daniel, the visionary practitioner who started Maryland's female only probation services unit, put it more bluntly: "For years people have assumed that all you have to do to make a program designed for boys work for girls is to paint the walls pink and take out the urinals" (Chesney-Lind 2000).

Indeed, emerging research has consistently found that girls confront different risk factors or challenges than boys. Summarizing U.S. and Canadian research, Corrado, Odgers, and Cohen (2000) argued that delinquent girls have high rates of physical and sexual victimization, drug addiction, poor academic achievement, and family conflict and abuse. In addition, studies conducted of runaway youth reveal high rates of sexual and physical abuse among girls, often higher rates than what is found among runaway boys. In a Toronto runaway shelter study, for example, 73 percent of girls and 38 percent of boys reported a history of sexual abuse. Sexual victimization among girls predicted higher rates of drug abuse, petty theft, and prostitution. Interestingly, the same correlation was not found for boys (McCormack, Janus, and Burgess 1986). A Seattle study of 372 homeless and runaway youth pointed to a similar pattern. In this study, 30 percent of girls and 15 percent of boys reported sexual victimization. In addition, girls were significantly more likely than boys to report being victimized in their homes and on the street after running away (Tyler, Hoyt, Whitbeck, and Cauce 2001).

The same trends seem to exist for institutionalized girls. In a Florida study of detained girls and boys, Dembo, Williams, and Schmeidler (1993) found that girls were more likely to have abuse histories than boys. In addition, in an expanded study of 2,104 youth in a Florida assessment center, Dembo, Sue, Borden, and Manning (1995) argued that girls' trajectory towards problem behaviors was different than boys'. Where boys' law violations reflected their involvement in a delinquent lifestyle, girls acting out related "to an abusive and traumatizing home life" (Dembo et al. 1995, 21). Similar findings came out of a California Youth Authority (CYA) study in which boys were likely to witness violence and girls were much more likely to be direct victims (Cauffman, Feldman, Waterman, and Steiner 1998).

Taken together, this research suggests that girls confront a separate pathway into the juvenile justice system, one that is marked by high rates of victimization and family turmoil. Therefore, girls seem to have unique needs that should be addressed with gender-specific programs. Increased attention to girls' experiences and the more precise map of their trajectory into delinquency is one of the positive developments in the last decade and suggests that there is a firm foundation upon which to build a better system for girls. Despite this promising picture, a closer look at girls' status in the juvenile justice system suggests that the work has only just begun. Regardless of the increased information available about girls and the greater attention given to girls' needs, several national juvenile justice trends in the past decade have made meeting the needs of the 1992 Reauthorization Act extremely difficult. In the next sections, we will outline some of these trends and link them to larger social changes, and argue how changes in girls' arrest, detention, and commitment rates complicate the effort to provide girls with equitable treatment.

Girls' Justice in the New Millennium

Despite three decades of legislative and research efforts to improve the situation of girls in the juvenile justice system, changes in the policing of girls in such intimate contexts as their families, peer groups, and schools have resulted in dramatic increases in their referral to juvenile courts, especially for "violent offenses."

As we have already noted, if you look at official statistics when we talk about delinquency, we are increasingly talking about girls. In 2004, girls accounted for nearly one-third of juvenile arrests: 30.5 percent (FBI 2005, 285). Two decades earlier, if one were to look at these same statistics, girls would have accounted for only about one-fifth of juvenile arrests (girls were 21.4 percent of youth arrests in 1983) (Sarri 1987, 181). This represents a 42.5 percent increase in girls' share of juvenile arrests. And as we have also documented, girls are increasingly arrested for violent offenses; in 2004, for example, girls' arrests for "other assaults" increased by 31.4 percent while boys' arrests for that offense decreased by 1.4 percent. That arrest category actually surpassed girls' arrests for "runaway," long seen as a female dominate.

More to the point, girls are now staying in the system after being arrested for these new "violent" offenses. Between 1985 and 2002, the number of delinquency cases coming into juvenile courts involving girls increased by 92 percent compared to a 29 percent increase for males (Snyder and Sickmund 2006). Looking at specific offense types, the report observed: "For females, the largest 1985–2002 increase was in person offense cases (202 percent)." As an example, during this period referrals of girls for "simple assault" increased by 238 percent and female referrals for "other person offenses" increased by 322 percent (the comparable male increases were 152 percent and 111 percent) (Snyder and Sickmund 2006, 160). Astonishingly, girls have proportionately more person offense referrals than boys: 26 percent compared to 23 percent. (Snyder and Sickmund 2006, 160). This pattern suggests that the social control of girls is once again on the criminal justice agenda, with a crucial change. In this century, the control is being justified by girls' "violence," whereas in the last century it was their "sexuality."

These trends in girls' arrests and referrals for violent offenses should not let us lose sight of the fact that large numbers of girls were also being arrested and referred to court for traditional female offenses, like runaway (where in 2004, girls' runaway arrests exceeded those of boys'—the only offense category where this is true) and larceny theft (the bulk of which for girls was shoplifting). These two offense categories account for one-third (31.4 percent) of female juvenile arrests but far less (15.5 percent) of boys' arrests (FBI 2005, 285). These simultaneous trends—arrest of girls for historically male and historically female offenses—have also further complicated the efforts to craft gender-specific or responsive ways to address girls' needs. Essentially, the juvenile justice system is being pressured to respond to the violent behavior of youth, including girls, while it still also faces all the complexities presented by more traditional girl offenders.

In fact, despite being labeled as "violent," girls' official delinquency differs from boys' in that it is less "chronic" and less often "serious" (see Figure 8.1). Based on an in-depth study of one large urban court system, 73 percent of females (compared to 54 percent of males) who enter the juvenile justice system never return on a new referral (Snyder and Sickmund 1999, 80). That same study noted that of the youth who came to court for delinquency offenses, only 3 percent of females had committed a violent offense by the age of 18 compared to 10 percent of the boys; likewise, only 5.5 percent of girls compared to 18.8 percent of boys had more than four referrals to court (Snyder and Sickmund 1999, 81).

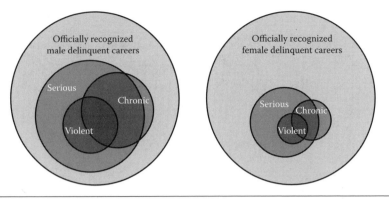

Figure 8.1 Offense profile of officially recognized male and female delinquents. (Snyder, H. N., and Sickmund, M., 1999. Juvenile Offenders and Victims: 1999 National Report. Washington, DC: U.S. Department of Justice, Office of Justice Programs, Office of Juvenile Justice and Delinquency Prevention.)

Girls' Detention Trends

The relabeling and upcriming of girls' delinquency has also had a dramatic and negative effect on girls' detention trends, undoing decades of "deinstitutionalization" trends. Between 1991 and 2003, girls' detentions rose by 98 percent compared to a 29 percent expansion seen in boys' detentions (see Figure 8.2); nearly one-third of girls (29 percent) were detained for a "technical violation" and 11 percent were detained for simple assault (Snyder and Sickmund 2006, 210).

In addition to a distinctly gendered pattern in these increases, there also seemed to be clear race-based differences. For example, a study conducted by the ABA and NBA (2001) revealed that nearly half of girls in secure detention in the United States were African-American. This is particularly interesting given that white girls made up a clear majority (65 percent) of the at-risk population (ABA and NBA 2001, 20).

More worrisome is the fact that despite the hype about violent girls, it was relatively minor offenses that actually *kept* girls in detention. Nearly half (40.5 percent) of all the girls in detention in the United States in 2001 were being held for either a status offense or a "technical violation" of the conditions of their probation, compared to only 25.3 percent of the boys (Sickmund, Sladky, and Kang 2004) (see Figure 8.3). Girls being detained for "violent" offenses

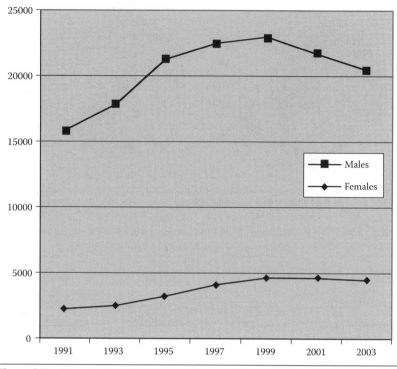

Figure 8.2 Trends in detention by gender. (Snyder, H. N. and Sickmund, M., 2006. Juvenile Offenders and Victims: 2006 National Report. Washington, DC: U.S. Department of Justice, Office of Justice Programs, Office of Juvenile Justice and Delinquency Prevention, p. 208.)

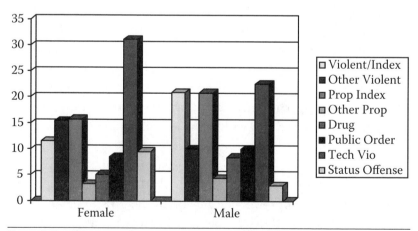

Figure 8.3 Offenses of detained by gender by percentage, 2003. (Snyder, H. N. and Sickmund, M., 2006. Juvenile Offenders and Victims: 2006 National Report. Washington, DC: U.S. Department of Justice, Office of Justice Programs, Office of Juvenile Justice and Delinquency Prevention, p. 210.)

were far more likely than boys to be held on "other person" offenses like simple assault (as opposed to more serious, part one violent offenses like aggravated assault, robbery, and murder). Well over half (57.3 percent) of the girls but less than a third of the boys in detention (32.4 percent) were held for these minor forms of violence (Sickmund et al. 2004).

Another troubling trend emerges in the use of detention was the reliance on private facilities since the early 1980s. The use of private facilities has a particular importance for girls, as they tend to make up a larger proportion of the institutionalized population in private versus public facilities. Also interesting to note is the fact that 45 percent of the girls in private settings were detained for status offenses in 1997 (Snyder and Sickmund 1999). This is compared to 11 percent of boys who were detained in private facilities for status offenses.

The use of private facilities presents some new and unique problems to the creation of equity in the juvenile justice system. Some have argued that the increasing trend to rely on private facilities has in essence created a bifurcated, or "two-track," juvenile justice system: one for white girls and another for girls of color. In 1997, whites made up 33 percent of the public detention population and 45 percent of individuals held in private facilities (Snyder and Sickmund 1999). This disparity might be explained by looking at how girls' cases are handled. In her study of one Los Angeles district from 1992 to 1993, Miller (1994) discovered that white girls were significantly more likely to be recommended for placement in treatment facilities than Latinas and African-American girls. In fact, 75 percent of white girls received treatment recommendations compared to only 34 percent of Latinas and 30 percent of African-American girls who received similar recommendations. Looking closely at probation officers' written reports, Miller found a surprising trend where white girls' offenses were more likely to be described as resulting from abandonment and low self-esteem and non-white girls' offenses were attributed to lifestyle choices (Miller 1994).

This trend has been corroborated in other studies. Robinson's (1990) examination of girls in a social welfare and a juvenile justice sample in Massachusetts revealed that 74 percent of girls in the welfare sample were white and 53 percent of girls in the juvenile justice sample were black. Although white girls seemed to be more likely to come into contact with the welfare rather than the juvenile justice system, Robinson found remarkably similar histories within both populations, especially with regard to their high rates of sexual victimization. One difference was that white girls tended to be charged with status offenses and non-white girls received criminal charges.

Another disturbing trend, present in the earlier data on the offenses for which girls were detained, might be described as the "re-detention" of girls. Essentially once girls were released on probation in the 1990s, they were more likely than boys to return to detention—usually for a technical violation of the conditions of their probation. A study by the ABA and NBA (2001, 20) not only found that girls were more likely than boys to be detained, but that they were more likely "to be sent back to detention after release. Although girls' rates of recidivism are lower than those of boys, the use of contempt proceedings and probation and parole violations make it more likely that, without committing a new crime, girls will return to detention."

Girls' Experiences in Detention

There is considerable evidence to suggest that girls confront vastly different environments and obstacles than boys while being detained. This trend has continued despite the fact that over half of all states have committed themselves to improving conditions for girls in the juvenile justice system, assessing girls' unique needs, and designing better programs for them. One enduring trend is that there continues to be a lack of programs for girls. In 1998, for example, Ohio judges reported that there were few sentencing options for girls. Two-thirds of judges surveyed disagreed with the statement that "there are an adequate number of treatment programs for girls," while less than one-third of judges disagreed with this statement regarding services for boys (Holsinger, Belknap, and Sutherland 1999). In a San Francisco study, Schaffner, Shorter, Schick, and Frappier (1996, 1) concluded that girls were "out of sight, out of mind" and that girls tended to linger in detention centers longer than boys. In fact, 60 percent of girls were detained for more than seven days, while only 6 percent of boys were detained that long.

Another concern noted by researchers examining the girls held in detention in Philadelphia was the "misdiagnosis of mental health issues" (Ambrose, Simpkins, and Levick 2000, 1). As the Female Detention Project found, 81 percent of the girls studied had reported experiencing a trauma of some sort (sexual abuse, physical abuse, witnessing violence, and abandonment). The girls were diagnosed with "Oppositional Defiant Disorder" (ODD) instead of "Post-Traumatic Stress Disorder" despite the fact that, according to the researchers, "many of the girls reported symptoms that are characteristics of Post-Traumatic Stress Disorder, but not ODD." Significantly, while ODD is "characterized by a persistent pattern of negativistic, hostile, disobedient and defiant—but not violent—behavior" most of these girls were detained for assaults, many school related. As a consequence of misdiagnosis, the girls were not getting the specific kind of treatment that they needed, many had used alcohol and other drugs, been hospitalized for psychiatric reasons, and about half had attempted suicide (Ambrose et al. 2000, 2).

The failure of detention facilities to provide girls with adequate mental health services was also the subject of a report on court involved girls in New York City. The study ran focus groups with some of these girls and reported that there was an "overwhelming sense of fear for their own physical safety while in facility care" due in large part to the "perceived lack of supervision and treatment of girls with mental health needs" (Citizen's Committee for Children 2006, 20). The girls also reported that there was a need for "high quality pre-natal care and health services for pregnant girls." The girls specifically suggested that the girl who had been in detention while pregnant had a "difficult time getting enough food and not being able to rest properly." Girls in detention also needed help to deal with the stress of pregnancy and the "frustration and depression" of being separated from their children (Citizen's Committee for Children 2006, 20).

There is also some evidence that girls are more vulnerable than boys to experiencing sexual abuse while being detained. In their study of 200 girls in California juvenile justice halls, Acoca and Dedel (1998, 6), found several examples of abuse including "consistent use by staff of foul and demeaning language, inappropriate touching, pushing and hitting, isolation, and deprivation of clean clothing." In addition, girls underwent strip searches while being supervised by male staff.

Lack of female staff seems to place girls in vulnerable positions while being detained. In addition to increasing the chances that female wards will be abused by male staff, the lack of female staff also limits the programs and activities available for girls. Staff shortages in the Miami-Dade County Juvenile Detention Center for girls, for example, resulted in decreased outdoor recreation for girls. Lederman and Brown (2000) reported that girls sometimes went as long as two weeks without outdoor recreation and were sometimes "locked down" due to shortage of staff. On some days, staff shortages resulted in girls' inability to attend school.

Why do girls languish in detention? The answers are not too hard to find, unfortunately, once one begins to review the literature on probation officers' (and other court officials') attitudes toward female delinquents. Research has consistently revealed that despite their less serious offense profile, girls in the juvenile justice system are regarded as "more difficult" to work with (Baines and Alder 1996; Belknap et al. 1997). A recent study of probation files in Arizona revealed stark gender and cultural stereotypes that worked against girls. Specifically, the authors found that "common images found in girls' probation files included girls fabricating reports of abuse, acting promiscuously, whining too much and attempting to manipulate the court system." Girls were universally seen as "harder to work with," "had too many issues," and were "too needy" (Gaarder, Rodriguez, and Zatz 2004, 14). Even when girls were abused, they were somehow partially responsible for the abuse in the eyes of probation officers:

> They feel like they're the victim. They try from, "Mom kicked me out" to "Mom's boyfriend molested me" or "My brother was sexually assaulting me." They'll find all kinds of excuses to justify their actions. Because they feel if I say I was victimized at home that justifies me being out on the streets…. (Gaarder et al. 2004, 16)

Gender and Training Schools—Girls' Victimization Continues

Girls' commitments to facilities increased by an alarming 88 percent between 1991 and 2003 while boys' commitments increased by only 23 percent. As a result, girls were 15 percent of youth "committed" to residential placements in 2003, up from 13 percent in 1991 (Snyder and Sickmund 2006, 208). Moreover, while girls can be "committed" to a variety of what are called "residential placements," the largest share end up in "long-term secure" facilities or training schools. Girls are also being committed to these facilities for different and less serious offenses than boys. In 2003, for example, well over one-quarter (29 percent) were committed for either status offenses or technical violations, compared to only 14 percent of boys. About half (46.74 percent) the girls committed for a "person" offense were committed for simple assault while only 22.2 percent of boys doing time for violent offenses were committed for these less serious assaults (Snyder and Sickmund 2006, 210).

Exactly how this works can be seen in a recent study of 444 incarcerated youth in Ohio (Holsinger, Belknap, and Sutherland 1999). These researchers found that girls were just as likely as boys to be incarcerated for violent offenses and that approximately one-half of the youths incarcerated reported being charged with violent offenses. On the surface, this suggests that incarcerated Ohio girls were just as violent as boys. Upon closer examination, however, researchers discovered glaring gender differences in the severity of violent offenses and, as Belknap et al. (1997) reported, focus group data with incarcerated girls revealed consistent accounts of girls being incarcerated for minor infractions, and in some cases for defending themselves. As a case in point, one girl revealed during a focus group interview that she was incarcerated for bringing a weapon to school. After being taunted and threatened by a boy at school and receiving no protection from school authorities, she hid a knife in her sock. While school authorities did not intervene in the boy's harassment, they did enforce the zero-tolerance for weapons policy against the girl (Belknap et al. 1997).

Several recent scandals suggest that like their adult counterparts (women's prisons), juvenile prisons are often unsafe for girls in ways that are uniquely gendered. Take a recent investigation of conditions in the Hawaii Youth Correctional Facility in the summer of 2003 by the American Civil Liberties Union (ACLU). According to the ACLU report, there were no female guards on duty at night in the girls' ward, one reported case of rape of a girl by a male guard, and several reports of girls exchanging sex for cigarettes. The report also noted that male guards made sexual comments to female wards, talked about their breasts, and discussed raping them. While wards noted that rape comments decreased after the rape incident, White (2003, 16) wrote, "wards expressed concern that the night shift is comprised entirely of male guards and they feel vulnerable after the rape because male guards could enter their cells at any time."

The ACLU report also discovered that wards reported being watched by male guards while they changed clothes and used the toilet. Male guards were also present when girls took showers. And, like their counterparts in detention, girls had not received outdoor recreation for a week due to lack of supervising staff and girls were told that the situation may last for up to a month (White 2003). While critics of the ACLU report commented that the wards made up stories and severely exaggerated tales of abuse, in April of 2004 the guard implicated in the rape charge pleaded guilty to three counts of sexual assault and one count of "terroristic threatening of a female ward" (Dingeman 2004). Although comprising a plea bargain, the legal rape case uncovered details indicating that the sexual abuse was more severe and alarming than wards originally reported to the ACLU.

More recently, the ACLU's Women's Rights Project and Human Rights Watch conducted an investigation of the conditions of girls sent to two juvenile facilities in New York (Lansing and Tryon, Human Rights Watch and ACLU 2006). They found many of the same problems identified in the Hawaii investigation, despite more limited access to wards and staff. Most notable among their findings was "use of inappropriate and excessive force by facilities staff against girls" (HWR and ACLU 2006, 4).

Girls who were former wards of the facility complained specifically about excessive use of a "forcible face down 'restraint' procedure" that often resulted in the girls having "rug burns" and other abrasions as well as broken limbs as a result of this restraint process. Said one young girl: "You see kids walking around with rug burns on their faces from their temple all the way to the bottom of their chin, with crutches, one girl was in crutches and a cast because they broke her arm and leg" (HWR and ACLU 2006, 48). While such procedures are supposed to be reserved for extreme situations, the girls alleged that staff used the procedure in response to all sorts of minor infractions (such as not eating something they were allergic to, "improperly making their bed or not raising their hands before speaking") (HWR and ACLU 2006, 5).

Girls also complained about sexual abuse at the hands of male staff as well as verbal abuse and degrading "strip searches," a severe lack of educational and vocational programming, and excessive idleness. As an example, "all girls are bound in some combination of handcuffs, leg shackles, and leather restraint belts any time they leave the facility" (HWR and ACLU 2006, 5).

Again, as we have seen in other profiles, African-American girls (who are only 18 percent of New York's youth population) comprised 54 percent of the girls sent to these facilities (HWR and ACLU 2006, 43). Many of these girls had histories of victimization and resultant mental heath issues. Roughly one-third of all the girls were incarcerated for "property" crimes (mainly larceny); of the girls imprisoned for "crimes against person," over one-third of these girls were there for "assaults," many of which involved family members (HWR and ACLU 2006, 36).

Finally, the report also notes that internal monitoring and oversight of the facilities are "dysfunctional" and independent, outside monitoring is "all but nonexistent" (HWR and ACLU 2006, 3-4). As a result, the two New York facilities, like virtually all youth facilities in the United States, are "shrouded in secrecy and the girls who suffer abuse have little meaningful redress" (HWR and ACLU 2006, 4). Sadly, scandals have long surfaced at girls' institutions (see Chesney-Lind and Shelden 2004), and all of these incidents suggest that while authorities often use institutionalization as a means of "protecting" girls from the dangers of the streets and in their homes, many of the institutions that house girls perpetuate the gendered victimization that pervades girls' lives outside of these institutions.

Explaining the Trends

The new millennium has signaled a dramatic reversal of previous decades of emphasis on the "deinstitutionalization" of girls. Today, as we have seen, girls are more likely to be arrested for violence and, once arrested, they were more likely to be detained or committed to residential facilities, often secure facilities with prison-like atmospheres and serious problems of abuse. Moreover, girls' detentions and commitments are longer now, and having served their time, girls are more likely than before to return to detention and residential placement, thanks to recent legislative changes. One feature of girls and justice has not changed. Girls continue to experience rampant abuse and neglect at the hands of their justice system protectors; abuse that is in violation of international standards of human rights (HWR and ACLU 2006). The persistence of neglect and abuse as well as the increase in girls' arrests, court appearances, detentions, and commitments seems truly ironic given that since the 1970s advocates, researchers, and legislators have pressed for increased services for and the decreased institutionalization, abuse, and neglect of girls. What happened to these efforts?

There are actually several forces at work that explain these troubling trends and that examine how the effort to defend and pay attention to girls has worked against them. As we have documented in other chapters, the trends include, "relabeling" (sometimes called "bootstrapping") of girls' status offense behavior, "rediscovery of girls' violence," and "upcriming" of minor forms of youth violence (including girls' physical aggression) (see Chesney-Lind and Belknap 2004 for a full discussion of these issues). Relabeling, rediscovery, and upcriming are all occurring as the juvenile justice system has become increasingly conflicted between its protective and its punitive role in the lives of youths.

Relabeling

As we noted in chapter 2, the rising arrest rates for girls is partly due to the rampant relabeling of behaviors that were once categorized as status offenses (non-criminal offenses like "runaway" and "person in need of supervision") into violent offenses. Specifically, we are seeing the relabeling of minor arguments that girls are having with their families into the crime of assault, which virtually always results in the arrest of the girl, even if the parent admits having hit the girl first (Buzawa and Hotaling 2006). Given the mounting pressure from advocates and legislators to cease arresting girls for status offenses like running away, incorrigibility, and truancy, parents and police, as we saw, were crafting new ways to control and discipline girls through arrest. In this era, such acts as throwing cookies or Barbie dolls at one's mother or brushing up against a parent while fleeing from a parent were likely to be classified as simple assaults rather than acts of incorrigibility or running away.

Rediscovery and Upcriming

As we have seen, girls have always been more violent than their stereotype as weak and passive "good girls" would suggest. A review of the self-report data discussed earlier clearly indicates that girls do get into fights and they even occasionally carry weapons. As an example, in 2005, over one-quarter of girls reported that they were in a physical fight, and nearly one in ten carried a weapon (Centers for Disease Control and Prevention 2006). In the past, girls' physical violence at school and in other contexts was often trivialized; the few girls who fought were seen as engaging in "cat fights" over trivial, "girlish" concerns (disparaging rumors, stolen boyfriends, or inappropriate flirting). Today, in the grips of a national awareness of youth violence problems and a specific campaign hyping girls' aggression, girls' fights are criminalized rather than trivialized. Law enforcement, parents, social workers, and teachers were once more concerned with controlling girls' sexuality than they were with their violence, but recent research suggests that is changing. So in part, the contemporary focus on girls' violence is actually a "rediscovery" of female violence that has always existed, although at much lower rates than boys' violence.

A related phenomenon, "upcriming," is likely also involved in the increases in girls' arrests, detentions, and incarcerations. Upcriming refers to policies like the zero-tolerance policies that we reviewed in chapter 7 that increase the severity of criminal penalties associated with particular offenses. Until very recently, schoolyard fights and other instances of bullying were largely ignored or handled informally by schools and parents, but today, in the post-Columbine period, there is extensive evidence suggesting that such behaviors are being handled formally.

These trends in girls' arrests for violent offenses should not let us lose sight of the fact that large numbers of girls were also being arrested and referred to court for traditional female offenses, like runaway (where in 2004 girls' runaway arrests exceeded those of boys'—the only offense category where this is true) and larceny theft (the bulk of which for girls was shoplifting). These two offense categories account for one-third (31.4 percent) of female juvenile arrests but far less (15.5 percent) of boys' arrests (FBI 2005, 285). These simultaneous trends—arrest of girls for historically male and historically female offenses—have also further complicated the efforts to craft gender-specific or responsive ways to address girls' needs. Essentially, the juvenile justice system is being pressured to respond to the violent behavior of youth, including girls, while it still faces all the complexities presented by more traditional girl offenders, who have always been the recipients of what Ruth Wells described as "throwaway services for throwaway girls" (Wells 1994). And, as we have already suggested, the two groups often share more in common with each other than conventional wisdom might predict.

The Protective/Punitive System

Clearly, relabeling, rediscovery, and upcriming help us understand why girls' arrests for violence have been increasing, but how can we account for the rising rates of girls' detentions and commitments? The answer is that girls in the new millennium are enduring the effects of a juvenile system that is becoming simultaneously more protective and more punitive of youth. The increasing punitive response towards youth misbehaviors can be readily seen in the zero-tolerance policies and practices in response to the youth violence epidemic and the spate of school shootings. What was also occurring for girls was a contradictory trend: a call to return to the protective policies and visions from the child-saving era.

The punitive turn in juvenile justice was often crafted in response to boys' violence, first as a way of controlling the "super-predators" of the youth violence epidemic and, eventually to apprehend the "school shooter" in the post-Columbine years. The protective trend, ironically, emerged in part due to the increasing attention given to girls after the Reauthorization Act. By the mid-1990s research agendas had made it clear that girls confronted an entirely different set of circumstances in and out of the system. The overwhelming presence of victimization at home or on the streets gave a clear indication that young female offenders had different histories and service needs than boys. The solution, sadly, was to develop services to meet girls' needs in the system and through arrest, detainment, and commitment, funnel girls into these services as a way of protecting them from victimization on the streets or in their own families.

An example of this trend can be seen in the 1995 Washington State "Becca's Bill" implemented in response to the murder of Rebecca Headman, a 13-year-old chronic runaway. After a series of runaway incidents and repeated calls to the police by her parents, Rebecca was murdered while on the streets. Under Becca's Bill, apprehended runaways could be detained in a crisis residential center for up to seven days. Between 1994 and 1997, youth detention rates increased by 835 percent in Washington State, and by 1997, girls made up 60 percent of the detained population (Sherman 2000). According to Sherman (2000), while there was Becca's Bill designed to save youths (mostly girls) from the streets in Washington by placing them in detention, there were no long-term community-based programs for runaway girls. In addition, as we have explained, detention centers were certainly not universally safe havens for girls.

According to Corrado et al. (2000), the reliance on detention rather than treatment in the community was a trend in Canada as well. Looking at delinquency data and sentencing practices leading up to girls' detentions, Corrado et al. (2000, 193) found that "the sentencing recommendations made by youth justice personnel are primarily based on the desire to protect female youth from high-risk environments and street-entrenched lifestyles." Furthermore, they argue that reliance on detention came partly because of the:

> … inability of community-based programs to protect certain female
> youth, the difficulties these programs have in getting young female

offenders to participate in rehabilitation programs, when they are not incarcerated, and the presence of some, albeit usually inadequate, treatment resources in custodial institutions. (Corrado et al. 2000, 193)

The balance between punitive and protective juvenile justice practices affects girls in another way. At the same time that detention and arrest were being used to protect girls from the dangers of the streets, many jurisdictions were cracking down on youths' probation and court order violations. Although designed to get tough on repeat index offenders, sentencing youth to detention for probation and court order violations, in practice, did not distinguish between status and index offenses. Therefore, girls were placed in a precarious position under this practice. Status offending girls could be swept into detention through policies designed to protect them from the dangers of the streets, and in the end, could be charged as criminal offenders through contempt of court and probation violations. In fact, as a study by the American Bar Association and National Bar Association (ABA and NBA 2001) found, this happened frequently in the 1990s. As we noted earlier, girls in the U.S. juvenile justice system were more likely than boys to not only be detained, but to return to detention after being released. This was in large part through contempt of court, probation, and parole violations.

There is an inherent irony in the protective–punitive confluence that underlies the arrest and detention rates of girls during the 1990s and early 2000s. On one hand, although practitioners are becoming increasingly aware of the challenges that girls uniquely confront, there are consistent reports of inadequate community-based programs to meet girls' needs. Therefore in some jurisdictions, detaining girls has become the only "program" available. On the other hand, we also find a system that has become increasingly intolerant and punitive of certain offenses, such as violent crimes and contempt of court and probation and parole violations. This sets up a troubling trajectory towards incarceration for girls, and one in which they were likely to find themselves either ignored and pushed aside when outside of the system, or set up for failure and certain punishment when they do become involved in the juvenile justice system.

In reviewing the data on detention practices, particularly the role played by minor aggressive offenses and technical violations, which are essentially proxies for status offenses, one can see the way in which the juvenile justice system has essentially married the protectionist logic to the new punitive emphasis in ways that distinctly disadvantage girls, particularly girls of color. And, while those in the system may argue that they are forced to detain girls "for their own protection," a review of the conditions in these facilities as well as the services provided suggests that they are anything but protective.

Girls and Juvenile Justice: What Does the Future Hold?

The Juvenile Justice and Delinquency Prevention Act of 2002 supports the continued focus on girls. Specifically, the act requires states, again, to create "a plan for providing needed gender-specific services for the prevention and treatment of juvenile delinquency" and denotes a category of funding for "programs that focus on the needs of young girls at risk of delinquency or status offenses" (Sharp and Simon 2004). Perhaps this time, as more girls enter the various juvenile justice systems, the states will take more seriously the unique needs of girls.

Reports from a number of national organizations such as the American Bar Association, the National Bar Association (ABA and NBA 2001), and the Child Welfare League (Sharp and Simon 2004) have, once again, focused critical attention on the unmet needs of girls in the juvenile justice. Beyond the continued claim that girls lack adequate gender-specific programming, there is also the undeniable fact that the girls in the juvenile justice system need considerable advocacy. As this chapter has indicated, girls are currently caught between multiple trends in the juvenile justice system—trends that confront them with new and more severe levels of disadvantage than they experienced in the 1970s and 1980s. In the arena of contemporary justice trends, girls, especially girls of color, are bearing the brunt of "tough-on-crime" policies specifically in the form of mandatory arrest and zero-tolerance initiatives towards youth violence. For example, where boys' arrest rates for violence peaked in 1994 (and have been declining since), girls' violence arrest rates have continued to climb since the early 1980s. In several twists and contortions of policies, laws, and initiatives meant to protect girls from victimization, we find that tough-on-violence responses have been deployed in ways that actually harm girls.

While the punitive turn in criminal justice has lashed out against girls in new ways, girls in the juvenile justice system continue to face the system's historic impulse to use correctional facilities to "protect" them. However traditional this protective pattern may be, it also confronts girls with a new set of challenges as legal initiatives like Washington State's Becca's Bill exemplifies. Instead of unabashedly sweeping up female status offenders into the system for their protection, as was a common practice critiqued by the 1994 and 2002 JJDPA Acts, legal initiatives like Becca's Bill turn status violators into criminal offenders. It seems that the juvenile court judges' desire to regain the ability to detain youth charged with status offenses has withstood the efforts of critics and reformers (Chesney-Lind and Pasko 2004).

Ultimately, the juvenile justice system's unfortunate return to its historic (and problematic) pattern of "protecting" girls, coupled with a simultaneous "get-tough" trend permeating the entire criminal justice system, has had very negative consequences for girls, particularly girls of color. We find that girls are systematically being reclassified from status offenders "in need of protection and supervision" into criminals deserving strict control and harsh punishment.

What are the prospects for gender-specific programming, assuming that we could get it right? It has also been three decades since the second wave of feminism presumably rekindled a national focus on women's rights, yet girls and women remain a very low priority when it comes to public as well as private funding.

Youth services all too often translate into "boys' services," as can be seen in a 1993 study of the San Francisco Chapter of the National Organization for Women. The study found that only 8.7 percent of the programs funded by the major city organization funding children and youth programs "specifically addressed the needs of girls" (Siegal 1995). Not surprisingly, then, a 1995 study of youth participation in San Francisco after school or summer sports programs found only 26 percent of the participants were girls (Siegal 1995).

Likewise, problems exist with delinquency programming; in a list of "potentially promising programs" identified by the Office of Juvenile Justice and Delinquency Prevention, there were twenty-four programs cited specifically for boys and only two for girls. One program for incarcerated teen fathers had no counterpart for incarcerated teen mothers (Girls Incorporated 1996). And things are apparently no better in the area of private funding. A 2003 study conducted by the Washington Women's Foundation reviewed 12,000 grants given by DC-area foundations in 2002 and 2003, and determined that only 7 percent of a total of $441 million dollars went to programs serving girls or women (E. Viner, personal communication, October 21, 2003). Clearly, the sexism that has long haunted public policy relating to girls programming haunts the world of private funding as well. In short, the prospects are about as dim as they were three decades ago in the area of programmatic funding.

What are some key themes that must be addressed to adequately meet the needs of girls in the juvenile justice system? While space does not permit a full discussion of the rich emerging literature on programming for girls, it is clear that the gendered pathways that bring girls into the system provide a good starting point for crafting gender responsive programming (see Chesney-Lind and Shelden 2002; OJJDP 1998).

Clearly, programs must address girls' unique problems with both physical and sexual victimization, a pattern that begins when they are very young and often continues. Dealing with the trauma associated with this victimization should focus on depression, issues of relational as well as direct aggression, self-medication with drugs, and the inevitable problems that arise with survival strategies that girls develop to deal with abuse (running away, depending on older, inappropriate, and often exploitative males). Girls, particularly girls of color, are also the victims of educational neglect and have severe housing and employment issues, often made more complicated by early motherhood and growing health problems.

Efforts to foreground gender, though, should avoid pathologizing girls and should also build on the considerable resilience that exists in this population. They should also seek to avoid stereotypical and dated notions of femininity that have long haunted juvenile justice programming (especially in girls' facilities), and remember that paying attention to a girl's cultural background is critical. Girls who enter this system are often very clear about their need to be heard, often eager to connect (especially with members of their own ethnic group who understand their problems and can provide culturally responsive ways to begin healing and reconnecting). Girls, according to those who enjoy working with them, are able to articulate their problems and are clear about needing to find spaces to rebuild lives that were often shredded by forces over which they had no control.

Advocacy for more of this sort of programming is critical, since it is clear that the girls in the juvenile justice system cannot wait another generation for things to change. As their numbers increase daily in the detention centers and training schools, and as the scandals in those facilities become more common, it is long past time to pay attention to girls. Imagine how different the juvenile justice system would look if we as a nation decided to take girls' sexual and physical victimization seriously and arrested the perpetrators rather than criminalizing girls' survival strategies and jailing them for daring to escape.

9

POLICING GONE WILD

Are girls going wild in this post-feminist era? Clearly, this book has argued that despite evidence from arrest data that girls are getting more violent, most of the other available data suggest that changes in the policing of girls, particularly in aspects of girls' lives that had previously been outside formal social control, explain the increases seen in arrests. Notably, increased social control of girls in the family, the peer group, and the school system have served to push increasing numbers of girls into the formal system of social control—the juvenile justice system—for offenses that were previously either ignored or labeled as non-violent offenses.

The most alarming aspect of the pattern that this book has documented is that the increased policing of girls' relatively minor behavior has resulted in dramatic increases in their arrest, detention, referral to court, and most recently, their incarcerations. Specifically, during the period between 2001 and 2003, the nation saw a 98 percent increase in the detentions of girls (compared to a 29 percent increase in boys' detentions), a 92 percent increase in girls' referrals to juvenile courts (compared to 29 percent among boys), and finally an 88 percent increase in girls' commitments (compared to only 23 percent increase in boys' commitments). Most significantly, more girls in court populations were there for "person" or violent offenses than boys (Snyder and Sickmund 2006).

We argue that the media as well as authors of popular books with titles like *See Jane Hit*, *Queen Bees and Wannabes*, and *Sugar and Spice and No Longer Nice* bear a significant responsibility for the patterns we have documented. We are particularly concerned that the media in recent decades have participated actively in the construction of girls as violent and mean. Both of these constructions are, we argue, inaccurate. But, more to the point, they serve important functions.

The mean girl construction serves to blame girls, particularly white girls, for their own problems. Specifically, the mean girl discourse relocates the well-documented problems of girlhood away from abusive families, schools that ignore and silence girls, and peer groups that reward hegemonic femininity to the girls themselves. Girls are simply mean to each other, and their "aggression" is as bad and injurious as male violence, we are told. So, if "girlworld" is toxic, it's girls' own fault. Their backstabbing, gossiping, and devious natures are responsible for the well-documented miseries of their gender, not institutional misogyny and sexism. The new millennium has seen increasing efforts to pathologize girls, even privileged girls, since this means that the well-documented social problems that haunt the lives of all girls can be neatly ducked or even better blamed on the girls themselves.

The role of the media in creating and perpetuating the violent girl myth, we argue, is a related trend. Here, the project is to warn girls and women that seeking social justice or equality with men has a "dark side" (Adler 1975). In short, they risk becoming more like men, more "violent," and "criminal." This backlash journalism has a long history, since it was first deployed to discredit the first wave of feminism (Pollock 1999), but it also dovetails neatly with racial agendas in the era of mass incarceration. Specifically, the demonization and masculinization of girls of color, particularly African-American girls, has its roots in America's sordid history of slavery. According to Paula Johnson, African-American women have always been seen through the "distorted lens of otherness" (9), constructed as "subservient, inept, oversexed and undeserving" (10); in short, just the "sort" of girls and women that belong in jail and prison. Constructing African-American girls and Latinas as violent serves a number of important functions. First, they serve to warn white women away from feminist goals (showcasing the unintended effects of seeking equality with men), and they simultaneously justify the jailing of large numbers of African-American and Latina girls since the public has been shown that they are just as violent and scary as their male counterparts.

We also document the ways in which both the media hype about girls' violence and books that purport to address the problem have actually created a self-fulfilling prophecy. Here, the media construct girls as "bad," and then books written by experts in the area of violence prevention craft the "solution." Often, but not always, these trade or popular books lay the foundation for increased funding to respond to the "problem," often purchasing interventions or programs crafted by the books' authors.

On the family front, the pathologizing of girlhood has ratified and bolstered parental insistence on girls' obedience to parental authority, complete with its often uncritical endorsement of the sexual double standard. Parents need to police their daughters, and if they are mean or defiant they are encouraged to seek out special programs to curb their willfulness; and programs don't come cheap. Rachel Simmons, author of *Odd Girl Out*, now runs a two-week summer program for girls to the tune of over $2,500 per girl (Simmons 2006).

More serious problems that girls have with families, particularly those that are physically and sexually abusive, can also be blamed on girls, with police and others advising parents to have their daughters arrested for domestic violence. As we have documented, huge numbers of girls in detention and training schools are committed for "violence" that might not only be family related, but might even have been self-defense. Decades earlier these would have been status offenses, which would not have resulted in incarceration, but in this backlash era, the relabeling girls' defiance makes this possible.

Schools, too, have become increasingly drawn into the formal control of girlhood. Violence prevention programs, spawned by the horrific school shootings, virtually all of which involved males, discovered "bullying." These bullying prevention programs, in turn, used the "discovery" of girls' parity in aggression to police girls in their peer groups, and worse, to equate this "meanness" with boys' physical violence. Here, we take specific issue with the construction of "aggression" that equates eye rolling with assault. Instead, we reviewed a growing list of literature which questions assertions that there is a gender gap in this behavior with girls more likely to engage in covert aggressions, that girls' aggression is extremely harmful, and that girls who engage in this behavior are "powerful." Finally, we even propose that some research suggests that youth who engage in this non-violent behavior may have higher social intelligence (Underwood, Galen, and Paquette 2001). Certainly, conflating physical violence and girls' non-violent relational aggression as similar forms of "bullying" is very disturbing, especially when schools are increasingly mandated by school boards to formally intervene and punish youth for this behavior.

This work has also discussed violence intervention programs, particularly the rise of "zero-tolerance" policies with reference to a wide range of youthful behaviors that have served to expand the formal control of girlhood. Schools, as we note, have always had a hidden system of social controlling and reproducing girlhood, but in recent years that hidden curriculum has been joined by a formal system of controls that has notably disadvantaged girls on the margin. Schools in low-income neighborhoods, in particular, have been encouraged by both federal and state officials to harshly police and punish and criminalize extremely minor forms of violence, as well as other behaviors like weapon carrying and drug use. While zero-tolerance policies appear on the surface to be equitable solutions, data were presented that indicate that youth of color, both boys and girls, have been the disproportionate targets of these enforcement efforts that in turn has produced an increase in girls' arrests and referrals to juvenile courts for "violence."

Arrests, referrals, detentions, and incarcerations of African-American and Latina girls for crimes of violence is clearly occurring in the juvenile justice system, a pattern that increasingly resembles an adult criminal justice system's approach to women's deviance. The number of women in U.S. prisons not only grew during the last century, but it increased *tenfold*, and African-American women bore the brunt of that shift, as current data show that African-American women account for "almost half (48 percent)" of all the women we incarcerate (Johnson 2003, 34). While the mass incarceration of adult women of color is largely a product of the war on drugs (Chesney-Lind 2004), the pattern seen in girls' incarceration is different. Here, we contend that the willingness of all to relabel and upcrime girls' minor forms of misbehavior (much of it family related) from "status offenses" to "person" offenses is moving the juvenile justice system into the same racialized patterns of incarceration that we see in the adult system.

The tragedy here is that the juvenile justice system thirty years ago charted a very different course; one that emphasized deinstitutionalization and diversion of minor offenders. The current trajectory is a dangerous reversal of that history, and it is one that is not warranted by the actual offenses committed by the girls we are incarcerating.

What is required, first and foremost, is a strong challenge to the myth that girls have become more violent. Beyond that, we must also challenge other efforts to repeatedly spread only "bad" news about girls and girlhood. Certainly, girls face challenges, as the young women we interviewed for this book told us, but they also survived and thrived, in part because of their friendship with other girls and women. They also correctly saw that it wasn't just mean girls, though they were in the mix, but it was also racism, sexism, and sexual violence that made girlhood challenging. As they told us about these challenges, though, they also told us incredible stories of resilience and determination. We will close with the words of Calle, a 25-year-old European-American, who discussed adolescent challenges and resilience when she described what being a successful young woman meant to her:

> My mom used to talk to me all the time, "You've got to make sure you keep your own identity. Keep your own things that you are into and not get rid of them." Because when you are in junior high, everything is just the end of the world. I think it's important to remember that it's not the end of the world. And in high school, you don't really have your own identity. Just make sure that you do what you want to do and not be afraid that you are going to be an outcast because you are so different. Just make sure that you are your own person. And I think that is success. You are happy doing what you are doing and being who you are.

References

ABC, *Primetime Live*, 1997, "Girls in the Hood," November 5, 1997.

Acker, J., Acker, B., Acker, K., and Acker, E., Joke, objectivity, and truth: Problems in doing feminist research, *Women's Studies International Forum*, 6(4): 423–435, 1983.

Acoca, L., Investing in girls: A 21st century challenge, *Juvenile Justice*, 6(1): 3–13, 1999.

Acoca, L. and Dedel, K., No place to hide: Understanding and meeting the needs of girls in the California juvenile justice system, San Francisco: National Council on Crime and Delinquency, 1998.

Adler, F., *Sisters in Crime: the Rise of the New Female Criminal*, New York: McGraw-Hill, 1975.

Adler, P. and Adler, P., *Peer Power: Preadolescent Culture and Identity*, New Brunswick: Rutgers University Press, 1998.

Adler, P. A. and Adler, P., Dynamics of inclusion and exclusion in preadolescent cliques, *Social Psychology Quarterly*, 58: 145–162, 1995.

Adler, P., Kless, S. J., and Adler, P., Socialization to gender roles: Popularity among elementary school boys and girls, *Sociology of Education*, 65: 169–187, 1992.

Advancement Project, Derailed: The Schoolhouse to Jailhouse Track, 2003.

Advancement Project, Education on Lockdown: The Schoolhouse to Jailhouse Track, 2005.

Alder, C. and Worrall, A., *Girls' Violence: Myths and Realities*, Albany, NY: SUNY Press, 2005.

Ambrose, A. M., Simpkins, S., and Levick, M., *Improving the Conditions for Girls in the Juvenile Justice System: The Female Detention Project*, Washington, DC: American Bar Association, 2000.

American Association of University Women, *Shortchanging Girls, Shortchanging America: A Call to Action*, Washington, DC: American Association of University Women, 1992.

American Association of University Women, *Hostile Hallways: The AAUW Survey on Sexual Harassment in America's Schools*, Washington, DC: American Association of University Women, 1993.

American Association of University Women, *Hostile Hallways: Bullying, Teasing, and Sexual Harassment in School*, Washington, DC: American Association of University Women, 2001.

American Bar Association and the National Bar Association, *Justice by Gender: The Lack of Appropriate Prevention, Diversion and Treatment Alternatives for Girls in the Justice System*, 2001.

American Correctional Association, *The Female Offender: What Does the Future Hold?* Washington, DC: American Correctional Association, 1990.

Anderson, E., *Code of the Street: Decency, Violence, and the Moral Life of the Inner City*, New York: Norton, 1999.

Andreou, E., Social preference, perceived popularity and social intelligence: relations to overt and relational aggression, *School Psychology International*, 27: 339–351, 2006.

Anonymous, The fight's not over, *New Republic*, 221(23): 9; 22112/06/99, December 6, 1999.

Anonymous, Pay closer attention: Boys are struggling academically, *USA Today*, December 3, 2004, p. 12A.

Arnold, R., The processes of victimization and criminalization of black women. In *The Criminal Justice System and Women*, Price. B. R. and Sokoloff, N. J. (Eds.), New York: McGraw-Hill, 1995.

Artz, S., *Sex, Power, and the Violent School Girl*, Toronto: Trifolium Books, 1998.

Artz, S., Blais, M., and Nicholson, D., Developing girls' custody units, Unpublished report, 2000.

Artz, S. and Riecken, T., What, so what, then what?: The gender gap in school-based violence and its implications for child and youth care practice, *Child and Youth Care Forum*, 26 (4): 291–303, 1997.

Backe-Hansen, E. and Ogden, T., Competent girls and problematic boys? Sex differences in two cohorts of Norwegian 10- and 13-year-olds, *Childhood*, 3: 331–350, 1996.

Baines, M. and Alder, C., Are girls more difficult to work with? Youth workers' perspectives in juvenile justice and related areas, *Crime & Delinquency*, 42: 3, 467–485, 1996.

Barnett, R. and Rivers, C., *Same Difference: How Gender Myths Are Hurting Our Relationships, Our Children, and Our Jobs*, New York: Basic Books, 2004.

Bartollas, C., Little girls grown up: The perils of institutionalization. In *Female Criminality: The State of the Art*, Culliver, C. (Ed.), pp. 469–482, New York: Garland Press, 1993.

Belenko, S., Sprott, J., and Petersen, C., Drug and alcohol involvement among minority and female juvenile offenders: Treatment and policy issues, *Criminal Justice Policy Review*, 15: 1 (March): 3–36, 2004.

Belknap, J., Dunn, M., and Holsinger, K., Moving toward juvenile justice and youth-serving systems that address the distinct experience of the adolescent female, Gender-Specific Work Group Report to the Governor, Office of Criminal Justice Services, Columbus, OH, February, 1997.

Belknap, J., Winter, E., and Cady, B., Assessing the needs of committed delinquent and pre-adjudicated girls in Colorado: A focus group study, A Report to the Colorado Division of Youth Corrections, Denver, CO, 36 pp. 2001.

Best, A. L., *Prom Night: Youth, Schools, and Popular Culture*, New York: Routledge, 2000.

Best, A. L., Girls, schooling and the discourse of self-change: Negotiating meanings of the high school prom. In *All About the Girl*, Harris, A. (Ed.), New York: Routledge, 2004.

Best, R., *We All Have Scars*, Bloomington: Indiana University Press, 1983.

Bettis, P. J. and Adams, N. G., Short skirts and breast juts: Cheerleading, eroticism and schools, *Sex Education*, 6: 121–133, 2006.

Beyette, B., Hollywood's teenage prostitutes turn tricks for shelter, food, *Las Vegas Review-Journal*, Aug. 21, 1988.

Bjorkvist, K., Sex differences in physical, verbal, and indirect aggression: A review of recent research, *Sex Roles*, 30: 177–188, 1994.

Bjorkqvist, K. and Niemela, P., New trends in the study of female aggression. In *Of Mice and Women: Aspects of Female Aggression*, Bjorkqvist, K. and Niemela, P. (Eds.), San Diego: Academic Press, 1992.

Bjorkqvist K. and Niemela, P., *Of Mice and Women: Aspects of Female Aggression*, San Diego: Academic Press, 1992.

Block, J. H., *Sex Role Identity and Ego Development*, San Francisco: Jossey-Bass, 1984.

Bloom, B. and Campbell, R., Literature and policy review, In *Modeling Gender-Specific Services in Juvenile Justice: Policy and Program Recommendations*, Owen, B. and Bloom, B. (Eds.), Sacramento: Office of Criminal Justice Planning, 1998.

Blumer, H., *Symbolic Interactionism; Perspective and Method*, Englewood Cliffs, N.J.: Prentice-Hall, 1969.

Blumstein, A., Youth violence, guns, and the illicit-drug industry, *Journal of Criminal Law & Criminology*, 86: 10–34, 1995.

Blumstein, A. and Cork, D., Linking gun availability to gun violence, *Law and Contemporary Problems*, 59, Winter: 5–24, 1996.

Blumstein, A. and Wallman, J., *The Crime Drop in America*, Cambridge: Cambridge University Press, 2000.

Bortner, M. A., *Delinquency and Justice: An Age of Crisis*, New York: McGraw-Hill, 1988.

Bourgois, P., In search of Horatio Alger: Culture and ideology in the crack economy, *Contemporary Drug Problems*, 16: 619–649, 1989.

Bourgois, P., In search of masculinity: Violence, respect and sexuality among Puerto Rican crack dealers in East Harlem, *British Journal of Criminology*, 36: 412–427, 1996.

Bourgois, P., *In Search of Respect: Selling Crack in El Barrio*, New York: Cambridge University Press, 2001.

Boyer, D. and James, J., Easy money: Adolescent involvement in prostitution. In *Justice for Young Women*, Davidson, S. (Ed.), Seattle: New Directions for Young Women, 1982.

Brener, N. D., Simon, T. R., Krug, E. G, and Lowry, R., Recent trends in violence-related behaviors among high school students in the United States, *Journal of the American Medical Association*, 282: 5, 330–446, 1999.

Brinson, S. A., Boys don't tell on sugar-and-spice-but-not-so-nice girl bullies, *Reclaiming Children & Youth*, 14: 169–174, 2005.

Brown, L. M., *Raising their Voices: The Politics of Girls' Anger*, Cambridge, MA: Harvard University Press, 1998.

Brown, L. M., *Girlfighting*, New York: New York University Press, 2003.

Brown, L. M., Chesney-Lind, M., and Stein, N., Patriarchy matters: Toward a gendered theory of teen violence and victimization, *Violence Against Women*. An earlier version of this article appeared in the *Wellesley Centers for Women, Working Paper Series*, 2004. No. 417 (in press).

Brown, L. M. and Gilligan, C., *Meeting at the Crossroads: Women's Psychology and Girls' Development*, New York: Ballantine, 1992.

Brumberg, J. J., *The Body Project: An Intimate History of American Girls*, New York: Vintage Books, 1997.

Bureau of Criminal Information and Analysis, Report on arrests for domestic violence in California, 1998. Sacramento: State of California, Criminal Justice Statistics Center, 1999.

Bureau of Justice Statistics, *Sourcebook of Criminal Justice Statistics*, 31st ed., 2003.

Bursik, R., Merten, J. D., and Schwartz, G. Appropriate age-related behavior for male and female adolescents: Adult perceptions, *Youth & Society* 17: 115–130, 1985.

Buzawa, E. S. and Hotaling, G. T., The impact of relationship status, gender, and minor status in the police response to domestic assaults police response to domestic assaults, *Victims and Offenders*. 1: 1-38, 2006.

Calahan, M., *Historical Corrections Statistics in the United States, 1850–1984*, Washington, DC: Bureau of Justice Statistics, 1986.

Cameron, M., *The Booster and the Snitch*, New York: Free Press, 1964.

Campagna, D. S. and Poffenberger, D. L., *The Sexual Trafficking in Children*, Dover, MA: Auburn House, 1988.

Campbell, A., *The Girls in the Gang*, London: Basil Blackwell, 1984.

Canaan, J., A comparative analysis of American suburban middle class, middle school, and high school teenage cliques, In *Interpretive Ethnography of Education: At Home and Abroad*, Spindler, G. and Spindler, L. (Eds.) 1987.

Canter, R. J., Sex differences in self-report delinquency, *Criminology*, 20: 373–393, 1982.

Cauce, A., Hiraga, Y., Graves, D., Gonzales, N., Ryan-Finn, K., and Grove, K., African-American mothers and their adolescent daughters: Closeness, conflict, and control. In *Urban Girls: Resisting Stereotypes, Creating Identities*, Leadbeater, B. and Way, N. (Eds.), New York: New York University Press, pp. 100–116, 1996.

Cauchon, D., Schools struggling to balance "zero tolerance," common sense, *USA Today*, April 13: 1A. 1999.

Cauffman, E., Feldman, S.S., Waterman, J., and Steiner, H., Posttraumatic stress disorder among female juvenile offenders, *Journal of the American Academy of Child and Adolescent Psychiatry*, 31: 11, 1209–1216, 1998.

CBS, "Girls in the Hood," *Street Stories*, August 6, 1992.

Centers for Disease Control and Prevention, 1992–2003, Youth Risk Behavior Surveillance—United States, 1991–2001, CDC Surveillance Summaries, U.S. Department of Health and Human Services, Atlanta: Centers for Disease Control.

Centers for Disease Control and Prevention, National Center for Injury Prevention and Control, Web-Based Injury Statistics Query and Reporting System (WISQARS) [online]. (2006) [cited 2006 July 18]. Available from: www.cdc.gov/ncipc/wisqars.

Chen, X., Tyler, K., Whitbeck, L., and Hoyt, D., Early sexual abuse, street adversity, and drug use among female homeless and runaway adolescents in the midwest, *Journal of Drug Issues*, Winter, 34: 1, 2004.

Chesney-Lind, M., *The Female Offender: Girls, Women, and Crime*, Thousand Oaks: Sage, 1997.

Chesney-Lind, M., Girls and violence, youth violence: Prevention, intervention and social policy, D. J. Flannery and C. H. Huff, *American Psychiatric Press*: 171–200, Washington, DC, 1999.

Chesney-Lind, M., Media misogyny: Demonizing "violent" girls and women. In *Making Trouble: Cultural Representations of Crime, Deviance, and Control*, Ferrel, J. and Websdale, N. (Eds.), New York: Aldine, pp. 115–141, 1999.

Chesney-Lind, M., What to do about girls? In *Assessment to Assistance: Programs for Women in Community Corrections*, McMahon, M. (Ed.), Lanham, MD: American Correctional Association, pp. 139–170, 2000.

Chesney-Lind, M., Are girls closing the gender gap in violence? *Criminal Justice*, Spring: 18–23, 2001.

Chesney-Lind, M., Criminalizing victimization: The unintended consequences of pro-arrest policies for girls and women, *Criminology and Pubic Policy*, 2: 81–90, 2002.

Chesney-Lind, M., The meaning of mean. Review of *Odd Girl Out: The Hidden Culture of Aggression in Girls* by Rachel Simmons, *The Secret Lives of Girls* by Sharon Lamb, and *Queen Bees and Wannabes* by Rosalind Wiseman, *Women's Review of Books*, November: 20–22, 2002.

Chesney-Lind, M., Delinquency in girls: An overview of key themes in female delinquency. Chapter for *OJJDP Girls Study Group Volume*. Zahn, M. (Ed.). Forthcoming.

Chesney-Lind, M. and Belknap, J., Trends in delinquent girls' aggression and violent behavior: A review of the evidence. In *Aggression, Antisocial Behavior and Violence among Girls: A Developmental Perspective*, Putallaz, M. and Bierman, P. (Eds.), New York: Guilford Press, 2004.

Chesney-Lind, M. and Brown, M., Girls and violence: An overview. In *Youth Violence: Prevention, Intervention, and Social Policy*, Flannery, D. J. and Huff, C. R. (Eds), Washington, DC: American Psychiatric Press, pp. 171–200, 1999.

Chesney-Lind, M. and Eliason, M., From invisible to incorrigible: The demonization of marginalized women and girls, *Crime, Media, and Culture*, 2: 1. 29–48, 2006.

Chesney-Lind, M. and Hagedorn, J. M. (Eds.), *Female Gangs in America: Essays on Gender, and Gangs*, Lakeview Press, 1999.

Chesney-Lind, M. and Irwin, K., From badness to meanness: popular constructions of contemporary girlhood. In *All About the Girl: Culture,*

Power, and Identity, Harris, A. (Ed.), New York: Routledge, pp. 45–56, 2004.

Chesney-Lind, M. and Irwin, K., Still "the best place to conquer girls:" Gender and juvenile justice. In *Women, Law and Social Control*, Pollock, J. and Merlo, A. (Eds.), Boston: Allyn and Bacon, 2005.

Chesney-Lind, M., Mayeda, D., Paramore, V., and Okamoto, S., Juvenile Robbery Arrests in Honolulu: An Overview, Honolulu: Crime Prevention and Justice Assistance Administration, Department of the Attorney General, January, 1999.

Chesney-Lind, M. and Paramore, V. V., Are girls getting more violent? Exploring robbery trends, *Journal of Contemporary Criminal Justice*, 17 (2): 142–166, 2001.

Chesney-Lind, M. and Pasko, L., *The Female Offender: Girls, Women and Crime*, 2nd ed., Thousand Oaks, CA: Sage, 2004.

Chesney-Lind, M. and Shelden, R .G., *Girls, Delinquency, and Juvenile Justice*, Pacific Grove, CA: Brooks/Cole, 1997.

Chesney-Lind, M. and Shelden, R. G., *Girls, Delinquency, and Juvenile Justice*, Belmont, CA: Wadsworth, 1998.

Chesney-Lind, M. and Shelden, R .G., *Girls, Delinquency and Juvenile Justice*, 2nd ed., Belmont: Thompson/Wadsworth, 2004.

Chessler, P., *Women's Inhumanity to Women*, New York: Nation Books, 2001.

Children's Defense Fund and Girls Incorporated, Overview of gender provisions in state juvenile justice plans, Washington, DC: *Children's Defense Fund and Girls Incorporated*, August 2002.

Cillessen, A. H. N. and Rose, A. J., Understanding popularity in the peer system, *Current Directions in Psychological Science*, 14: 102–105, 2005.

Citizen's Committee for Children of New York, *Girl in the Juvenile Justice System: Understanding Service Needs and Experiences*, New York: Citizen's Committee for Children, 2006.

Coleman, J., *The Adolescent Society*, Glencoe, IL: Free Press, 1961.

Conlin, M., The new gender gap, *Business Week*, May 26: 74, 2003.

Cook, P. J. and Laub, J. H., The unprecedented epidemic in youth violence. In *Youth Violence. Crime and Justice: A Review of Research*, Tonry, M. and Moore, M. H. (Eds.), Chicago: University of Chicago Press, pp. 27–64, 1998.

Coolbaugh, K. and Hansel, C. J., The comprehensive strategy: Lessons learned from the pilot sites, *OJJDP Juvenile Justice Bulletin*, Washington, DC: U.S. Department of Justice, Office of Justice Programs, Office of Juvenile Justice and Delinquency Prevention, 2000.

Corrado, R., Odgers, C., and Cohen, I. M., The incarceration of female young offenders: Protection for whom? *Canadian Journal of Criminology*, 2: 189–207, 2000.

Corsaro, W. A., *Friendship and Peer Culture in the Early Years*, Norwood, NJ: Ablex, 1985.

Cowan, G., and Hoffman, C. D., Gender stereotyping in young children: Evidence to support a concept-learning approach, *Sex Roles*, 14: 211–224, 1986.

Craig, W. M., The relationship among bullying, victimization, depression, anxiety, and aggression in elementary school children, *Personality and Individual Differences*, vol. 123–140, 1998.

Crick, N. R., Relational aggression: The role of intent attributions, feelings of distress, and provocation type, *Development and Psychopathology*, 7: 313–322, 1995.

Crick, N. R., The role of overt aggression, relational aggression, and prosocial behavior in the prediction of children's future social adjustment, *Child-hood Development*, 67: 2317–2327, 1996.

Crick, N. R., Childhood aggression and gender: A new look at an old problem. In *Gender and Motivation*, Bernstein, D. (Ed.), Lincoln: University of Nebraska Press, pp. 75–141, 1999.

Crick, N. R. and Bigbee, M. A., Relational and overt forms of peer victimization: A multiinformant approach, *Journal of Consulting and Clinical Psychology*, 66: 337–347, 1998.

Crick, N. R., Bigbee, M. A., and Howes, C., Gender differences in children's normative beliefs about aggression: How do i hurt thee? Let me count the ways, *Child Development*, 67: 1003–1014, 1996.

Crick, N. R. and Grotpeter, J. K., Children's treatment by peers: Victims of relational and overt aggression, *Development and Psychopathology*, 8: 367–380, 1996.

Crick, N. R. and Grotpeter, J. K., Relational aggression, gender, and social–psychological adjustment, *Child Development*, 66: 710–722, 1995.

Crittenden, D., You've come a long way, moll, *Wall Street Journal*, January 25: A 14. 1990.

Croll, P. and Moses, D., *One in Five: The Assessment and Incidence of Special Educational Needs*, New York: Routledge, 1985.

Currie, D., De-coding femininity: Advertisements and their teenage readers. *Gender and Society*, 11, No. 4 (August): 453–477, 1997.

Currie, D., Kelly, H., Deirdre M., and Pomerantz, S., The geeks shall inherit the earth: Girls' agency, subjectivity, and empowerment, *Journal of Youth Studies*, 9: 419–436, 2006.

Currie, E., *Crime and Punishment*, New York: Metropolitan Books, 1998.

Dabney, D.A., Hollinger, R.C., and Dugan, L., Who actually steals? A study of covertly observed shoplifters, *Justice Quarterly*, 21(4): 681–692, 2004.

Dart, B. and Clark, J., Sexism in schools: A new look, *Educational Review*, 40: 41–49, 1988.

Datesman, S. and Scarpitti, F., Unequal protection for males and females in the juvenile court. In *Juvenile Delinquency: Little Brother Grows Up*, Ferdinand, T. N. (Ed.), Newbury Park, CA: Sage, 1977.

Davies, B., *Frogs and Snails and Feminist Tales: Pre-School Children and Gender*, Boston: Allen and Unwin, 1989.

De Beauvoir, S., *The Second Sex*, New York: Knopf, 1952.

Deem, R., *Schooling for Women's Work*, Boston: Routledge and Kegan Paul, 1980.

DeKeseredy, W., *Women, Crime and the Canadian Criminal Justice System*, Cincinnati: Anderson, 2000.

Delamont, S., *Sex Roles and the School*, New York: Methuen, 1981.

De Los Reyes, A. and Prinstein, M. J., Applying depression-distortion hypotheses to the assessment of peer victimization in adolescents, *Journal of Clinical Child and Adolescent Psychology*, 33: 325–335, 2004.

Dembo, R., Sue, S. C., Borden, P., and Manning, D., Gender Differences in Service Needs among Youths Entering a Juvenile Assessment Center: A Replication Study. Paper presented at the annual meeting of the Society of Social Problems, Washington, DC, August, 1995.

Dembo, R., Williams, L., and Schmeidler, J., Gender differences in mental health service needs among youths entering a juvenile detention center, *Journal of Prison and Jail Health*, 12: 73–101, 1993.

Deschanes, E. and Esbensen, F-A., Violence among girls: Does gang membership make a difference? In *Female Gangs in America: Essays on Gender, and Gangs*, Chesney-Lind, M. and Hagedorn, J. M. (Eds.), Lakeview Press, pp. 277–294, 1999.

DeVoe et al., Indicators of School Crime and Safety. National Center for Education Statistics, Bureau of Justice Statistics, 2004.

DeVoe et al., Indicators of School Crime and Safety, National Center for Education Statistics, Bureau of Justice Statistics, 2005.

Deyken, E. Y. and Buka, S. L., Prevalence and risk factors for posttraumatic stress disorder among chemically dependent adolescents, *American Journal of Psychiatry*, 154: 752–757, 1997.

Dietrich, L. C., *Chicana Adolescents: Bitches, 'Ho's, and Schoolgirls*, Westport, CT: Praeger, 1998.

Dilulio, J. J., The Coming of the Super-Predators, *The Weekly Standard*, 27: 23, November, 1995.

Dilulio, J. J., *How to Stop the Coming Crime Wave*, New York: Manhattan Institute, 1996.

Dingeman, R., Ex-guard guilty in sex assault. *Honolulu Advertiser*. Posted April 30, 2004, on http://the.honoluluadvertiser.com/article/2004/apr/30/in/in14a.html.

Durham, M. G., Dilemmas of desire: Representations of adolescent sexuality in two teen magazines, *Youth and Society*, 29: 369–389, 1998.

Eaton, D. K. et al., Youth Risk Behavior Surveillance—United States 2005, *Morbidity and Mortality Weekly Report Surveillance Summaries*, 55: 1–108, 2006.

Edelhard, C., Bringing on the boys, *Honolulu Advertiser*, November 17: E2–E3, 2003.

Eder, D., The cycle of popularity: Interpersonal relations among female adolescents, *Sociology of Education*, 58: 154–165, 1985.

Eder, D. and Enke, J. L., The structure of gossip: Opportunities and constraints of collective expression among adolescents, *American Sociological Review*, 56(191): 494–508, 1991.

Eder, D. and Parker, S., The central production and reproduction of gender: The effect of extracurricular activities on peer-group culture, *Sociology of Education*, 60: 200–213, 1987.

Ehrhart, J. K. and Sandler, B. R., Looking for More than a Few Good Women in Traditionally Male Fields, Washington, DC: Project on the Status and Education of Women, 1987.

Elder, G. H., Appearance and education in marriage mobility, *American Sociological Review*, 34: 519–533, 1969.

Elizabeth, J., Girl bullies don't leave black eyes, just agony, *Pittsburgh Post-Gazette*, April 10, A1, 2002.

Elliott, D. and Voss, H., *Delinquency and Dropout*, Lexington: DC Heath, 1974.

Elliott, D., Olweus, D., Limber, S., and Mihalic, S., *Book Nine: Bullying Prevention Program*, Boulder: Center for the Study and Prevention of Violence, Institute for Behavioral Sciences, University of Colorado, Boulder, 2002.

English, K., Self-reported crime rates of women prisoners, *Journal of Quantitative Criminology*, 9: 357–382, 1993.

Fagot, B., The child's expectations of differences in adult male and female interactions, *Sex Roles*, 11: 593–600, 1984.

Fairtest, 2006: Gender Bias in College Admissions Tests, www.fairtest.org/facts/genderbias.htm.

Faludi, S., *Backlash: The Undeclared War against American Women*, New York: Crown, 1991.

Federal Bureau of Investigation, *Crime in the United States 1990*, Washington, DC: U.S. Government Printing Office, 1991.

Federal Bureau of Investigation, *Crime in the United States 1994*, Washington, DC: U.S. Government Printing Office, 1995.

Federal Bureau of Investigation, *Crime in the United States 1995*, Washington, DC: U.S. Government Printing Office, 1996.

Federal Bureau of Investigation, *Crime in the United States 1996*, Washington, DC: U.S. Government Printing Office, 1997.

Federal Bureau of Investigation, *Crime in the United States 1997*, Washington, DC: U.S. Government Printing Office, 1998.

Federal Bureau of Investigation, *Crime in the United States 1998*, Washington, DC: U.S. Government Printing Office, 1999.

Federal Bureau of Investigation, *Crime in the United States 1999*, Washington, DC: U.S. Government Printing Office, 2000.

Federal Bureau of Investigation, *Crime in the United States 2000*, Washington, DC: U.S. Government Printing Office, 2001.

Federal Bureau of Investigation, *Crime in the United States 2001*, Washington, DC: U.S. Government Printing Office, 2002.

Federal Bureau of Investigation, *Crime in the United States 2002*, Washington, DC: U.S. Government Printing Office, 2003.

Federal Bureau of Investigation, *Crime in the United States 2003*, Washington, DC: U.S. Government Printing Office, 2004.

Federal Bureau of Investigation, *Crime in the United States 2004*, Washington, DC: U.S. Government Printing Office, 2005.

Federal Bureau of Investigation, *Crime in the United States 2005*, Washington, DC: U.S. Government Printing Office, 2006.

Feld, B. C., The juvenile court meets the principle of offense: Punishment, treatment and the difference it makes, *Boston University Law Review*, 68: 821–915, 1988.

Feld, B. C., *Bad Kids: Race and the Transformation of the Juvenile Court*, New York: Oxford University Press, 1999.

Female Offender Resource Center, *Little Sisters and the Law*, Washington, DC: American Bar Association, 1977.

Ferguson, A. A., *Bad Boys: Public Schools in the Making of Black Masculinity*, Ann Arbor: University of Michigan Press, 2001.

Fine, G. A., The social organization of adolescent gossip: The rhetoric of moral evaluation. In *Children's Worlds and Children's Language*, Cook-Gumperz, J., Corsaro, W. A. and Streeck, J. (Eds.), New York: M. de Gruyter, 1986.

Fine, G. A., *With the Boys: Little League Baseball and Preadolescent Culture*, Chicago: University of Chicago Press, 1987.

Fine, M., Working the hyphens: Reinventing self and other in qualitative research. In *Handbook of Qualitative Research*, Denzin, N. K. and Lincoln, Y. (Eds.), Thousand Oaks, CA: Sage, pp. 70–82, 1994.

Finkelhor, D., Current information on the scope and nature of child sexual abuse, *The Future of Children*, 4(2): 31, 46–48, 1994.

Fisher, M., School expels 8th-grader who gave classmate Midol, *Dayton Daily News*, Pg. 1A, October 4, 1996.

Ford, R., The Razor's Edge, *Boston Globe Magazine*, 13, 22–28, May 24, 1998.

Francis, B., *Boys, Girls, and Achievement: Addressing the Classroom Issues*, New York: Routledge Falmer, 2000.

Franklin, A., Criminality in the workplace; a comparison of male and female offenders. In *The Criminality of Deviant Women*, Adler, F. and Simon, R. (Eds.), Boston: Houghton Mifflin, 1979.

Freitas, K. and Chesney-Lind, M. Difference doesn't mean difficult: Workers talk about working with girls, *Women, Girls, & Criminal Justice*, 65–78, August/September, 2001.

French, J. and French, P., Gender imbalance in the primary classroom: An interactional account, *Educational Research*, 26: 127–136, 1984.

Friere, P., *Pedagogy of the Oppressed*, translated by Myra Bergman Ramos, New York: Continuum, 1970/1993.

Fuller, M., Black girls in a London comprehensive school. In *Schooling for Women's Work*, Deem, R. (Ed.), Boston: Routledge and Kegan Paul, pp. 52–65, 1980.

Gaarder, E. and Belknap, J., Tenuous borders: Girls transferred to adult court, *Criminology*, 40: 481–518, 2002.

Gaarder, E., Rodriguez, N., and Zatz, M. S., Criers, liars and manipulators: Probation officers' views of girls, *Justice Quarterly*, 21: 547–578, 2004.

Galen, B. R. and Underwood, M., A developmental investigation of social aggression among girls, *Developmental Psychology*, 33: 589–599, 1997.

Galton, M., Hargreaves, L., Comber, C., Wall, D., and Pell, A., *Inside the Primary Classroom: 20 Years On*, New York: Routledge, 1999.

Garbarino, J., *See Jane Hit: Why Girls are Growing More Violent and What We Can Do About It*, New York: Penguin Press, 2006.

Garland, D., *The Culture of Control: Crime and Social Order in Contemporary Society*, Chicago: University of Chicago Press, 2001.

Garvey, J., Kids killing kids: Does Columbine tell us anything, *Commonweal*, June 4, 1991.

Gelsethorpe, L., *Sexism and the Female Offender*, Aldershot, UK: Gower, 1989.

Gilbert, S. C., Keery, H., and Thompson, J. K., The media's role in body image and eating disorders. In *Featuring Females: Feminist Analyses of Media*, Cole, E. and Daniel, J. H. (Eds.), Washington, DC: American Psychological Association, pp. 41–56, 2005.

Gilligan, C., *In a Different Voice*, Cambridge, MA: Harvard University Press, 1982.

Gilligan, C. and Brown, L. M., *Meeting at the Crossroads: Women's Psychology Girls' Development*, Cambridge, MA: Harvard University Press, 1992.

Girls Incorporated, *Prevention and Parity: Girls in Juvenile Justice*, Indianapolis: Girls Incorporated National Resource Center, 1996.

Glaser, B. G. and Strauss, A., *Discovery of Grounded Theory: Strategies for Qualitative Research*, Chicago: Aldine, 1967.

Goodwin, M., *He-Said-She-Said*, Bloomington: Indiana University Press, 1990.

Goodwin, M. H., Exclusion in girls' peer groups: Ethnographic analysis of language practices on the playground, *Human Development*, 45: 392–415, 2002.

Grant, L., Race and the schooling of young girls. In *Education and Gender Equality*, Wrigley, J. (Ed.), Washington, DC: Falmer Press, pp. 94–114, 1992.

Griffiths, V., *Adolescent Girls and Their Friends: A Feminist Ethnography*, Brookfield, VT: Ashgate, 1987.

Grotpeter, J. K. and Crick, N. R. Relational aggression, overt aggression, and friendship, *Child Development*, 67: 2328–2338, 1996.

Grunbaum, J. et al., Youth risk behavior surveillance—United States 2001, *Morbidity and Mortality Weekly Report Surveillance Summaries*, 51: 1–64, 2002.

Guido, M., In a new twist on equality, girls crimes resemble boys, *San Jose Mercury*, pp. 1B–4B, June 4, 1998.

Gurian, M. and Stevens, K., *The Minds of Boys: Saving Our Sons from Falling Behind in School and Life*, San Francisco: Jossey-Bass, 2005.

Guthrie, B. J., Young, A. M., Boyd, C. J., and Kintner, E. K., Ebb and flow when navigating adolescence: Predictors of daily hassles among African-American adolescent girls, *Journal for Specialists in Pediatric Nursing*. 7 (4): 143–152, October–December, 2002.

Hadley, M., Relational, indirect, adaptive, or just mean: Recent studies on aggression in adolescent girls—Part II, *Studies in Gender and Sexuality* 5(3): 331–350, 2004.

Hagan, F. E., *Introduction to Criminology*, Chicago: Nelson-Hall, 1987.

Hagedorn, J. and Devitt, M., Fighting female: The social construction of female gangs. In *Female Gangs in America: Essays on Gender, and Gangs*, Chesney-Lind, M. and Hagedorn. J. M. (Eds.), Lakeview Press, pp. 256–276, 1999.

Hall, R. M and Sandler, B. R., The Classroom Climate: A Chilly One for Women? Project on the Status and Education of Women, Association of American Colleges, 1982.

Hammersley, M., An evaluation of two studies of gender imbalance in primary classrooms, *Educational Research Journal*, 16: 125–143, 1990.

Hansen, S., A Girl's Best Friend, *New York Times Book Review*, p. 8., May 22, 2005.

Harding, S., *The Science Question in Feminism*, Ithaca, NY: Cornell University Press, 1986.

Harms, P., Detention in Delinquency Cases, 1989–1998, OJJDP Fact Sheet, No. 1, Washington, DC: U.S. Department of Justice, 2002.

Harris, A., *Future Girl: Young Women in the Twenty-First Century*, New York: Routledge, 2004.

Harvard Civil Rights Project, Opportunities Suspended: The Devastating Consequences of Zero Tolerance and School Discipline, report from A National Summit on Zero Tolerance, Washington, DC, June 15–16, 2000.

Hayward, K. J., *City Limits: Crime, Consumer Culture, and the Urban Experience*, London: Glasshouse Press, 2004.

Heimer, K., Changes in the gender gap in crime and women's economic marginalization. In *Criminal Justice 2000: Vol. 1, The Nature of Crime: Continuity and Change*, Washington, DC: National Institute of Justice, 2000.

Hennington, C. et al., The role of relational aggression in identifying aggressive boys and girls, *Journal of School Psychology*, 36: 457–477, 1998.

Hesse-Biber, S. N., *The Cult of Thinness*, New York: Oxford, 2007.

Hill, S. A. and Sprague, J., Parenting in black and white families, *Gender and Society*, 13(4): 480–502, 1999.

Hoff-Sommers, C., *The War Against Boys: How Misguided Feminism Is Harming Our Young Men*, New York: Simon and Schuster, 2000.

Holsinger, K., Belknap, J., and Sutherland, J. L., Assessing the Gender Specific Program and Service Needs for Adolescent Females in the Juvenile Justice System, A Report to the Office of Criminal Justice Services, Columbus, OH, 1999.

Horowitz, R. and Pottieger, A. E., Gender bias in juvenile justice handling of seriously crime-involved youths, *Journal of Research in Crime and Delinquency*, 28: 75–100, 1991.

Horswell, C., Girl's parents fight pain of suspension over Advil: School officials to uphold punishment, *Houston Chronicle*, Tuesday, October 22, 1996.

Huizinga, D., Over-time changes in delinquency and drug use: The 1970s to the 1990s. Unpublished report, Washington, DC: Office of Juvenile Justice and Delinquency Prevention, 1997.

Human Rights Watch and American Civil Liberties Union, *Custody and Control: Conditions of Confinement in New York's Juvenile Prisons for Girls*, New York: Human Rights Watch and ACLU, 2006.

Hyde, J. S., *Half the Human Experience: The Psychology of Women*, Lexington, MA: Heath, 1985.

Inness, S., *Millenium Girls: Today's Girls around the World*, Lanham: Rowman & Littlefield, 1998.

Irvine, J. J., Teacher–student interactions: Effects of student race, sex, and grade level, *Journal of Educational Psychology*, 78: 14–21, 1986.

Joe Laidler, K. A. and Chesney-Lind, M., Running away from home: Rhetoric and reality in troublesome behavior, *Journal of Contemporary Criminal Justice*, 12(2), May, 1996.

Joe, K. and Chesney-Lind, M., Just every mother's angel: An analysis of ethnic and gender variations in youth gang membership, *Gender and Society*, 9(4): 409–431, August, 1995.

Johnson, P. C. *Inner Lives: Voices of African American Women in Prison*, New York: New York University Press, 2003.

Kandiyoti, D., Patriarchal bargains, *Gender and Society*, 2: 274–290, 1998.

Kann, L. et al., Youth Risk Behavior Surveillance—United States 1993, *Morbidity and Mortality Weekly Report Surveillance Summaries*, 44: 1–55, 1995.

Kann, L. et al., Youth Risk Behavior Surveillance—United States 1995, *Morbidity and Mortality Weekly Report Surveillance Summaries*, 45: 1–83, 1996.

Kann, L. et al., Youth Risk Behavior Surveillance—United States 1997, *Morbidity and Mortality Weekly Report Surveillance Summaries*, 45: 1–89, 1998.

Kann, L. et al., Youth Risk Behavior Surveillance—United States 1999, *Morbidity and Mortality Weekly Report Surveillance Summaries*, 49: 1–96, 2000.

Kataoka, S., Zima, B., Dupre, D., Moreno, K., Yang, X. and McCracken, J., Mental health problems and service use among female juvenile offenders, *Journal of the American Academy of Child and Adolescent Psychiatry*, 40(5): 549–555, 2001.

Katz, P., The development of female identity. In *Becoming Female: Perspectives on Development*, Kopp, C. (Ed.), New York: Plenum Press, 1979.

Kaufman, P. et al., Indicators of School Crime and Safety, National Center for Education Statistics, Bureau of Justice Statistics, 1998.

Kaufman, P. et al., Indicators of School Crime and Safety, National Center for Education Statistics, Bureau of Justice Statistics, 2000.

Kehily, M. J., Gender and sexuality: Continuities and change for girls in school. In *All About the Girl*, Harris, A. (Ed.), New York: Routledge, 2004.

Kelly, A., Gender differences in teacher–pupil interactions: A meta-analytic review, *Research in Education*, 39: 1–24, 1988.

Kelly, D. M., *Last Chance High: How Girls and Boys Drop In and Out of Alternative Schools*, New Haven, CT: Yale University Press, 1993.

Kelly, P. and Morgan-Kidd, J., Social influences on the sexual behaviors of adolescent girls in at-risk circumstances, *Journal of Obstetric, Gynecologic, and Neonatal Nursing*, 30(5): 481–489, 2001.

Kempf-Leonard, K. and Sample, L. L., Disparity based on sex: Is gender-specific treatment warranted?, *Justice Quarterly*, 17, 89–128, 2000.

Kenny, L. D., *Daughters of Suburbia: Growing Up White, Middle Class and Female*, New Brunswick: Rutgers University Press, 2000.

Kersten, J., The institutional control of girls and boys. In *Growing Up Good: Policing the Behavior of Girls in Europe*, Cain, M. (Ed.), London: Sage, pp. 129–144, 1989.

Ketchum, O., Why jurisdiction over status offenders should be eliminated from juvenile courts. *In Status Offenders and the Juvenile Justice System*, Allinson, R. (Ed.), Hackensack, NJ: National Council on Crime and Delinquency, 1978.

Keys, R., *Is There Life after High School?* Boston: Little, Brown, 1976.

Kinney, D. A., From nerds to normals: The recovery of identity among adolescents from middle school to high school, *Sociology of Education*, 66: 21–40, 1993.

Klein, J., An invisible problem: Everyday violence against girls in schools, *Theoretical Criminology*, 10: 147–177, 2006.

Klemesrud, J., Women terrorists, sisters in crime, N.Y.T. News Service, *Honolulu Star Bulletin*, C1, January 16, 1978.

Kluger, J., Taming wild girls, *Time Magazine*, 54, May 1, 2006.

Koester, S. and Schwartz, J., Crack, gangs, sex and powerlessness: A view from Denver, In *Crack Pipe as Pimp: An Ethnographic Investigation of Sex-for-Crack Exchanges*, Ratner, M. S. (Ed.), New York: Lexington Books, 1993.

Komorosky, M., *Women in the Modern World*, Boston: Little, Brown, 1953.

Kruse, M., Girl Arrested for Butter Knife in Backpack, *St. Petersburg Times*, October 25, 2005, www.sptimes.com/2005/10/25/Hernando/Girl_arrested_for_but.shtml.

Kuhn, D., Churnin Nash, S., and Brucken, L., Sex role concepts of two- and three-year-olds, *Child Development*, 49(2): 445–451, 1978.

Laidler, K. J. and Hunt, G., Accomplishing femininity among girls in the gang, *British Journal of Criminology*, 41: 656–678, 2001.

Lamb, S., *The Secret Lives of Girls: What Good Girls Really Do—Sex Play, Aggression, and Their Guilt*, New York: The Free Press, 2001.

Lamb, S., Not with my daughter: Parents still have trouble acknowledging teenage sexuality, *Psychotherapy Networker*, May/June, 27(3), 2003.

Lamb, S. and Brown, L. M. *Packaging Girlhood: Rescuing Our Daughters from Marketers' Schemes*, New York: St. Martin's Press, 2006.

Lambart, A. M., The sisterhood. In *The Process of Schooling: A Sociological Reader*, Hammersley, M. and Woods, P. (Eds.), London: Routledge and Kegan Paul, pp. 152–159, 1976.

Lauderback, D., Hansen, J., and Waldorf, D., Sisters are doin' it for themselves: A black female gang in San Francisco, *The Gang Journal*, 1: 57–72, 1992.

Leadbetter, B., Ross, J., and Way, N., *Urban Girls: Resisting Stereotypes, Creating Identities*, New York: New York University Press, 1996.

Lease, A. M., Kennedy, C. A., and Axelrod, J. L., Children's social constructions of popularity, *Social Development*, 11: 87–109, 2002.

Leavitt, I., Hazing's horror related, *Glenview Announcements*, May 8, 2003.

Leblanc, L., *Pretty in Punk: Girls' Gender Resistance in a Boys' Subculture*, New Jersey: Rutgers University Press, 1999.

Lederman, C. S. and Brown, E. N., Entangled in the shadows: Girls in the juvenile justice system, *Buffalo Law Review*, 48(3), 2000.

Lee, F. R., For gold earrings and protections, more girls take road to violence, *New York Times*, A1, November 25, 1991.

Lees, S., *Ruling Passions: Sexual Violence, Reputation, and the Law*, Buckingham: Open University Press, 1997.

Leslie, C., Biddle, N., Rosenberg, D., and Wayne, J., Girls will be girls, *Newsweek*, 44, August 2, 1993.

Leventhal, T. and Brooks-Gunn, J., The neighborhoods they live in: The effects of neighborhood residence on child and adolescent outcomes, *Psychological Bulletin* 126(2): 309–337, 2000.

Lever, J., Sex differences in the games children play, *Social Problems* 23: 478–487, 1976.

Lewis, N., Delinquent girls achieving a violent equality in DC, *Washington Post*, A1, A14, December 23, 1992.

Lipsey, M., Juvenile delinquency treatment: A meta-analytic inquiry in the variability of effects. In *Meta-Analysis for Explanation: A Casebook*, Cook, T. A. et al. (Eds.), New York: Russell Sage, 1992.

Loeb, R. C. and Horst, L., Sex differences in self- and teachers' reports of self-esteem in preadolescents, *Sex Roles*, 4: 779–788, 1978.

Longfellow, H. W., There was a little girl. In *Familiar Quotations*, 16th ed., Bartlett, J. and Kaplan, J. (Eds.), Boston: Little Brown & Co., 1992.

Lott, B., *Women's Lives: Themes and Variations in Gender Learning*. Pacific Grove, CA: Brooks/Cole, 1987.

Lovekin, K., Settlement reached on clippers, *Temecula-Murrieta*, B01, June 15, 1995.

Mac an Ghaill, M., Beyond the white norm: The use of qualitative methods in the study of black youths' schooling in England. In *Gender and Ethnicity in Schools: Ethnographic Accounts*, Woods, P. and Hammersley, M. (Eds.), New York: Routledge, pp. 145–165, 1993.

Maccalair, D., School House Hype: Two Years Later, San Francisco: Center for Juvenile and Criminal Justice, www.cjcj.org/pubs/schoolhouse/shh2.html, 2000.

Maccoby, E., *The Development of Sex Differences*, Palo Alto, CA: Stanford University Press, 1966.

Macpherson, P. and Fine, M., Hungry for an us: Adolescent girls and adult women negotiating territories of race, gender, class and difference, *Feminism and Psychology*, 5: 181–200, 1995.

Madigan, E., Bullying by school kids gets lawmakers' attention, Stateline.org. Retrieved June 19, 2004 from www.stateline.org/stateline/.

Mahaffy, K. A., Girls' low self esteem: How is it related to later socioeconomic achievements?, *Gender and Society*, 18: 308–327, 2004.

Maher, L. and Daly, K., Women in the street level drug economy: Continuity or change? *Criminology*, 34, 465–491, 1996.

Males, M., *The Scapegoat Generation: America's War on Adolescents*, Monroe, ME: Common Courage Press, 1996.

Males, M., And now... superpredatrixes? More fact-bending hype about the spike in girl violence, *Youth Today*, 15(5): 34, May, 2006.

Males, M. and Shorter, A., *To Cage and Serve*, unpublished manuscript, 2001.

Mann, C. R., *Female Crime and Delinquency*, Tuscaloosa: University of Alabama Press, 1984.

Marini, M. M., Sex differences in the determination of adolescent aspirations: A review of research, *Sex Roles*, 4: 723–753, 1978.

Mauer, M., *Race to Incarcerate*, New York: The New Press, 1999.

Mauer, M. and Chesney-Lind, M., *Invisible Punishment: The Collateral Consequences of Mass Imprisonment*, New York: New Press, 2002.

May, D., Juvenile shoplifters and the organization of store security: A case study in the social construction of delinquency, *International Journal of Criminology and Penology*, 6: 137–160, 1978.

Mayeda, D. T., Chesney-Lind, M., and Koo, J., Talking story with Hawaii's youth: Confronting violent and sexualized perceptions of ethnicity and gender, *Youth and Society*, 33: 99–128, 2001.

Mayer, J., Girls in the Maryland juvenile justice system: Findings of the female population task force, presentation to the Gender Specific Services Training Group, Minneapolis, MN, July 1994.

McCarthy, B., Felmlee, D., and Hagan, J., Girl friends are better: gender, friends, and crime among school and street youth, *Criminology*, 42: 805–835, 2004.

McCormack, A., Janus, M., and Burgess, A. Runaway youths and sexual victimization: Gender differences in an adolescent runaway population, *Child Abuse and Neglect*, 10: 387–395, 1986.

McRobbie, A., Working class girls and the culture of femininity. In *Women Take Issue: Aspects of Women's Subordination*, Women's Studies Group (Eds.), London: Hutchinson, 1978.

Meadows, S. and Johnson, D., Girl fight: Savagery in the Chicago suburbs, *Newsweek*, 37, May 19, 2003.

Melton, G. B. et al., Violence among Rural Youth: A Final Report to the Office of Juvenile Justice and Delinquency Prevention, Unpublished report, Washington, DC: U.S. Department of Justice, Office of Justice Programs, Office of Juvenile Justice and Delinquency Prevention, 1998.

Merten, D. E., The meaning of meanness: Popularity, competition, and conflict among junior high school girls, *Sociology of Education*, 70: 175–191, 1997.

Metcalf, F., She devils, *Courier Mail*, L 06, June 22, 2002.

Miller, J., Race, gender and juvenile justice: An examination of disposition decision-making for delinquent girls, In *The Intersection of Race, Gender and Class in Criminology,* Schwartz, M. D. and Milovanovic, D. (Eds.), New York: Garland Press, 1994.

Miller, J., Up it up: Gender and the accomplishment of street robbery, *Criminology,* 36(1) (February): 37–65, 1998.

Miller, J., *One of the Guys: Girls, Gangs, and Gender,* New York: Oxford University, 2001.

Miller, P., Danaher, D., and Forbes, D., Sex-related strategies for coping with interpersonal conflict in children aged five and seven, *Developmental Psychology,* 22: 543–548, 1986.

Mills, J. S., Polivy, J., Herman, C. P., and Tiggeman, M., Effects of exposure to think-media images: Evidence of self-enhancement among restrained eaters, *Personality and Social Psychology Bulletin,* 28: 1687–1699, 2002.

Miranda, M. K., *Homegirls in the Public Sphere,* Austin: University of Texas Press, 2003.

Money, J., Hampson, J. L., and Mapson, J. G., Imprinting and the establishment of gender role, *AMA Archives of Neurology and Psychology,* 77: 333–336, 1957.

Moore, J., *Going Down to the Barrio: Homeboys and Homegirls in Change,* Philadelphia: Temple University Press, 1991.

Morash, M. and Chesney-Lind, M., Girls violence in context, Chapter for *OJJDP Girls Study Group Volume,* Zahn, M., (Ed.), forthcoming.

Morris, A., *Women, Crime, and Criminal Justice,* New York: Basil Blackwell, 1987.

Morris, E., "Tuck in that shirt!" Race, class, gender and discipline in an urban school, *Sociological Perspectives,* 48(1): 25–48, 2005.

MSNBC.com chat, "Rachel Simmons Mean Girl," April 10, 2002.

Murphy, S., Waldorf, D., and Reinarman, C., Drifting into dealing: Becoming a cocaine seller, *Qualitative Sociology,* 13: 321–343, 1991.

Myhill, D., Bad boys and good girls? Patterns of interaction and response in whole class teaching, *British Educational Research Journal,* 28: 340–352, 2002.

Nadon, S., Koverola, C., and Schludeermann, E., Antecedents to prostitution: Childhood victimization, *Journal of Interpersonal Violence,* 13(2), April: 206–221, 1998.

Nansel, T. R. et al., Bullying behaviors among U.S. youth, *Journal of the American Medical Association,* 285: 2094–2100, 2001.

National Association for the Advancement of Colored People Legal Defense Fund, Dismantling the National Center on Addiction and Substance Abuse Prevention, Criminal School-to-Prison Pipeline, 2005. Neglect: Substance Abuse, Juvenile Justice and the Children Left Behind, www.casacolumbia.org/supportcasa/item.asp?cID=12&PID=81, 2004.

National Conference of State Legislators, www.ncsl.org/programs/educ/Sch-BullyingLegislation.htm. Retrieved December 15, 2006.

National Council on Crime and Delinquency, The Juveniles Taken into Custody Research Program: Estimating the Prevalence of Juvenile Custody by Race and Gender, San Francisco: National Council on Crime and Delinquency, 1993.

National Women's Law Center, Title IX and Equal Opportunity in Vocational and Technical Education: A Promise Still Owed to the Nation's Young Women, June, 2002.

NBC, Fighting with friendship: Understanding the secret warfare girls wage on each other, *Dateline*, April 9, 2002.

Nilan, P., Exclusion, inclusion, and moral ordering in two girls' friendship groups, *Gender and Education*, 3: 163–182, 1991.

Office of Juvenile Justice and Delinquency Prevention, *Guiding Principles for Promising Female Programming: An Inventory of Best Practices*, Nashville, TN: Green Peters, 1998.

Offill, J. and Schappell, E., *The Friend Who Got Away: Twenty Women's True-Life Tales of Friendships That Blew Up, Burned Out, or Faded Away*, New York: Doubleday, 2005.

Olweus, D., Aggression and peer acceptance in adolescent boys: Two short-term longitudinal studies of rating, *Child Development*, 48: 1301–1313, 1977.

Olweus, D., *Aggression in the Schools, Bullies and Whipping Boys*, Washington, DC: Hemisphere Press: Wiley, 1978.

Olweus, D., Stability of aggressive reaction patterns in males: A review. *Psychological Bulletin*, 86: 852–875, 1979.

Olweus, D., *Bullying at School: What We Know and What We Can Do*, Cambridge: Blackwell, 1993.

Olweus, D., Annotation: Bullying at school: Basic facts and effects of a school based intervention program, *Journal of Child Psychology and Psychiatry*, 35: 1171–1190, 1994.

O'Reilly, P., Learning to be a girl. In *Educating Young Adolescent Girls*, O'Reilly, P., Penn, E., and deMarrais, K. (Eds.), Mahwah, New Jersey: Lawrence Erlbaum Associates, pp. 11–28, 2001.

Orenstein, P., *Schoolgirls: Young Women, Self-Esteem and the Confidence Gap*, New York: Anchor, 1994.

Osler, A. and Vincent, K., *Girls and Exclusion: Rethinking the Agenda*, New York: Routledge, 2003.

Owens, S. L., Smothers, B. C., and Love, F. E., Are girls victims of gender bias in our nation's schools?, *Journal of Instructional Psychology*, 30: 131–138, 2003.

Paquette, J. A. and Underwood, M. K., Gender differences in young adolescents' experiences of peer victimization: Social and physical aggression, *Merrill-Palmer Quarterly*, 45: 242–266, 1999.

Parker, J. G. and Gottman, J. M., Social and emotional development in a relational context: Friendship interaction from early childhood to adolescence. In *Peer Relationships in Child Development*, Berndt. T. J. and Ladd, G. W. (Eds.), Somerset, NJ: John Wiley and Sons, 1989.

Pettit, B. and Western, B., Mass imprisonment and the life course: Race and class inequality in U.S. incarceration, *American Sociological Review*, 69: 151–169, 2004.

Pipher, M., *Reviving Ophelia: Saving the Selves of Adolescent Girls*, New York: Ballantine, 1994.

Pittsburgh Post-Gazette, Just between us girls: Not enough sugar, too much spite, June 5, 2002, pp. 5–3.

Platt, A. M., *The Child Savers*, Chicago: University of Chicago Press, 1969.

Polivy, J. and Herman, C. P., Sociocultural idealization of thin female body shapes: An introduction to the special issue on body images and eating disorders, *Journal of Social and Clinical Psychology: Special Body Image and Eating Disorders*, 234: 1–6, 2004.

Pollak, O., *The Criminality of Women*, Philadelphia: University of Pennsylvania Press, 1950.

Pollock, J. *Criminal Women*, Cincinnati: Anderson, 1999.

Portillos, E. L., Women, men and gangs: The social construction of gender in the barrio. In *Female Gangs in America*, Chesney-Lind, M. and Hagadorn, J. (Eds.), Chicago: Lake View Press, 1999.

Presser, H., Sally's corner: Coping with unmarried motherhood, *Journal of Social Issues*, 36: 107–129, 1980.

Prezbindowski, K. and Prezbindowski, A. K., Educating young adolescent girls about lesbian, bisexual and gay issues. In *Educating Young Adolescent Girls*, O'Reilly, P., Penn, E., and deMarrais, K. (Eds.), Mahwah, NJ: Lawrence Erlbaum Associates, pp. 47–80, 2001.

Prinstein, M. J., Boergers, J., and Vernberg, E. M., Overt and relational aggression in adolescents: Social-psychological adjustment of aggressors and victims, *Journal of Clinical Child Psychology*, 30: 479–491, 2001.

Project on Equal Education Rights (PEER), Computer Equity Report, Sex Bias at the Computer Terminal—How Schools Program Girls, Washington, DC, 1984.

Prothrow-Stith, D. and Spivak, H. R., *Sugar and Spice and No Longer Nice: How We Can Stop Girls' Violence*, San Francisco: Jossey-Bass, 2005.

Putallaz, M., Kupersmidt, J., et al., Overt and Relational Aggression: Aggressors, Victims, and Gender, Biennial Meeting of the Society for Research in Child Development, Symposium on Social Relationships and Two Forms of Aggression: Gender Considerations, Albuquerque, NM, 1999.

Puzzanchera, C., Stahl, A., Finnegan, T., Tierney, N., and Snyder, H., Juvenile Court Statistics 1999, Washington, DC: Office of Juvenile Justice and Delinquency Prevention, 2003.

Rabban, M. L., Sex role identification in young children in two diverse social groups, *Genetic Psychological Monographs*, 42: 81–158, 1950.

Rafter, N. H., *Partial Justice: Women, Prisons and Social Control*, New Brunswick, NJ: Transaction Books, 1990.

Ray, D., Letter to Glenda MacMullin, American Bar Association, Re: National Girl's Institute, March 20, 2002.

Ray, J. A. and Briar, K. H., Economic motivators for shoplifting. In *Crime and Criminals: Contemporary and Classic Readings*, Scarpitti, F. and Nielsen A. L. (Eds.), Los Angeles: Roxbury, 1999.

Reitsma-Street, M. and Artz, S., Girls and crime: Issues and perspectives on young offenders in Canada. Winterdyk, J. A. (Ed.), Toronto: Harcourt, pp. 61–87, 2000.

Reitsma-Street, M. and Offord, D. R., Girl delinquents and their sisters: A challenge for practice, *Canadian Social Work Review*, 8: 11–27, 1991.

Renzetti, C. M. and Curran, D. J., *Women, Men, and Society*, Boston: Allyn and Bacon, 2003.

Reyes, O. and Jason, L. A., Pilot study examining factors associated with academic success for Hispanic high school students, *Journal of Youth and Adolescence*, 22: 57–71, 1993.

Rhodes, J. E. and Fischer, K., Spanning the gender gap: Gender differences in delinquency among inner city adolescents, *Adolescence* (Winter): 1–7, 1993.

Robinson, R., Violations of Girlhood: A Qualitative Study of Female Delinquents and Children in Need of Services in Massachusetts, unpublished PhD dissertation, Brandeis University, 1990.

Roecker Phelps, C., Children's responses to overt and relational aggression, *Journal of Clinical Child Psychology*, 30: 240–252, 2001.

Roper v. Simmons, 125 S. Ct. 1183, 2005.

Rose, A. J., Swenson, L. P., and Waller, E. M., Overt and relational aggression and perceived popularity: Developmental differences in concurrent and prospective relations, *Developmental Psychology*, 40: 378–387, 2004.

Rosenberg, M., *Society and the Adolescent Self-Image*, Princeton, NJ: Princeton University Press, 1965.

Rotherman-Borus, M. J., Suicidal behavior and risk factors among runaway youths, *American Journal of Psychiatry*, 150: 103–107, 1993.

Rubin, L., *Worlds of Pain: Life in the Working Class Family*, New York: Basic Books, 1976.

Russ, H., The war on catfights, *City Limits*, February: 19–22, 2004.

Rys, G. S. and Bear, G. G., Relational aggression and peer relations: Gender and developmental issues, *Merrill-Palmer Quarterly*, 43: 87–106, 1997.

Sadker, M. and Sadker, D., *Failing at Fairness: How America's Schools Cheat Girls*, New York: Maxwell Macmillan International, 1994.

Salmivalli, C., Kaukiainen, A., and Lagerspetz, K., Aggression and sociometric status among peers: Do gender and type of aggression matter? *Scandinavian Journal of Psychology*, 41: 17–24, 2000.

Sarri, R., *The Woman Client*, Burden, D. and Gottlieb, N. (Eds.), New York: Tavistock, 1987.

Savoye, C., Putting rock-solid faith in zero tolerance, *Christian Science Monitor*, June 20: 12, Op. 1C, 2001.

Scelfo, J., Bad girls go wild, *Newsweek*, June 13: 66, 2005.

Schaffner, L., Shorter, A. D., Shick, S., and Frappier, N. S., *Out of Sight, Out of Mind: The Plight of Girls in the San Francisco Juvenile Justice System*, San Francisco: Center for Juvenile and Criminal Justice, 1996.

Schwartz, G. and Merten, D., *Love and Commitment*, Beverly Hills, CA: Sage, 1980.

Sedlak, A. and Broadhurst, D., Executive Summary of the Third National Incidence Study of Child Abuse and Neglect, Washington, DC: National Center on Child Abuse and Neglect, U.S. Department of Health and Human Services, 1996.

Sharp, C. and Simon, J., *Girls and the Juvenile Justice System: The Need for More Gender Responsive Servi*ces, Washington, DC: Child Welfare League, 2004.

Sherman, F., What's in a name? Runaway girls pose challenges for the justice system, *Women, Girls and Criminal Justice*, 1: 2, 19–20, 2000.

Sickmund, M., Sladky, T. J., and Kang, W., Census of juveniles in residential placement databook, Washington, DC: U.S. Department of Justice, available at www.ojjdp.ncjrs.org/ojstabb/cjrp/, 2004.

Siegal, N., Where the girls are, *San Francisco Bay Guardian*, October 4: 19–20, 1995.

Silvern, L. E., Masculinity–femininity in children's self-concepts: The relationship to teachers' judgments of social adjustment and academic ability, classroom behaviors, and popularity, *Sex Roles*, 6: 929–949, 1978.

Simmons, R., *Odd Girl Out: The Hidden Culture of Aggression in Girls*, New York: Harcourt, 2002.

Skiba, R. and Peterson, R., The dark side of zero tolerance, *Phi Delta Kappan*, 80: 372–379, 1999.

Skolnick, J., *How to Encourage Girls in Math and Science*, New Jersey: Prentice Hall, 1982.

Slayer, S., Outcast no more, *HeraldNet* May 19, 2003, www.heraldnet.com/stories/03/5/19/16964394.cfm, retrieved June 9, 2003.

Smart, C., *Women, Crime and Criminology: A Feminist Critique*, London: Routledge and Kegan Paul, 1976.

Smith, A., Michigan's verbal assault law abused students: A student's view, Detroit news on-line, November 23, 2003. www.detnews.com/2003/editorial/0311/23/a15-332160.htm retrieved July, 13, 2005.

Snyder, H. N., Law Enforcement and Juvenile Crime, Juvenile Offenders and Victims: A National Report. Washington, DC: U.S. Department of Justice, Office of Justice Programs, Office of Juvenile Justice and Delinquency Prevention, 2001.

Snyder, H. N., Juvenile Arrests 2002, Washington, DC, Juvenile Justice Bulletin, Office of Juvenile Justice and Delinquency Prevention, U.S. Department of Justice, 2004.

Snyder H. N. and Sickmund, M., Juvenile Offenders and Victims: A National Report, Washington, DC: U.S. Department of Justice, Office of Justice Programs, Office of Juvenile Justice and Delinquency Prevention, 1995.

Snyder, H. and Sickmund, M., Juvenile Offenders and Victims: 1999 National Report, Office of Juvenile Justice and Delinquency Prevention: National Center for Juvenile Justice, 1999.

Snyder, H. N. and Sickmund, M., Juvenile Offenders and Victims: 2006 National Report (NCJ 178257), Washington, DC: U.S. Department of

Justice, Office of Justice Programs, Office of Juvenile Justice and Delinquency Prevention, 2006.

Snyderman, N. L. and Streep, P., *Girl in the Mirror: Mothers and Daughters in the Years of Adolescence*, New York: Hyperion, 2002.

Sobieraj, S., Taking control: Toy commercials and the social construction of patriarchy. In *Masculinities and Violence*, Bowker, L. (Ed.), Thousand Oaks: Sage, 1998.

Soriano, F. I., Lourdes, M. R., Williams, K. J., Daley, S. P., and Reznik, V. M., Navigating between cultures: The role of culture in youth violence, *Journal of Adolescent Health*, 34: 169–176, 2004.

Stahl, A., Delinquency Cases in Juvenile Courts, OJJDP Fact Sheet #31 (September), Washington, DC: U.S. Department of Justice, 2003.

Stanley, J., Sex and the quiet school girl. In *Gender and Ethnicity in Schools: Ethnographic Accounts*, Woods, P. and Hammersley, M. (Eds.), New York: Routledge, pp. 34–48, 1993.

Stanworth, M., *Gender and Schooling: A Study of Sexual Divisions in the Classroom*, London: Hutchinson, 1983.

Steele, Claude M., A threat in the air: How stereotypes shape intellectual identity and performance, *American Psychologist*, 52: 613–619, 1997.

Steffensmeier, D. et al., An assessment of recent trends in girls' violence using diverse longitudinal sources: Is the gender gap closing? *Criminology*, 43: 355–406, 2005.

Steffensmeier, D. J. and Steffensmeier, R. H., Trends in female delinquency: An examination of arrest, juvenile court, self-report, and field data, *Criminology*, 18: 62–85, 1980.

Stein, N., Sexual harassment in K-12 schools. In *The Gendered Society Reader*, Kimmel, M. (Ed.), pp. 216–229, New York: Oxford University Press, 2000.

Stein, N., Bullying or sexual harassment? The missing discourse of rights in an era of zero tolerance, *Arizona Law Review*, 43(3): 783–799, 2003.

Stein, N. D., *Classrooms and Courtrooms: Facing Sexual Harassment in K-12 Schools*, New York: Teachers College Press/Columbia University, 1999.

Stone, G., Student suspended for handing out cough drop, *Charleston Gazette*, November 6: P1A, 1997.

Storch, E. A. et al., Peer victimization and social-psychological adjustment in Hispanic and African-American children, *Journal of Child and Family Studies*, 12: 439–452, 2003.

Storch, E. A., Werner, N., and Storch, J. B., Relational aggression and psychosocial adjustment in intercollegiate athletes, *Journal of Sport Behavior*, 26: 155–167, 2003.

Sullivan, O.L., Respect the key ingredient in Pittsburgh Middle School initiative, *Morning Sun*, January 24, 2003.

Sutton, J. R., *Stubborn Children: Controlling Delinquency in the United States, 1640–1981*, Berkeley: University of California Press, 1988.

Swan, J. and Graddol, D., Gender inequalities in classroom talk, *English in Education*, 22: 48–65, 1988.

Talbot, M., Girls just want to be mean, *New York Times Magazine*, February 24: 24–64, 2002.

Tappan, M., Internalized oppression as mediated action: Implications for critical pedagogy, unpublished manuscript, November, 2002.

Taylor, J., Cultural stories: Latina and Portuguese daughters and mothers. In *Urban Girls: Resisting Stereotypes, Creating Identities*, Leadbeater, B. and Way, N. (Eds.), New York: New York University Press, pp. 117–131, 1996.

Taylor, J. M., Gilligan, C., and Sullivan, A. M., *Between Voice and Silence: Women and Girls, Race and Relationship*, Cambridge: Harvard University Press, 1995.

Thomas, W. I., *The Unadjusted Girl*, Montclair, NJ: Patterson Smith, 1923.

Thompson, J., *Women, Class, and Education*, New York: Routledge, 2000.

Thorne, B., Girls and boys together, but mostly apart: Gender arrangements in elementary schools. In *Relationships and Development*, Hartup, W. and Rubin, Z. (Eds.), Hillsdale, NJ: Lawrence Erlbaum, pp. 167–184, 1986.

Thorne, B., *Gender Play: Girls and Boys in School*, New Brunswick, NJ: Rutgers University Press, 1994.

Thorne, B. and Zella, L., Sexuality and gender in children's daily worlds, *Social Problems*, 33: 176–190, 1986.

Tolan, P. H., Guerra, N. C., et al., A developmental-ecological perspective on antisocial behavior in children and adolescents: Towards a unified risk and intervention framework, *Journal of Consulting and Clinical Psychology*, 63: 579–584, 1995.

Tyler, K., Hoyt, A. D., Whitbeck, L., and Cause, A., The impact of childhood sexual abuse on later sexual victimization among runway youth, *Journal of Research on Adolescence*, 11(2): 151–176, 2004.

Tyre, P., The trouble with boys, *Newsweek*, January 30, 2006, www.msnbc.msn.com/id/10965522/site/newsweek/.

U.S. Department of Education, Violence and Discipline Problems in the U.S. Public Schools: 1996–1997, Office of Educational Research and Improvement, National Center for Education Statistics, 1998.

U.S. Department of Education, Elementary and Secondary Education Survey, National and State Projections, Office of Civil Rights, Washington DC, 2000.

U.S. Department of Education, Revenues and Expenditures for Public Elementary and Secondary Education: School Year 2002–2003, National Center for Education Statistics 2005.

U.S. Department of Health and Human Services, Youth Violence: A Report of the Surgeon Gender, Rockville, MD: Department of Health and Human Services, Centers for Disease Control and Prevention, National Center for Injury Prevention and Control; Substance Abuse and Mental Health Services Administration, Center for Mental Health Services; and National Institute of Mental Health, 2001.

Underwood, M. K., The comity of modest manipulation: The importance of distinguishing among bad behaviors, *Merrill-Palmer Quarterly*, 49: 373–389, 2003.

Underwood, M. K., Galen, B. R., and Paquette, J. A., Top ten challenges for understanding gender and aggression in children: Why can't we all just get along? *Social Development*, 10: 248–266, 2001.

Viner, E., personal communication with the author (Chesney-Lind), October 21, 2003.

Vossekuil, B. et al., The final report and findings of the safe school initiative: Implications for the prevention of school attacks in the United States, United States Secret Service and United States Department of Education, Washington, DC, 2002.

Wacquant, L., Deadly symbiosis: When ghetto and prison meet and mesh, *Punishment and Society*, 3: 95–134, 2001.

Wald, J., Zeroing in on rule-breakers "one strike and you're out" rules are doing more harm than good, *Boston Globe*, August 13, 2000, p. F1, 3rd edition.

Wald, J. and Losen, D. J., Defining and redirecting a school-to-prison pipeline, *New Directions for Youth Development*, Fall: 9–15, 2003.

Walker, L. J., Sex differences in the development of moral reasoning: A critical review, *Child Development*, 55: 677–691, 1984.

Ward, J., Raising resisters: The role of truth telling in the psychological development of African-American girls. In *Urban Girls: Resisting Stereotypes, Creating Identities*, Leadbeater, B. and Way, N. (Eds.), New York: New York University Press, pp. 85–99, 1996.

Ward, L. M. and Harrison, K., The impact of media use on girls' beliefs about gender roles, their bodies, and sexual relationships: A research synthesis. In *Featuring Females: Feminist Analyses of Media*, Col, E. and Daniel, J. H. (Eds.), Washington, DC: American Psychological Association, pp. 3–23, 2005.

Weiler, J. D., *Codes and Contradictions: Race, Gender Identity, and Schooling*, Albany: State University of New York Press, 2000.

Weisfeld, C. C., Female behavior in mixed-sex competition: A review of the literature, *Developmental Review*, 6: 278–299, 1986.

Wells, R., America's delinquent daughters have nowhere to turn for help, *Corrections Compendium*, 19: 4–6, 1994.

Werner, N. E. and Crick, N. R., Relational aggression and social-psychological adjustment in a college sample, *Journal of Abnormal Psychology*, 108: 615–623, 1999.

White, B., American Civil Liberties Union report on the Hawaii Youth Correctional Facility, June 3–23, 2003, available at www.acluhawaii.org/pages/news/030826youthcorrection.html.

Whitney, I. and Smith, P. K., A survey of the nature and extent of bullying in junior/middle and secondary schools, *Educational Research*, 35: 3–25, 1993.

Widom, C. S., The cycle of violence, Washington, DC: National Institute of Justice, U.S. Department of Justice, 1992.

Widom, C. S., Victims of childhood sexual abuse—later criminal consequences, Washington, DC: National Institute of Justice, U.S. Department of Justice, 1995.

Wilkinson, S., Focus groups: A feminist method. In *Feminist Perspectives on Social Research*, Hesse-Biber, S. N. and Yaiser, M. L. (Eds.), New York: Oxford University Press, 2004.

Wilson, W. J., *When Work Disappears: The World of the New Urban Poor*, New York: Alfred A. Knopf, 1996.

Wing, B. and Keleher, T., Zero tolerance: An interview with Jesse Jackson on race and school discipline, *Colorlines*, 3(1): 1–3, 2000.

Wiseman, R., *Queen Bees and Wannabes: Helping Your Daughter Survive Cliques, Gossip, Boyfriends and Other Realities of Adolescence*, New York: Crown, 2002.

Wolpe, A. M., *Within School Walls: The Role of Discipline, Sexuality and the Curriculum*, New York: Routledge, 1988.

Xie, H. S., Dylan, C., Beverley D., and Cairns, R. B., Aggressive behaviors in social interaction and developmental adaptation: A narrative analysis of interpersonal conflicts during early adolescence, *Social Development*, 11: 205–224, 2002.

Younger, M., Warrington, M., and Williams, J., The gender gap and classroom interactions: Reality and rhetoric? *British Journal of Sociology of Education*, 20: 325–341, 1999.

Zahn-Waxler, C., The development of empathy, guilt, and internalization of distress: Implications for gender differences and externalizing problems. In *Anxiety, Depression, and Emotion: Wisconsin Symposium on Emotion*, Vol. II, Davidson, R. J. (Ed.), New York: Oxford University Press, pp. 222–265, 2000.

Zerointelligence, 11-year-old girl arrested at school for shoving match that happened previous week, February 4, 2005, www.zerointelligence.net/archives/000535.php.

Appendix

Speaking of Girls: Study Participants

Pseudonym	Ethnicity[1]	Age	SES/Parents' Occupation	Home State[2]	Interview Type
Clare	Asian American: Chinese	22	Middle Class	HI	Face-to-Face
Tina	European American: English and Irish	22	Teacher	CO & Europe	Face-to-Face
Hauʻoliʻipo	Native Hawaiian: Hawaiian	20	Home Health Care Nurse	HI	Face-to-Face
Shane	European American	20	Middle Class	CA	Face-to-Face
Simone	Asian American: Japanese	20	Middle Class	HI	Face-to-Face
Vivian	Asian American: South Asian	22	Military	NY/LA/CA	Face-to-Face
Mia	Asian American: Filipino	21	Working Class	HI	Face-to-Face
Violet	European American: Italian American	21	Middle Class: Small Business Owner	CA	Face-to-Face
Katelin	European American: French and Portuguese	21	Small Business Owner	HI	Face-to-Face
Jasmine	Latina: Puerto Rican	21	Middle Class	NY	Face-to-Face
Calle	European American: White	25	Small Business Owner	CA	Face-to-Face
Susie	African American	26	Middle Class	IL	Face-to-Face
April	Mixed: Native American and Irish	25	Working Class	IL/HI	Face-to-Face
Red	Latina: Mexican	20	Middle Class	CA	Face-to-Face
Jade	European American	25	Middle Class	MT	Face-to-Face
Mina	Asian American: Japanese	24	Teacher	HI	Focus Group 1

215

Pseudonym	Ethnicity[1]	Age	SES/Parents' Occupation	Home State[2]	Interview Type
Zoey	Asian American: Filipino	21	Doctor & Real Estate Agent	HI	Focus Group 1
Casey	Mixed: Caucasian and Japanese	30	Military	TX	Focus Group 1
Grace	European American: Caucasian	21	Military	AZ/TX/CA/HI	Focus Group 1
Mila	Asian American: Japanese	20	Public School Office Worker	HI	Focus Group 1
Candice	European American: White	19	Management Consultant and Nurse	WI/OH	Focus Group 2
Claudia	Asian American: Filipino	23	Real Estate Agent	CA/HI	Focus Group 2
Lexi	Asian American: Korean	21	CPA and Real Estate Broker	NY	Focus Group 2
Jane	Asian American: Japanese	21	Public School Administrative Assistant	HI	Focus Group 2
Ally	European American: Jewish Caucasian	26	Wealthy, Philanthropy Political Activism	CA	Focus Group 3
Linda	European American: White and Jewish	26	Filmmaker	CA	Focus Group 3
Erica	European American: White	26	Lower Class: Truck Driver and Clerk	TX	Focus Group 3

NOTES

Chapter 2

1. Although we share Osler and Vincent's (2003) view that girls are uniquely disadvantaged in school disciplinary policies designed to control boys' violence, we depart slightly from their analysis. Where they call specific attention to the link between relational bullying among girls and their voluntary exclusion from school, in this book, we question many of the popular and scholarly claims about girls' relational aggression. Not only do we suggest that girl-on-girl meanness is a symptom, not the source, of developmental challenges confronting girls, but we question whether girls are in fact the primary culprits of relational aggression and wonder why girls are receiving considerable blame for this brand of incivility.

Chapter 3

1. Our choice to include adults in this study does not mean that we view all research with adolescents or children as exploitative or problematic, although it does present clear ethical issues and challenges (not the least of which is that one must secure parental permission to talk to youth, which means that girls who are estranged from or in conflict with their parents may not speak to you). Many critical research projects in the past have been conducted with girls and the results of these studies have gone a long way to improve girls' lives (see Brown 2005; Orenstein 1994). The issue for us came down to the balance of potential risks versus benefits. Given the purpose of our study, to allow young women to "talk back" to the popular media about relationships in girls' lives, we felt that the benefits of our study for girls were fairly abstract and intangible. We might succeed in changing or challenging popular representations and constructions of girls, but it was not clear if we could improve concrete material conditions for girls. These benefits, in our minds, did not warrant the need for intrusion into adolescents' lives. We felt very confident, however, that 18- to 22-year-olds were close enough to adolescence to be able to describe their experiences accurately.

2. During our first focus group, we discovered that one participant was 30 years old. Because she was a college student with a very youthful appearance, we assumed that she was in her early or, at most, mid-twenties. Of course, we did not want to exclude her from the focus group and, as it turns out, she had considerable insights on racism and bullying, having

grown up mixed race in a predominantly white community. Although she is certainly an outlier in terms of age, the average age of our respondents was 22.5 years of age.

3. Hawaii is an expensive place to live and, although the financial resources to claim a middle-class status are more difficult to amass here compared with other places on the mainland, families have a strong stake in appearing middle class.

4. Here too, we lean more towards feminist than traditional scientific goals. Many researchers may wonder if our choice to interview students from our classes may inject bias into our sample, given that the young women from our classes had researched, read, or listened to lectures about feminist perspectives. Like our other study choices, we believe that our decision to talk with students who were interested in and educated about gender issues in adolescence actually enhanced the quality of our data and methods, rather than detracted from it. Our methods are, from the outset, subjective and not objective and we believe, like many feminist researchers, that perception of and pressure to be objective often mask a specifically masculine history of social science (see Harding 1986) and, more specifically, lead to a scientific endeavor that benefits men and boys more than women and girls. Here, we draw from the perspective of feminist research as being collaborative (Acker, Barry, and Esseveld 1983, 427) where "the research process becomes a dialogue between the researcher and researched ..." That being said, it is important to note that power distinctions between researchers and participants are always present to challenge the ability of researchers and subjects to create knowledge as equals. The task, therefore, is to minimize and acknowledge power distinctions as much as possible, which we feel is better served through acknowledging and even celebrating our subjective stance, rather than trying to strive for objectivity. Our goal was to let young women speak for themselves, construct their own subjective stance, and for us to respect their perspectives and opinions.

5. The names of people and, in many cases, the names of places have been changed to maintain interviewees' anonymity. Also, in some cases, details of individuals' life stories have been slightly changed or deleted to hide interviewees' identities. These changes, however, have not altered the meanings of their stories.

6. The idea that some girls would prefer to be "one of the guys" rather than "one of the girls" has emerged in other studies of adolescent girls. For example, Miller (2001, 182) found female gangsters that she interviewed joined gangs to escape the limitations of girlhood. According to Miller (2001, 182), being "one of the guys" allowed the girls in her study to be "tough and physically aggressive and not ... preoccupied with 'feminine concerns.'" In her study of punk-rock girls, Leblanc (1999) found that being "punk" allowed these girls to break out of multiple "feminine" stereotypes, such as being weak, frail, and overly concerned with a girlish appearance.

Chapter 4

1. The media's role in shaping girls' development is an important topic to explore, but demonstrating a direct effect of cultural messages in the media to girls' developmental outcomes is an extremely difficult task and demands careful analysis and rigorous scientific methods that are beyond the scope of our thesis (see Mills, Polivy, Herman, and Tiggemann 2002; Polivy and Herman 2004). Our argument is that girls have been policed particularly vigilantly since the 1980s. Our focus on the media as an agent of control over girlhood, therefore, focuses on its contribution to public fears and a moral panic about girlhood that, in the end, funnels girls into formal social control systems. We do not deny that the media also controls girlhood through cultural messages that are consumed by girls themselves. This, however, would take this book in another direction, into girls' internalization of damaging cultural messages (i.e., psycho-social regulation) and away from the formal policing of girlhood (i.e., institutional regulation).

Chapter 5

1. For example, of all of the youth homicides occurring between 1992 and 2000, only 0.9 percent occurred either on school grounds or while students were traveling to or from school sessions or school sponsored events (DeVoe et al. 2004). In 1994, 93 percent of serious juvenile assaults and 96 percent of juvenile robberies occurred outside of school (Snyder and Sickmund 1995).
2. The behavioral benefits were also difficult to ignore. Some of the most effective violence prevention programs, for example, did more than reduce violence among students. The most effective programs reduced students' conduct problems, aggressiveness, and hyperactivity in the classroom and improved their academic performances, relationships with teachers, and likelihood of graduating. Although some teachers balked at the extra time and energy required to implement these prevention programs, many noted that the programs did work. Students became better learners and teachers spent less time attending to classroom disruptions. In fact, teachers sometimes found that teaching became easier and more enjoyable after a violence prevention program was in place.
3. They were complex and required highly coordinated efforts. Administrators, teachers, and community members needed to be in full support of the program, the school needed to locate implementation resources, and teachers or other instructors were required to receive regular training. Because teachers were often not paid for the extra time required to implement the program, as we have suggested, securing teacher support was a difficult challenge. Some programs required schools to hire additional staff to coordinate and monitor them (see Coolbaugh and Hansel 2000).
4. This is the price quoted by the Quantum Opportunities Program.

5. Although bullying has been conflated with harassment, Olweus defined it somewhat differently than sexual harassment. Bullying is consistent negative treatment that includes physical, verbal, and indirect attacks. Indirect bullying includes ostracism from a group or even such subtle acts as rolling one's eyes at someone. In terms of perpetration, boys are overwhelmingly the perpetrators of physical bullying and girls and boys perpetrate indirect bullying. Sexual harassment, on the other hand, was defined by the AAUW study as "unwanted and unwelcome sexual behavior that interferes with your life" (AAUW 2001, 2).

Chapter 6

1. Brinson (2005) even argues that while same-sex bullying has received considerable attention, girls who bully boys have been overlooked. We argue that cross-gender bullying needs considerably more attention, but we would urge researchers to look closely at girls' victimization by boys.

2. Research on popularity and aggression sheds light on this phenomenon by suggesting a positive correlation between popularity and indirect aggression for boys and girls (Lease et al. 2002; Rose et al. 2004). Not all popular students, however, are aggressive. To date, research tends to demonstrate differences between well-liked and not well-liked popular youths (Cillessen and Rose 2005), with some indication that aggressive and popular boys are more accepted (Andreou 2006; Salmivalli et al. 2000) or more well liked than relationally aggressive and popular girls (see Cillessen and Borch 2006).

3. These divergent findings might be due to an age effect. Relational aggression among youths might look different at different stages of child and adolescent development.

4. This section of the chapter owes much to Lyn Mikel Brown and Meda Chesney-Lind. 2005. "Growing Up Mean: Covert Aggression and the Policing of Girlhood." This essay also draws on themes that earlier appeared in Brown's *Girlfighting*.

Chapter 7

1. There are several debates circulating around the topic of gender differences in teacher attention. Studies in the 1980s (Brophy 1985; Brophy and Good 1970; French and French 1984; Irvine 1986; Kelly 1988; Swan and Graddol 1988), for example, tended to support the idea that boys receive more attention than girls, suggesting that girls are "invisible" in the classroom. This assumption, however, has been challenged (see Dart and Clark 1988; Galton et al. 1999; Hammersley 1990). Looking at the types of attention received and the groups receiving attention, it

looks as if a small group of academically struggling and disruptive boys dominate teachers' time (see Croll and Moses 1985; Younger et al. 1999). Elaborating on the idea that boys dominate in a negative way, some have suggested that boys were falling behind girls in school (see Gurian and Stevens 2005) and were being held up to a feminized image of the model student that is difficult for them to achieve (see Backe-Hansen and Ogden 1996; Francis 2000). Adding to this debate, Myhill (2002) questions whether girls' typically non-disruptive and agreeable behavior in school reflects female privilege. She notes that few political or business leaders, but plenty of administrative assistants, are rewarded for compliance, conformity, and ability to follow rules.

2. Other studies of race and education explain why this might be occurring. For example, Weiler's (2000) study of 9th-grade African-American, Puerto Rican, and white working-class girls found that African-Americans and Puerto Rican girls saw school in instrumental terms (see also Fuller 1980; Grant 1992) and as a chance to enter the job market. In contrast, white working-class girls tended to have traditional views of romance and family as central to their future lives. Weiler (2000) argued that this is due to the lack of male bread-winner role models in Puerto Rican and African-American girls' lives.

3. This calculation uses the national average per student funding for elementary and secondary public schools, which was 6,912 for the 1999–2000 school year. Of course, school districts vary in the funds that they receive per student, so this is a very rough estimate.

Chapter 8

1. This phrase is taken from an inmate file by Rafter (1990, 169) in her review of the establishment of New York's Albion Reformatory.

Appendix

1. Hawaii's race and ethnic diversity makes ethic classifications difficult, although, arguably the geo-political history of race and ethnic categorizations (for example, the emergence and divergent meanings of terms like Hispanic or Latino), suggests that designating race and ethnicity is always complicated in any region of the globe. To resolve some of these problems, we provided two designations. The first term used is our own classification based upon contemporary terminologies circulating in the sociological literature and the second is respondents' own responses when asked to identify their ethnic identity and heritage. In many cases, interviewees' terms matched our own and there is only one designation provided.

2. This indicates the state in which interviewees grew up.

INDEX

A

AAUW, *see* American Association of University Women

ABA, *see* American Bar Association

Abusive homes, 6

Academic self-esteem, 131

Acculturative stress, 48

ACLU, *see* American Civil Liberties Union

Adolescence
  challenge of, 49
  difficulty of, 33, 99
  girls' loss of voice in, 68
  self-esteem lost during, 1

Adolescent(s)
  drinking, 48
  social aggression and, 113

Advanced placement classes, 60

Advil, student suspended for carrying, 152

African-Americans
  construction of as violent, 184
  displacement in labor market, 144
  incarceration of, 186
  schools-to-jails track and, 9
  self-esteem of, 131
  study of stress in, 134
  violence of, 17

Aggression, *see also* Relational aggression
  boys', research focus on, 99
  boys' and girls', 7
  covert, 108, 120
  day-to-day, 112
  definition of, 108
  differences in definition of, 111
  equality of relational and physical, 113
  female, discovery of, 109
  gender differences of, 108
  girls', feminist perspective of, 8
  indirect, 109

  pro-social response to, 120
  psychological concept of, 107
  psychologist definition of, 19, 107
  research, failure of, 125
  social, 113
  sports and, 24
  violence prevention programs and, 90

Alcohol abuse, 48

All About Eve, 21

Alternative schools, 132

American Association of University Women (AAUW), 130, 131, 142

American Bar Association (ABA), 178, 179

American Beauty, 107

American Civil Liberties Union (ACLU), 172

Anger, expression by indirect acts, 127

Anti-bullying legislation, 7, 103

Anti-bullying programs, relational aggression and, 107

Anti-bullying strategies, 91

Anti-violence campaign, image of youth violence and, 93

Anti-violence movement, *see* Girlhood, policing of

Arrest(s)
  girls', trend in, 29
  girls outpacing boys in, 25
  increases in, 183
  juvenile, 25
  juvenile robbery, 149
  lethal violence, 23
  runaway, 164
  violent offenses, 25, 163

Asianness, 136

Assaults, pattern of, 86

B

Backlash, 13

Backlash journalism, 155

Back-stabbing girl, 123
Bad femininity, 14
Bad girl
  hype, 2, 29
  hypothesis, 13
  media lover affair with, 13
Beauty
  ideals, hetero-eroticized, 77
  importance of, 74
  standards, 58
Becca's Bill, 177, 180
Best practices prevention programs,
  implementation of, 90
Betrayal, 33, 44, 47
Blaming, girl, 2, 132
Blondes, the, 57, 58
Body image
  distorted, 84
  girls' preoccupation with, 155
  problems with, 78
Body Project, The, 99
Body weight, 58
Bootstrapping, 29, 87, 174
Boy(s)
  aggression, research focus on, 99
  arrest rates, 26
  crisis, educational achievement
    and, 155
  expression of affect, 71
  girls seeking equality with, 1
  interpersonal skills of, 64
  Latino, 136
  loser, 115
  mean, 115
  popular, 115
  war against, 89
  winner, 115
  youth research focused on, 89
Bullying, 11, *see also* Peer groups,
  policing of
  behaviors, intervention in, 98
  categories of, 100
  definition of, 105
  emergence as social problem, 90
  indirect, 7, 102
  intolerance for, 105
  link between youth violence and, 97
  mean girl narrative and, 55

  minority experience of, 42
  moral panic about, 92
  playground, schoolboy driven to
    death by, 92
  prevention program(s), 7, 19
    addressing problems unique to
      girls, 102
    failure of, 125
    flaw of, 100
    gender responsive, 106
    idea touted by, 99
    logic of, 100
    punishments leveled against, 104
    relational aggression and, 7
    relevance of, 24
    school surveillance and, 105
    school definition of, 96
    school shootings and, 18, 94
    schools making parents aware of, 101
    school violence and, 101
    Secret Service report fueling
      interest in, 7
    students at risk for, 96
    suicide and, 91, 95
    targets of, 20
    victims, low self-esteem of, 101
Bullying at School, 91

C

California Youth Authority (CYA), 162
Carrie, 21
Cat fights, 126, 175
CDF, *see* Children's Defense Fund
Centers for Disease Control and
  Prevention, Youth Risk Behavior
  Survey, 26
Challenge grant activity, JJDPA, 160
Cheerleaders, white, 58
Child(ren)
  common form of aggression
    among, 112
  custody battles over, 159
  education as universal right for, 144
  sexual abuse, victims of, 83
  working-class, standards of, 142
Children's Defense Fund (CDF), 160

Child Welfare League, 179
Chilly classroom, 130, 132
Class
  biased society, 3
  differences, gender and, 77
Clique(s)
  dynamics, 74
  interpersonal dynamics in, 53
  member, rule broken by, 11
  popularity and, 74
  single-sex, 140
Cognitive development, 70
College preparatory classes, 60
Columbine High School massacre, 18,
  see also Peer groups, policing of
  concern about bullying after, 7
  legislation passed after, 103
  school surveillance techniques
    developed after, 105
  sympathy for, 95
  zero-tolerance strategies expanded
    after, 152
Concealed social attack, 113
Conflict avoidance, 49, 127
Connection tradition, girls', 49
Controversial group, 116
Covert aggression, 108, 120
Crack markets, introduction of, 24
Crime control agenda, schools co-opted
  into, 145
Crisis residential center, detention
  in, 177
Cultural capital, 136
Culturelessness, girlhood, 136
Custody battles, children caught in, 159
Cutting, 55
Cutting school, 134
CYA, *see* California Youth Authority

D

Dating rituals, 139
Daughters of Suburbia, 136
Deinstitutionalization
  juvenile justice system's
    abandonment of, 10
  reversal of, 174
  trends, 165

Delinquency
  familial patriarchy and, 118
  law and order strategies to
    control, 144
  official statistics, 163
  prevention, federal money for, 158
  programming
    advocacy for, 182
    problems of, 181
    self-reported, 27
Department of Education (DOE), 149
Depression, 68, 84
  bullying and, 101, 102
  cause of, 55
  relational aggression and, 117
Derogatory terms, 57, 119
Designer clothing, 57
Detention
  abuse while in, 169, 170, 173
  attitudes toward girls in, 170
  facilities, failure to provide mental
    health services, 169
  forcible face down restraint
    procedure, 172
  protective–punitive confluence, 178
  treatment vs., 177
  trends, girls', 165–173
    experiences in detention, 168–170
    gender and training schools,
      171–173
Differential socialization hypothesis, 70
Divorces, custody battles and, 159
DOE, *see* Department of Education
Domesticity, ideology of, 140
Domestic violence, 6, 86
Drinking, adolescent, 48
Drive-by shootings, 15
Drug(s), 16, 18
  abuse, sexual victimization and, 162
  possession at school, 146
  self-medication with, 181
  war on, incarceration and, 186

E

Early pregnancy, 79, 181
Eating disorders, 68, 78
Educational neglect, victims of, 134, 181

Emancipation, new violent girl and, 118
Emancipatory research program, 123
Empower Program, 117
Equality
    dark side of women's movement
        for, 15
    gangs and, 16
    women's demand for, 13
Equal opportunity crime sprees, 15
Ethic of care, 67
Ethnic difference, gender and, 77
Exclusion, 56, 59

F

Faithful friends, 44
Familial patriarchy, ideology of, 118
Families, regulation of girlhood and,
    67–88
    assaults and domestic violence,
        85–88
    class and culture, 77–80
    gender in girlhood, 69–73
    policing of girls' sexuality, 73–77
    running away, 80–85
Family
    control, girls seeking to avoid, 6
    disharmony, sexual double standard
        and, 75
    disputes, assaults and, 85
    social control of girls in, 183
    trauma, coping with, 80
    turmoil, juvenile justice system
        and, 162
Favored sex, girls as, 132
Federal Bureau of Investigation, arrest
    statistics, 16, 23
Female(s)
    beauty, markers of, 57
    competition paradigm, 40
    defiance, masculinization of, 3
    inherent duplicity of, 8
    revolutionary figures, 12
    traits, criticism of traditional, 46
Feminine double standards, 54, 57
Feminine goals, challenging of, 56
Femininity

attitudes condemning, 76
constraints of, 63
double bind between achievement
    and, 141
girls who broke rules of, 63
good girl, 129
heterosexualized, 139
standards of, 99
taint of, 50
teen, 140
Feminism, 13, 89d, 180
Feminists, negative press and, 45
Films, mean girls in, 21
Focus groups, 34, 39
Friend(s)
    abandonment by, 36
    betrayal from, 47
    faithful, 44
    victimization by, 84
Friendship(s)
    adolescent, 49
    heartbreaks, 40
    pro-social behavior and, 119
Friend Who Got Away, The, 125

G

Gang(s)
    attire, 146
    banging girls, 29
    media hype about, 17
    violence, 16
    women's equality and, 16
Gangsta girl, media-driven, 31
Gangster girls, 1
Gender
    bias, arrests and, 87
    children affected by, 69
    class differences in, 77
    development, stages in, 69
    equity, as goal in schools, 130
    school failure and, 132
    specific programming, 69
    stereotypes
        peer groups and, 133
        probation files and, 170
        services reinforcing, 161

Gendered control, vehicles for, 157
Gender-specific programming,
  prospects for, 180
"Getting ready" rituals, 139
Girl
  bashing, 45, 50
  blaming, 142
  problems, books hyping, 23
  socially powerful, 41
  supporting, 46
  throwaway, 176
Girlfighting, 20, 127
Girl-focused research, flaw in, 122
Girl-on-girl meanness, 61, 117, 155
Girlhood, *see also* Families, regulation
  of girlhood and
  blaming girls for problems of, 103
  challenges, 187
  control of, 2, 10, 31
  culturelessness of, 136
  false dichotomy in imagining, 63
  family pathologizing of, 185
  intervention to control, 88
  poisoned, 99
  school policing of, 135
  vilifications of, 63
  vulnerability, anxiety about, 126
Girlhood, policing of, 129–155
  girlworld and girl blaming, 142–143
  paying attention to and punishing
    girls, 154–155
  pretty and popular, 138–142
  punitive control in schools, 143–148
  racism, educational neglect, and
    white privilege, 134–138
  reproducing gender at school,
    130–134
  upcriming of youth violence,
    148–150
  violence control, 150–154
Girl in the Mirror, 99
Girlworld
  frightening, 33
  toxic, 184
Glenbrook High School hazing
  incident, 30
"Going with" rituals, 139
Good femininity, 14

Good girl femininity, violations of, 129
Gossip, 52, 120
Grain alcohol, 152
Grooming issues, 57
Group meaning making, 35
Gun-Free Schools Act, 146

H

Hazing incident, 30
Heathers, 21, 40
Hetero-eroticized beauty ideals, 77
Heterosexualized femininity, 139
High school, *see* School
Hijacking, 149, 150
Hispanic students, academic
  achievement of, 138
HIV/AIDS, 82
Homecoming queens, 58
Homeless youth, sexual victimization
  of, 162
Horizontal violence, 118, 123, 124
Hospital injury data, 27
Hostile attribution bias, 117
Hostile Hallways, 142
*Hostile Hallways: The AAUW Survey on
  Sexual Harassment in America's
  Schools*, 103
*Hostile Hallways, Bullying, Teasing, and
  Sexual Harassment in School*, 103
Human rights, international standards
  of, violation of, 174
Hype
  bad girl, 2, 29
  meanness as, 39
  media
    control of girlhood and, 10
    girls and gangs, 17
    monitoring of girls and, 4–5
    self-fulfilling prophecy and, 184
Hyper policing hypothesis, 28

I

Incarceration, racialized patterns
  of, 186
In a Different Voice, 67

Indirect aggression, *see* Relational aggression
Indirect bullying, 7
    girls' aggression and, 108
    intolerance for, 105
    major culprits of, 102
Initiation rituals, brutal, 12
Inner city(ies)
    crack markets in, 24
    migration of jobs out of, 18
    neighborhoods, youth violence in, 17
    schools, violence confronting girls in, 142
Institutionalized girls, abuse histories of, 162
Institutional racism, 65
Institutional review board (IRB), 38
Interpersonal skills, boys', 64
Interviews
    girl-on-girl meanness described during, 5
    identifying information, 39
    interviewee recall, 35
    purpose of, 34
    refusal to participate in, 38
    sharing of personal information in, 36
    snowball sampling techniques, 37
IRB, *see* Institutional review board

J

Jawbreakers, 21
JJDPA, *see* Juvenile Justice and Delinquency Prevention Act
Justice legislation, girls', 158
Juvenile arrests, 25
Juvenile Justice and Delinquency Prevention Act (JJDPA), 69, 80, 157, 158, 160, 179, 180
Juvenile justice system, 2, 157–182
    abandonment of commitment to deinstitutionalization, 10
    century of girls' justice legislation, 158–163
    detention trends, 165–173
    enforcement of girls' place in society, 3
    explanation of trends, 174
    future of juvenile justice, 179–182
    girls' status in, 163
    legislation calling for more equitable treatment of girls in, 157
    new millennium of girls' justice, 163–164
    protective/punitive system, 176–179
    rediscovery and upcriming, 175–176
    relabeling, 175
    schools-to-jails track, 9
    two-track, 167
    youth violence and, 176
Juvenile robbery, 148, 149

K

Kids killing kids, 18

L

Latina(s)
    conflicts with mothers, 80
    construction of as violent, 184
    students, 60
Latinos
    policed behavior of, 136
    violence of, 17
Law Enforcement Assistance Administration, 158
Law enforcement personnel, violent offenses at schools handled by, 149
Law-and-order solutions, violence prevention and, 97
Lethal violence, girls' arrests for, 23, 29
Life lessons, 52
Lifelong damages, girls inflicting, 20
Loser boys, 115
Low-income girls, school life for, 78

M

Male infidelity, 76
Male privilege, culture of romance perpetuating, 139
Marijuana, 48

Masculinization hypothesis
    alternative to, 28
    equality and, 12
    media and, 14
    women's violence and, 13
Mean boy story, 115
Mean girl, *see also* Mean and violent
  girls, construction of
    books, 100
    media
        disturbing aspect of, 33
        narratives, 3
Meanness
    acknowledging, 33
    destructiveness of, 50
    discovery of girls', 12
    effect of, 50
    as experience and hype, 39
    girl-on-girl, 61
    girls', discovery of, 109
    intensity of girls', 23
    programs focusing on curbing, 126
    stories about, 41
    talking about, 34
Mean and violent girls, construction of,
  11–31
    films, 21
    gangs, guns, and emancipation,
        17–18
    popular constructions, 13–17
    queen bees as bad girls, 18–21
    savagery in the suburbs, 22–24
    trends in girls' violence, 24–29
    violence, 21–22
    youth violence, bad girl hype, and
        consequence, 29–31
Media
    attack of feminist goals by, 13
    claims, gap between real lives
        and, 2
    hype
        control of girlhood and, 10
        girls and gangs, 17
        monitoring of girls and, 4–5
        self-fulfilling prophecy and, 184
    masculinization hypothesis and, 14
    mean girl, 33
    narratives, mean girl, 3

talking back about claims in, 34
    violent girl myth and, 184
Mental health issues, misdiagnosis
    of, 169
Miami-Dade County Juvenile
    Detention Center, 170
Midol, student expelled for giving, 152
Mildred Pierce, 21
Military-style boot camp, student
    facing time in, 152
Minority students, metal detector
    checks at schools with, 150
Misogynistic culture, 76
Misogynistic popular narratives, 4
Model student, feminized depiction
    of, 155
Moral panics paradigm, 2
Moral reasoning, 67
Mother(s)
    adolescent intimacy with, 72
    Latina conflict with, 80
Motherhood, state supported, 78

N

National Bar Association (NBA),
    178, 179
National Conference of State
    Legislatures, 95
National "get tough" attitude, school
    violence and, 150
National Organization for Women, 180
National Youth Survey, 81
NBA, *see* National Bar Association
Negative stereotypes, 3, 45
No-exception punishments, 9
Non-serious violence, 148

O

ODD, *see* Oppositional Defiant
    Disorder
Odd Girl Out, 5, 8, 11, 19, 36, 102
Odd girl out, 40
Office of Juvenile Justice and
    Delinquency Prevention, 98, 181

Olweus Bullying Prevention Program, 9, 98, 101, 108
Open competition, taboo towards, 20
Oppositional Defiant Disorder (ODD), 169
Ostracism, 11, 22
Other person offenses, 167
Outsider identity, 42
Out of wedlock births, 68
Oversocialization hypothesis, 72

P

Pack journalism, 15
Parental authority, girls' obedience to, 88
Parents
    anger at, 62
    child-rearing practices, 70, 71
    daughters oversocialized by, 72
    incriminating phone messages left for, 11
    influence of, peer groups and, 75
    male, abusive, 118
    socialization patterns of, 70, 75
    uneasiness about daughters' sexuality, 6, 76
Parity hypothesis, *see* Masculinization hypothesis
Partner abuse, 17
Passive stereotype, 29
Patriarchy, collective bargains with, 50
Peer(s)
    culture research, 120
    girls' emotional ruthlessness with, 40
    nominations
        classmates' behavior traits and, 121
        relational aggression and, 111
    pressure, 132
    rejection from, 50
    -related hassles, 134
Peer group(s)
    African-American, 59
    controversial, 116
    emotional support from, 6
    ethnographic literature on, 56
    experiences, misunderstood, 122

gender stereotypes and, 133
    interviews of women in, 5
    literature, ethnographic, 45
    name for, 44
    parental influence and, 75
    policing of, 89–106
        bullying, depression, and sexual harassment, 102–104
        bullying prevention, 98–102
        Columbine and moral panic about bullying, 92–94
        emergence of bullying as social problem, 90–92
        gender responsive or gender blaming, 90
        policing and punishing of bullies, 104–106
        school shootings, 94–98
    pro-social behavior in, 120
    Puerto Rican, 59
    racism within, 56
    rival, 42
    same-sex, 141
    scrutiny of, 31
    teacher behavior and, 138
Penal state, shift from welfare state to, 144
Perfect police, 20
Person offenses, 86
Person-to-person offenses, 86
Peyton Place, 21
Physical aggression
    relational aggression and, 113, 114
    theme in, 118
Physical attractiveness, 57
Physical bullying, intolerance for, 105
Physical ideal, 57
Playground
    bullying, schoolboy driven to death by, 92
    interactions, significance of, 138
Poisoned culture, 143
Policing, 183–187
    arrest increases and, 183
    challenge, 187
    family front, 185
    mean girl construction, 184
    media, 183, 184

minorities, 186
schools, 185
violence intervention programs,
186
Popularity
backstabbing and, 1
cliques and, 74
conditions surrounding rules
of, 64
contests, 61
girls' vs. boys', 139
hair and makeup issues, 44
obedience to rules of, 47
power and, 117
purchasing behaviors and, 58
relational aggression and, 117
standards for, 59
success and, 54
transformation into power, 40
Power
popularity and, 117
relations, boy-girl, 133
transformation of popularity
into, 40
Predatory violence, arrest data and, 29
Prestige, opportunities to gain, 124
Pretty power hierarchy, 57
Pro-arrest statute, 86
Probation
services unit, gender stereotyping
and, 161
technical violation of, 165, 168
Programmatic funding, sexism
in, 181
Property crimes, incarceration
for, 173
Pro-social behavior, 116, 119, 122
Prostitution, 80, 83, 85, 162
Puberty, adjusting to, 69
Punishment, school, 154–155
Punk-rock subculture, 42

Q

Queen bees, 11, 40, 116
Queen Bees and Wannabes, 5, 11, 19,
21, 183

R

Race biased society, 3
Racial stereotyping, effect of, 137
Racism, 56
classroom, 60
educational neglect and, 134
institutional, 65
school personnel and, 61
sexism and, 61
Racist stereotypes, future aspirations
and, 5–6
Rape, 17, 82, 172
Rebecca, 21
Re-detention, 168
Reform school, 30
Rehabilitative welfare programs,
agenda to replace, 152
Rejection, self-esteem and, 55
Relabeling, 29, 174
Relational aggression, 107, 111
bullying prevention programs and, 7
conflicting images, 117
gender differences, 111
harm of, 112
interviewees devastated by, 51
literature, 8, 122
loneliness and, 110
media construction of, 116
physical aggression and, 113, 114
popularity and, 117
pro-social, 113
punishment by, 127
repeated, 112
thankfulness for, 51–52
violence prevention and, 107–127
fact and myth about relationally
aggressive girls, 115–117
girl-on-girl violence, 117–119
girls' friendships, 119–122
girls' friendships in context,
122–125
harm of relational aggression,
112–115
research on girls' aggression,
108–112
Relational victimization, 5
Relationship

aggression, 12
violence, physical, 21
Research, gender bias in, 122
Residential placements, 171
Resilience, underestimates of, 55
Resistance strategies, race-related, 79
Reviving Ophelia, 1, 2, 99, 143
Revolutionary figures, female, 12
Risk amplification, 83
Robbery, juvenile, 148, 149
Romance, culture of, 139
Roper v. Simmons Supreme Court
  decision, 51
Ruined lives, 50
Runaway(s)
    arrests, 164
    behavior, theme in, 118
    chronic, 6
    sexually abused, 83, 162
Running away, 80, 157, 175
    petitioned status offenders charged
      with, 81
    responses to, 82

S

Safe and Drug Free Schools and
  Communities Act (SDFSCA), 96,
  97, 98
Salable commodities, girls seeing
  themselves as, 85
Same Difference, 63
Savagery in the suburbs, 1
School(s)
    alternative, 132
    boards, zero-tolerance policies of, 145
    control of girlhood by, 185
    crimes, reporting of to police, 147
    culture, how to read, 141
    definition of bullying, 96
    disruption, students causing, 146
    dress code, 135
    drug possession at, 146
    failure, gender and, 132
    gender equity as goal in, 130
    girls, social control of, 130
    girls disengaged from, 133

hazing incident, 30
hidden curriculum, 129, 130, 154
information-gathering techniques, 94
-to-jails track, 9, 144
law enforcement representatives
  stationed at, 150
law and order approaches of, 9
loss of funding, 147
minority enrollment, 150
officials, hypervigilance in
    patrolling of noncriminal
    behavior, 129
posted rules inside classrooms, 137
public perception of, 145
punitive control in, 143
racism in, 60
safety survey, 147, 151
sexism in, 61
sexual harassment in, 7
shooters, description of, 95
shootings
    bullying and, 94
    perpetrators of, 7
    significant feature of, 93
    tough-on-youth-crime agenda
      and, 143
social exclusion at, 41
social hierarchy of, 47
socially competitive, 52
student regimes of terror, 153
surveillance, bullying prevention
    programs and, 105
suspensions, 30
targets of bullying at, 20
tension between white and
    Mexican-American students, 59
violence, 93
    bullying and, 101
    control, 150
prevention programs, 19
wealthy, white community, 58
zero-tolerance policies
    transfer to reform school under, 30
    weapon carrying prohibited by,
      147
SDFSCA, *see* Safe and Drug Free
  Schools and Communities Act
Second Sex, The, 123

Secret Service report, school shooting analysis, 7
See Jane Hit, 4, 22, 183
Self-confidence, easily shaken, 33
Self-destructive behaviors, 55
Self-esteem
  academic, 131
  of bullying victims, 101
  drop in, 68
  explanation for drop in, 131
  loss of, 84
  low, white girls' offenses resulting from, 167
  male approval and, 140
  rejection and, 55
Self-fulfilling prophecy, media hype and, 184
Self-medication, 181
Self-report(s)
  data, 23
  studies, girls' violence, 26
  of victimization, 111
Sex-appropriate behaviors, pressure from parents for, 71
Sexism, *see* Girlhood, policing of
Sexual abuse, 62, 65
  injuries caused by, 6
  patterns for, 118
Sexual capital, 84
Sexual double standard, 140
  durability of, 82
  family disharmony and, 75
  family endorsement of, 185
  girls' aggressions and, 20
  parental concern about girls, 73
  parental reasons for enforcing, 82
Sexual harassment
  AAUW report on, 142
  bullying and, 102, 103
  bullying prevention and, 104
  civil rights victories and, 106
  de-gendering of, 104
  legal protections from, 143
  problems, degendering of, 7
  school, 7
Sexuality, girls'
  concern with control of, 175
  policing of, 73

regulator of, 77
Sexually promiscuous girls, 4
Sexual victimization, 56
  drug abuse and, 162
  girls' unique problems with, 181
  history of, detention and, 168
  risk amplification and, 83
Shape of a Girl, The, 21
Shoreham-Wading River (SWR) Middle School, 136
Shortchanging Girls, Shortchanging America, 130, 142
Shoving incident, 152
Single-sex cliques, 140
Sisters in Crime, 13
Social aggression, definition of, 113
Social control
  girlhood control involving, 31
  mechanisms of, 3
Social exclusion
  school, 41
  victimization reports and, 121
Social hierarchy, school, 47
Social intelligence, indirect aggression and, 114
Socialization
  practices, parental, 75
  process, developmental stages in, 69
  sex differentiation in, 70
Socially powerful girl, 41
Social punishment, 43
Social welfare programs, political agenda and, 144
Sowing wild oats, 88
Speaking of girls, 33–65
  acknowledging meanness, 33–34
  meanness as experience and hype, 39–45
  not the end of the world, 50–56
  sexual victimization, racism, and exclusion, 56–62
  supporting girls, 46–50
  talking about meanness, 34–39
Sports
  aggression and, 24
  girls' participation in, 130
Standard intimate partner violence, 86

Starvation, 53, 55
Status
    opportunities to gain, 124
    symbols, 57
Status offenders
    deinstitutionalization of, 158
    in violation of valid court order, 159
Status offenses
    deinstitutionalization of, 85
    gendered control and, 157
Stereotypes, aggression and, 109
Street women, 78
Strip searches, 173
Student
    model, feminized depiction of, 155
    sexual cultures, importance
        of, 141
Study participants, 215–216
Suburbs
    savagery in, 22
    victimization endured by white girls
        in, 142
    white-collar, 73
Sugar and spice mythology, 43
Sugar and Spice and No Longer Nice,
    22, 183
Suicide, 53
    attempted, 84
    bullying and, 91, 95, 101
Super-hero, feminization of, 23
Super-predator, 9, 24
Survival sex, 84, 85
SWR Middle School, *see* Shoreham-
    Wading River Middle School

T

Targeted events, 93
Teacher(s)
    behavior, peer groups and, 138
    complaint about African-American
        girls, 135
Teen femininity, girls pushed into
    cultivating, 140
Teen parenthood, 115
Teen sex, zero tolerance for, 76
Television
    images of mean girls, 19
    stories on girls in gangs, 16
Therapeutic liberalism, zero tolerance
    as blow to, 153
Third National Incidence Study, 82
Throwaway girls, 176
Tiny traps, peer groups called, 44
Title IX, 130
Tomboys, 72
Tough-on-crime policies, girls bearing
    brunt of, 179
Toxic culture, 24
Training schools, gender and, 171
Truancy, 81, 157, 175
Truth-telling, 79
Tyranny of nice, 8, 106, 131, 155

U

Underground drug markets, 18
Uniquely juvenile offenses, 81
University of Hawaii, Committee on
    Human Subjects, 37, 38
Upcriming, 29, 148, 175
Uppity voice research, 35

V

Valid court order, status offenders in
    violation of, 159
Vandalism, 51
Verbal bullying, intolerance for, 105
Victimization
    girl-to-girl, 119
    girls blamed for their own, 104
    girls' vulnerability to, 99
    relational vs. physical, 5
    reports, social exclusion and, 121
    student self-reports of, 111
    studies, 4, 29
Videotape, girls gone bad, 22
Violence
    control, school-based, 150
    domestic, 86
    forcing driving, 17
    gang, 16

gender gap in, 24
girl-on-girl, 117, 155
horizontal, 118, 123, 124
in inner-city neighborhoods, 17
lethal
    arrests for, 23, 29
    trends in, 27
non-serious, 148
predatory, arrest data and, 29
prevention, *see also* Relational
    aggression, violence prevention
    and
prevention programs
    aggression and, 90
    best practice, high cost of, 98
    disadvantages of, 97
rise in girl-on-girl, 22
school, bullying and, 101
self-report studies, 26
standard intimate partner, 86
trends in, 24
women's, masculinization theory
    of, 13
youth, epidemic of, 24
Violent girls, *see* Mean and violent girls,
    construction of
Violent offenses, arrests for, 163, 176

W

Wannabes, 11
War against boys, 89
War on drugs, incarceration and, 186
Washington Women's Foundation, 181
Weapons
    possession, 6th grader arrested
        for, 152
    violations, students charged
        with, 151
We've All Got Scars, 115
White lies, system of, 137
Whiteness, 136

White people's turf, 62
White privilege, educational neglect
    and, 134
Winner boys, 115
Womanhood, passive, 14
Women, internalized notions of being
    female, 20
Working-class backgrounds,
    adolescents from, 77
Working-class children,
    standards of, 142

Y

Year of the Woman, 14
Youth(s)
    bias against, arrests and, 87
    high-risk, survey of, 26
    homeless, sexual victimization
        of, 162
    relationally aggressive, conflicting
        images of, 117
    runaway, sexual victimization
        of, 162
    socially marginal, 117
    violence, epidemic of, 24

Z

Zero tolerance
    as blow to therapeutic liberalism, 153
    codes, rule violators of, 9
    penalties
        students exempted from, 153
        unambiguous, 154
    policies
        anti-bullying legislation and, 95
        legal challenges to, 153
        punitive responses of, 176
        transfer to reform school under, 30
        students expelled under, 153